THE BATTLE OF
STALINGRAD
THROUGH
GERMAN EYES

OTHER BOOKS
BY JONATHAN TRIGG

THE BATTLE OF STALINGRAD THROUGH GERMAN EYES

The Death of the Sixth Army

JONATHAN TRIGG

AMBERLEY

For Tony – keep on smiling and playing – you're missed.

Page 1. This is how *Signal* magazine portrayed the defiant last stand at the railway embankment of Generals Max Pfeffer, Alexander von Hartmann, Richard Stempel and *Oberst* Crome. It was pure propaganda and absurd fantasy.

Page 3. The reality of *6.Armee*'s surrender. A filthy, starving, frozen *landser* is taken prisoner. Obviously, this is a Soviet propaganda photo emphasising the difference between the miserably attired Germans and the well-equipped Soviets. Nevertheless, the comparison was accurate. (Courtesy of Bundesarchiv_Bild_183-E0406-0022-011)

First published 2022

Amberley Publishing
The Hill, Stroud
Gloucestershire, GL5 4EP

www.amberley-books.com

Copyright © Jonathan Trigg, 2022

The right of Jonathan Trigg to be identified as the Author of this work has been asserted in accordance with the Copyright, Designs and Patents Act 1988.

ISBN 978 1 3981 1071 7 (hardback)
ISBN 978 1 3981 1072 4 (ebook)

British Library Cataloguing in Publication Data. A catalogue record for this book is available from the British Library.

1 2 3 4 5 6 7 8 9 10

Typesetting by SJmagic DESIGN SERVICES, India. Printed in the UK.

CONTENTS

ACKNOWLEDGEMENTS

As usual there are a host of people to whom I owe an enormous debt of gratitude for all the help they've given. I would like to especially thank all the veterans who've given so freely of their time and been so hospitable. For them to agree to talk about some of the most horrific experiences any human could endure is greatly appreciated, and so thank you to Ivar Corneliussen, Rudolf von Ribbentrop and Werner Block. Thank you as well to Patrick Eriksson for all his expert advice on the Luftwaffe on the Eastern Front, especially on details of the Stalingrad airlift. I also wish to tip my hat to James Beringer, who has quietly and diligently persevered with the biography of his grandfather-in-law, Dr Stephen Ritli. Over several years of conversations with Stephen, and a huge amount of patience in going through his papers after Stephen sadly passed away, James has been able to produce a book that is both testament to Stephen Ritli the man, and a unique insight into the life and times of an officer in the Second Hungarian Army who served on the Eastern Front as a military chaplain and somehow survived the horror of the Stalingrad fighting. I hope that Stephen Ritli's story is heard by a wider audience.

I would also – once again – like to pay tribute to the *Museumsstiftung Post und Telekommunikation Briefsammlung* – the letter collections of the Museum Foundation for Post and Telecommunications in Berlin. Their collection of German *Feldpost* letters was instrumental in my last book; *Barbarossa Through German Eyes*, and I am hugely pleased to say that the same can be said for this book. If anything, it was even more satisfying to follow on from the events of *Barbarossa* and continue reading the stories of German veterans as they continued their service into 1942 and the summer offensive. Having said that, it was also profoundly sad to know that for so many of the young men, whose letters home I was so avidly reading, their stories would end in Stalingrad. The Museum's work continues, and I can only assume it is a Sisyphean task, given that the number of letters sent back and forth between members of the Wehrmacht and their families runs into the tens of millions. It is clearly a task worth doing and so I both applaud them for what they've achieved thus far and wish them well for the future. In the meantime, the ability to read so very many letters from ordinary serving members of the Wehrmacht is a gift for which I am incredibly grateful.

INTRODUCTION

Stalingrad. In popular imagination the battle that was fought in the eponymous city in the latter half of 1942 and early 1943 is seen as the turning point of the Second World War. The standard narrative is that the Nazis – having seen their attempt to defeat the Soviet Union in 1941 collapse in the ice and snow of winter – tried once more to win the war in the East by launching yet another huge offensive in the summer of 1942, only this time with the goal of seizing the far-off oilfields of the fabled Caucasus. Initially, the victorious Germans advanced headlong once more, repeating the successes of the previous year as their panzers ate up the miles and columns of dispirited Red Army PoWs trudged into an uncertain captivity.

Then – just when final victory was tantalisingly close – the Germans found themselves among the shattered buildings and twisted debris of an industrial ruin on the River Volga; a city whose name became a byword for destruction, horror and suffering. There, among the smoke and rubble, the masters of the operational art of war found themselves drawn into a claustrophobic meat-grinder where their superior tactics, weapons and training were useless against an enemy completely at home amidst the alleyways and sewers of an urban battlefield. In this greatest of battles the German soldier as a fighting man was found wanting, as the Soviet commander in Stalingrad, Vasily Chuikov, gloatingly recalled:

> They didn't have the spirit to look an armed Soviet soldier in the eye. You could locate an enemy soldier in a forward post from a long way off … every five to ten minutes he would fire a burst from his tommy gun, obviously to boost his morale. Our soldiers could find such 'warriors', creep up and finish them with bullet or bayonet.

The shovel-faced Chuikov would have felt validated in his belief by the words of one particular *landser* (German nickname for a frontline soldier akin to the British 'Tommy') who wrote home saying: 'At the slightest rustle I pull the trigger and fire off tracer bullets in bursts from the machine-gun… If only you could understand what terror is.' It is telling, though, that Chuikov also said during the last few weeks of the battle that 'They [the German defenders] continued to live in hope and put up a desperate resistance, often literally to the last bullet. We practically took no prisoners as the Nazis just wouldn't surrender.' The Soviet marshal's former assertion sounds more like a propaganda statement than a description of reality, whereas the latter has the exasperated ring of truth.

However, the standard narrative then continues by outlining that the Red Army, in a masterstroke, used masses of fresh, well-equipped troops to slice through the enemy's vulnerable flanks, manned as they were by Romanians, Italians and Hungarians – Axis allies of dubious quality and commitment. As these lukewarm comrades threw down their weapons and ran away pell-mell through the snow, the hunter became the hunted as the German Wehrmacht's powerful *6. Armee* (Sixth Army) found itself trapped in the very city it had fought so long to conquer. Hitler and his lazy and incompetent air force chief – Hermann Goering – then turned defeat into catastrophe by overruling the military experts and insisting the encircled troops stay put through a Russian winter and be supplied with all their needs by air. That airlift turned out to be a disaster, with hardly a trickle of the promised supplies ever arriving, and as the winter cold bit hard the besieged Germans began to starve to death even as the battle raged.

As the weeks rolled by, so life in the Stalingrad Pocket became ever more wretched, especially when the much-heralded ground offensive to relieve the city failed to break through. Refused permission to surrender, the enfeebled Germans fought on until the inevitable capitulation, following which endless thousands shuffled into a nightmarish captivity from which only a bare handful ever returned. It was a defeat the Germans never recovered from; the losses so huge it crippled their war effort from then onwards. This is the popular picture of Stalingrad and in many respects it is searingly accurate. The airlift was a disaster and never a serious military proposition and the Red Army's *Uranus* counter-offensive to encircle 6. *Armee* was a brilliant operation, but this isn't the whole story, and that story is more fascinating still.

Selecting any one battle in the Allies' long and costly struggle to defeat the evils of Nazi Germany and saying with absolute certainty that this was the turning point of the war is a bold move; after all, there's a strong case to be made that the German defeat at Kursk in the summer of 1943 was of greater importance. It is hard though, to look beyond the failure of Nazi Germany's invasion of the Soviet Union back in 1941 – *Operation Barbarossa* – as the crucial battle. As the panzer commander Ewald von Kleist said of *Barbarossa*, 'Hopes of victory were largely built on the prospect that the invasion would produce a political upheaval in Russia ... and that Stalin would be overthrown by his own people if he suffered heavy defeats.' Kleist's point is well made. Perhaps the only criticism of it would be that Hitler believed that the military defeat of the Red Army, and not a popular rising, would cause the collapse of the Soviet state. Regardless of the veracity of Kleist's comments, what is hardly disputed is that when Hitler's infamous declaration that all the Wehrmacht needed to do was kick in the door and the whole rotten structure would come crashing down didn't materialize, Nazi Germany's strategy in the East was left beached. How then to win the war?

In truth, the Germans didn't know. Every country they had invaded up until then had capitulated, their governments either suing for peace or going into enforced exile. When Great Britain and her Empire stood firm, Hitler had no answer, and he had none in the Soviet Union either. All Germany, from Hitler downwards, thought in terms of an impending final victory – the long awaited *Endsieg* – which would leave the Third Reich in control of a continent-spanning empire that would have all the resources it would need to not have to worry about Great Britain's dominance of the world's shipping lanes. Berlin could then deal with London at its leisure, probably by coming to some sort of deal when Churchill had been sent packing and the muddle-headed fools in Whitehall accepted the inevitable. But to reach that point the Nazis first had to secure their empire by destroying the Soviet Union, and most thought that goal was in their grasp. As the smooth-faced SS intelligence head Walter Schellenberg said: 'We still stood on the dizzy heights and the Nazi leaders believed that victory was in sight.'

Interestingly, in his own memoirs Schellenberg wrote that he felt strongly that some sort of political accommodation with Stalinist communism was the way forward, but it's difficult to see this as anything other than hindsight. In reality, Hitler was in no mood for any sort of settlement with either the Soviet dictator or his subject peoples, about whom the Nazi overlord felt nothing but a fathomless loathing. Pathologically unable to climb over his own ideology to find a political solution, the Nazi supremo only had the military option, and by presenting Stalin with a choice of either extermination or victory it wasn't difficult to guess the Soviet leader would choose the latter.

Not that Hitler was solely culpable for the lack of a feasible strategy for German victory in the East in 1942. The General Staff had no idea either. Just as unable – and unwilling – to articulate a political way forward and having failed to achieve a comprehensive military victory in 1941, Nazi Germany's military brains trust was at a loss. Our old friend Ewald von Kleist addressed exactly the same point when he admitted that 'There were no plans for a prolonged struggle. Everything was based on the idea of a decisive result before the end of autumn 1941.' Having failed to achieve that 'decisive result', the generals' only answer was more of the same, another major offensive – but where, and to achieve what? Far more comfortable with conducting operations rather than grand strategy, the generals deferred to Hitler, who discounted the capture of Moscow or the wholesale destruction of the Red Army as strategic goals and instead settled on the subject he was confident he understood and his generals – to whom he felt a distinct intellectual inferiority, didn't – economics. While the 'gentlemen of the Greater German General Staff' talked of advances, envelopments and encirclements, he would talk of coal, steel and above all, oil. So as the weather warmed in the new year of 1942, the Wehrmacht took the offensive once more, although, inexplicably in Soviet eyes, the Nazis did not try to take Moscow but struck in the south, advancing towards the petroleum *Shangri-la* of the mysterious and mountainous Caucasus.

Effectively a huge land bridge between Europe and Asia Minor, bounded in the west by the Black Sea and in the east by the Caspian, the Caucasus is a vast region steeped in history and home to a multitude of peoples and ethnicities, both Christian and Moslem. A remote land, its most frequent visitors from the outside for a hundred years had been explorers and adventurers until the armies of the Romanov tsars had gobbled up piece after piece in the nineteenth century. Attempts to break free from Russian – then Soviet – domination had ended in bloody repression by the Kremlin, which became ever more determined to hang onto the region's mountains and valleys when it was discovered that under so much of it were endless lakes of oil. It was that natural bounty which had fuelled much of the Soviet Union's latent industrialisation, making her almost as oil-rich as the United States.

The Caucasus was, however, a long way away from even the *Ostheer*'s (German Army in the East) most forward positions. In fact, the distance from Gerd von Rundstedt's foremost units to the petroleum city of Baku on the Caspian was some 800 miles – a tad further than the old warhorse had managed to advance during

Barbarossa. To achieve such vast distances the Nazis massed a great host, made up not only of the best the Reich had to offer in this the third year of the war but also including four entire allied armies, armies that would play an enormously important role in the fighting to come.

Yet, as with *Barbarossa*, Berlin would underestimate what a successful offensive would require, and when the Red Army showed it had learnt its lessons from the previous summer and refused to stand and be annihilated in huge encirclements, the Germans found themselves in a cul-de-sac of their own making. Denied a single, shattering victory, the Nazi penchant for operational profligacy reared its head once more, as men and machines were sent in different directions with wildly differing objectives. Stalingrad was never one of those goals. The fact it became one was more due to happenstance and Hitler's innate stubbornness than any strategic plan. The fight for the city took on a life of its own. 6. *Armee* and its commander, Friedrich Paulus, would accidentally become the point of the spear, or *schwerpunkt*, in Germany's war in the East.

As it happened, Germany's 6. *Armee* was a martial machine of immense power, however the fighting in Stalingrad exposed the contradictions of what was then the Wehrmacht's largest field formation and also of its leader, an officer who excelled at staff work but was wildly out of his depth in Stalingrad. It was his conduct of the battle that hamstrung his army, not his soldiers' fragility in the white-hot heat of street fighting.

Paulus's answer to winning the battle throughout the autumn was the bludgeon and not the rapier, using immense firepower and sledgehammer assault to try and win through. Countering such a strategy wasn't easy, but neither was it complicated, and as the Red Army adapted, the Germans – and more specifically their commander – didn't. An operational machine of huge power and poise was wasted in piecemeal battles whose only real outcome was bloodletting on a titanic scale. The fastidious Paulus ended up burning out his divisions in a series of offensives that owed more to the attritional tactics of the First World War than the manoeuvre operations of the Second. It was those battles across the autumn months of September and October that fatally weakened 6. *Armee* and left it ripe for destruction.

Paulus's lack of imagination was in stark contrast to that of the Soviets as the Red Army launched *Operation Uranus* to cut off 6. *Armee* in mid-November. The success of *Uranus* has always been cited as showing the feeble nature of Nazi Germany's allies, but the reality is far more nuanced, with a number of Romanian units in particular putting up a stiff fight before their lack of air support and heavy weapons left them retreating in chaos.

Soviet success with *Uranus* should also be viewed in the context of the bloody failure of the offensive's big brother – *Operation Mars* – launched at much the same time and aimed at destroying *Heeresgruppe Mitte*'s (Army Group Centre) 9. *Armee* to the north. Far bigger than *Uranus*, *Mars* became an attritional blood bath for the Red Army with the German commander Walter Model acting with all the decisiveness and guile that Paulus so distinctly lacked, while the Soviets displayed the type of pig-headedness that the Nazis showed down south regarding Stalingrad.

With Paulus's army now surrounded, the chimera of an airlift appeared as the solution to the predicament. The subject of the Stalingrad airlift is just as complex and contradictory as much of the other major facets of the battle. The myth that it was Hitler's brainchild and that he rabidly insisted on sticking with it, turns out to be exactly that – a myth. Senior Luftwaffe figures were deeply implicated in what was obviously a flawed strategy but were keen to distance themselves from it when it inevitably went wrong, as were a number of army generals who initially felt the alternative break-out plan would be a costly mistake.

The second falsehood with the airlift is that it was the lack of food flown in that sealed the fate of 6. *Armee*. This is a vast simplification. Much more injurious to the trapped soldiers was the lack of ammunition and fuel. Those two items – far heavier and bulkier than loaves of *kommissbrot* (German Army ration bread) – were the key to 6. *Armee*'s survival. Most of the men could just about survive on the meagre rations available, at least initially, but with no bullets to fire or gasoline to move them and their heavy weapons around the battlefield, they were condemned to immobility and the occasional pot-shot at their besiegers. Artillery ammunition especially was the key. Gunners are invaluable in both defence and attack, and it is their high explosive and deadly shrapnel that dominate a static battle such as Stalingrad, but as their stocks of shells disappeared, so did 6. *Armee*'s hopes. In the end, the trapped survivors, Germans, Romanians, Croats and *Hiwis* (*Hilfswillige* – literally *willing helpers*),[1] had nothing left to fight with.

The battle they had fought was a grisly epic. Soviet losses were gargantuan and never truly admitted to, and for the Axis a total of five separate armies disappeared in the conflagration: two Romanian and one each from Germany, Italy and Hungary. Yet Germany fought on – as did her allies – and had another opportunity to turn the tide in the East the following summer at Kursk. Oil – ostensibly the reason for the 1942 summer offensive but one almost casually cast aside – remained a huge problem for the Nazis. Nevertheless, they survived until spring 1945 without the bounty from the Caucasus.

So, was Stalingrad the turning point so many thought it was, or was it not? Karl Dönitz, who would head Germany's Navy before taking over the government as head of State after Hitler's suicide, believed it was: 'After Stalingrad ... it was clear that we couldn't hope to win the war against Russia.' He was far from alone in his view. An internal security report compiled by the SS *Sicherheitsdienst* (SD – the SS security service) and dated 4 February 1943, just days after 6. *Armee*'s surrender, stated that 'There is a general conviction [among the civilian population] that Stalingrad signifies a turning point in the war.'[2] This is perhaps the most telling reflection of all on the battle. So grievous was the disaster for Germany that hardly a family in the country was untouched, everyone had a son, a father, uncle, cousin or nephew who perished at Stalingrad or who disappeared into a Soviet labour camp – tantamount to a death sentence. For the German people, for so long used to an almost endless enumeration of victories,

Stalingrad left an indelible mark on the national consciousness and struck at the very foundation stone of their belief in final victory.

Turning point or not, nothing can detract from the fact that even amid the unparalleled savagery of the Russo-German war on the Eastern Front, Stalingrad has a special place of horror in the human imagination. It wasn't a battle fought out in the middle of the open steppe, desert or jungle, but in the houses, factories and streets that so many of us today recognise in our own urban existence. The very name Stalingrad conjures up images of smoke, fire and rubble, with twisted girders lying atop mounds of shattered bricks – there's nothing glorious or romantic in it. This is the total and utter destruction of an entire army of men and their machines. This is the battle through the eyes of the Germans and their allies who fought it. This is Stalingrad.

NOTES ON THE TEXT

The Germans didn't actually reach the city of Stalingrad until August 1942, but I felt that to begin the narrative at that point was to do the whole campaign, of which Stalingrad was a part, a huge disservice, as well as to short-change the reader. To try and understand what happened at Stalingrad it is absolutely necessary to pick up the story months earlier, when all the key decisions were made that would end with 6. *Armee*'s destruction, not least the appointment of Friedrich Paulus as its commander. From then on, a chain of events would occur that seemed almost inevitably to lead to the final surrender in the snow. Which hazards the question, was the annihilation of 6. *Armee* inevitable? I don't believe so, but I will leave it to the reader to make his or her own judgement on that most vexed question. In such a battle as Stalingrad where the discussions and disagreements between senior military and political leaders is so relevant and so voluminous, I have taken the view that not to include much of what Hitler and his generals said or wrote at the time would be unhelpful, but at the same time I have been steadfast in my commitment to outweigh those mutterings with the words of those whose lives and deaths were – for me – the essence of the battle.

In terms of the narrative itself I have chosen to adopt a number of devices which, I hope, both improve the text itself and help the reader with the ebb and flow of the story. I appreciate that some readers may not agree with one or more of these, but I ask for forgiveness if that is the case.

Firstly, during the war most Germans used the term 'Russians' to cover everyone in the now-dissolved Soviet Union's Red Army and State, despite the multitude of nationalities and ethnic groups within it; for ease, I have followed suit.

Many place names have changed since the war; most notably in the former Soviet Union and regions that have since become part of other states; for example, those parts of what was the Soviet Union that are now modern Ukraine. I have applied a mix and match approach to this situation, with most place names given using their spelling at the time and then their modern name in brackets afterwards. There are some exceptions to this; I have kept Leningrad as the name of the besieged city in northern Russia rather than St Petersburg, and for obvious reasons I have used Stalingrad throughout rather than its modern name of Volgograd.

I have also adopted a similar approach to the writing of numbers. So, for some numbers I have used figures; '3, 512', while for others I have used words; 'half a million'. Again, I accept that this may be perplexing for some readers, but I ask for forbearance. My reasoning is that a narrative that is stuffed full of exact numbers gains in accuracy, but equally, loses as much, if not more, in its flow.

Regarding German military units I have used German nomenclature, for example the *71st Infantry Division* is written as *71. Infanterie-Division* or shortened to *71.ID*, and *kompanie*, *bataillon* for *company* and *battalion* when appropriate. I have also opted to use German ranks, so *Captain* is *Hauptmann*, *Colonel* is *Oberst* etc. The exception is where the holders are Waffen-SS members, and there I've used that organisation's own designation of *SS-Hauptsturmführer* and so on. There are a table of comparative German and British Army ranks in the appendix, although I have omitted a comparative table of Waffen-SS ranks as they are very rarely used here.

I also thought it would be helpful if readers understood in broad terms what German units looked like in terms of numbers. Units – or sub-units when we talk of companies, battalions and so on – have so-called 'establishments', this is the strength the sub-unit or unit is meant to have on paper and against which equipment tables, ration rolls etc are measured. However, helpful though it is to know what the establishment is, the fact remains that numbers in a military formation are more useful as a guide rather than a hard-and-fast rule, especially during a conflict like the Russo-German one where often appalling casualties were a constant fact of life. Having said that, although a guide may not be accurate to the exact number, it is still useful.

A German Army would usually be composed of anywhere between two to five Corps, with a Corps comprising two to three divisions. Each infantry division (the mainstay of the Army) would contain between 12-17,000 men, although occasionally the odd one may be larger and edge towards 19-20,000 men. Each division would comprise three infantry regiments with an artillery regiment and supporting sub-units of engineers, signals, logistics and so on. Panzer divisions would be different, as were light infantry (*jäger*) or specialist mountain divisions. A German regiment was about the same size as a British brigade, with three battalions of approximately 800-1,000 men each, although a battalion's strength could be as low as six hundred. Each battalion would be led by a *Major* (major) and would dispose of four rifle companies of 200 men each, with an additional support company equipped with heavy weapons including mortars, machine-guns, light cannons and anti-tank guns. A company – usually commanded by a *Hauptmann* (captain) – would have four platoons each of around 40 men with a single officer in charge – a *Leutnant* (lieutenant) – though in many cases the platoons would be led by a senior NCO such as a sergeant as no officer was available to command.

I

BARBAROSSA FAILS

His fingers were steepled under his chin, his gaze fixed intently on the wall opposite, but without focus, as he mulled over the document lying on the vast desk in front of him. He removed the round-rimmed spectacles that no-one outside his inner circle knew he wore; no photographer was allowed to snap him wearing them to maintain his carefully cultivated public image of invulnerability. Then he sat back, absently leafing through the double-spaced pages with their oversized type, not really looking at them, the details already imprinted in his memory.

The report bore the official stamp of the *Fremde Heere Ost* (FHO – Enemy Armies East) department, and its new boss, the vulpine-featured *Oberstleutnant* Reinhard Gehlen, drafted in to replace Eberhard Kinzel, whose manifest failures during the previous year's *Barbarossa* campaign had seen him banished to the *Führerreserve* (pool of semi-retired officers awaiting reassignment – which sometimes never came). Those failures were manifold and included a chronic underestimate by the monocled Kinzel of VVS numbers (*Voyenno-Vozdushnye Sily*, literally 'Military Air Forces' – the Red Airforce) and the existence of the superlative Soviet T-34 tank, but it was his inability to foresee Moscow's rapid mobilisation of millions of men with barely a fortnight's training, armed with one rifle between two and ropes instead of trouser belts, that was most damning. The Red Army had then suffered losses on a scale never before seen in the history of warfare, but those same ill-equipped masses had blunted the Nazi invasion force, wearing it down and exhausting it even before it made its last-gasp lunge at Moscow.

That final offensive – *Operation Taifun* (Typhoon) – had failed utterly. Its strike force *Heeresgruppe Mitte* [Army Group Centre] had been caught in the winter snows without food, fuel, ammunition or proper clothing, and a Soviet counter-offensive made them pay the price. The *Barbarossa* invasion host – without doubt the strongest force the Wehrmacht ever assembled in the war – died in those snows, its best formations in the air and on the ground left decimated. Against his generals' advice, Hitler ordered his panicking troops to hold where they were, digging into the frozen earth of the open steppe if they had to. His decision saved the army, but German casualty lists were jaw-dropping, and there were further 'losses' as swathes of senior officers were sacked by a dictator who had lost faith in the officer corps.

The axed generals included the likes of Gerd von Rundstedt, the doyen of the old Prussian military caste that had formed the backbone of the German state since before Bismarck's unification wars, and Heinz Guderian, the self-appointed father of Germany's much vaunted *panzerwaffe* (panzer arm). Among the other 40-odd officers sent packing were Fedor von Bock and Wilhelm von Leeb – Rundstedt's fellow army group commanders – and Erich Hoepner, a panzer army leader like Guderian. The biggest beast of them all though was undoubtedly Walther von Brauchitsch, the *Oberbefehlshaber* (Commander-in-Chief) of the Army itself. The totally dispirited Brauchitsch was replaced in post by none other than Hitler himself who believed his intuition - and First World War frontline experience as a messenger with the rank of corporal - made him the ideal candidate to wield such immense power. Adolf Hitler was now the self-proclaimed *Oberkommandierender der Wehrmacht* (Supreme Commander of the Armed Forces).

Just as his nemesis Stalin had done in the 1930s – though without resorting to show trials and wholesale executions – Hitler had now purged his army of a cohort of its most senior figures and left the remainder cowed and unwilling to challenge him.

Accepting that *Barbarossa* had failed, before they were sacked Rundstedt and Leeb had called for the Wehrmacht to withdraw back to the old Polish frontier and perhaps even seek some sort of settlement with Moscow, but their perceived failure and subsequent enforced retirement had muted their voices. With only Alfred Jodl and Wilhelm Keitel, *Lakeitel* (*lackey*, a pun on his name) as he was known, whom even Hitler described as having the 'brains of a movie usher' left in his entourage, the last man standing in military terms who had any real hope of influencing the Nazi leader was Franz Halder. A thoroughly professional officer, Halder was also prone to erratic mood swings, oscillating wildly between an ecstatic belief in total victory and portents of ruinous defeat. Deeply compromised already by his failure to stand up to Hitler at any point, his advice for the *Ostheer* to hold where it was in the East and use the year to consolidate their gains was easily brushed aside. Hitler, and Hitler alone, would make the final decision as to what the *Ostheer* would do in 1942, and his decision was enshrined in the leather-bound report sitting on his desk.

Now, with the Soviet bear finally floundering in the spring thaw, a momentous decision faced the man who was now Nazi Germany's highest military as well as political leader. With the next campaigning season just round the corner, what strategic choices would Nazi Germany make? The French Mediterranean and Atlantic coasts were both secure and RAF Bomber Command's raids over the Reich were a nuisance but nothing more. The Wehrmacht was involved in a bitter insurgency against communist Partisans in the dismembered limbs of Yugoslavia, but locally raised fascist militias, collaborators and the Italians were doing the bulk of the fighting. The only theatre of note that German forces were engaged in outside of the Soviet Union was in North Africa, where Erwin Rommel's *Panzerarmee Afrika* was going backwards and forwards across Egypt and northern Libya dependent on when reinforcements and resupply arrived. The *Kriegsmarine* was trying to interdict Great Britain's vital supply routes across the Atlantic, and at the same time sink Allied aid convoys to Soviet ports, but Hitler was an elephant and not a whale and had no affinity with the warfare of the sea. That left Russia, where the situation was messy to say the least.

Georg von Küchler's *Heeresgruppe Nord* (Army Group North) – forever the runt of the *Ostheer* litter – was embroiled in a battle on the River Volkhov as the Soviets tried to break the siege of Leningrad, while Günther von Kluge's *Heeresgruppe Mitte* was still burying its dead and counting the cost of *Taifun*'s failure. That left *Heeresgruppe Süd* (Army Group South), in many ways the odd man out of the *Ostheer*'s three major military groupings. Odd, because it alone had more or less achieved its *Barbarossa* objectives, having captured Ukraine and annihilated the bulk of the forces facing it at the cataclysmic battle of Kiev, and odd because its order of battle included all the major allied Axis formations involved in the East.

Gehlen's report didn't talk about Axis forces in the East however, his branch of intelligence was specifically assigned to assess and analyse Moscow's military machine, so Hitler and his generals could decide on an appropriate course of action, and Gehlen was clear: the lengthy string of defeats in the 1941 campaign had gutted Soviet strength. The Wehrmacht genius for destructive encirclement battles (in German *vernichtungsschlachten*) had resulted in a staggering twenty-two of them across the western republics of the Soviet Union, with the Red Army losing over 25,000 guns and well in excess of 14,000 tanks. The human cost had been colossal: at least two million dead and wounded to add to the three million-plus who'd shuffled into captivity only to be left to die of starvation, thirst and disease by a German military administration which turned neglect into near genocide. Gehlen's main point was that as a result of these losses, Soviet frontline strength had been reduced to around four million men, and that Germany could now finally see the bottom of Moscow's manpower barrel, with as few as two million men left to call up in eligible age classes.[1] He went on to expound on his view that the Red Army's winter counter-offensives had, in fact, fatally weakened it with unprecedented losses among its ranks, which Moscow was struggling to fill. Indeed, the diminutive intelligence officer was so convinced of this analysis he briefed the students of Berlin's War Academy that 'the enemy can no longer withstand losses such as he took in the battles of Bialystok and Vyazma-Bryansk [June and October 1941]. He also cannot ... throw reserves onto the scales the way he did in the winter.'

This view would prevail throughout the summer and beyond with a follow-on FHO report from 9 September further claiming the Soviets had no reserves left worth speaking of. As a senior SS officer said at the time, 'Our Wehrmacht leaders, confident in their offensive power and the superiority of their strategic and tactical commands, still underestimated the ... strength of the Red Army ... the immense area of the Russian steppes and the climatic conditions of the country.'

Gehlen's hugely over-optimistic report was exactly what Hitler wanted to hear. He had no interest in a thorough examination and analysis of what had gone wrong with *Barbarossa* – the truth would be unpalatable – instead, he wanted to believe that the Nazis were within an ace of victory, and his intelligence boss was telling him exactly that. When one senior officer contradicted this view and told Hitler that credible sources were saying that the Soviet Union was now outproducing Germany in tanks, with more than 600 a month rolling off Soviet production lines, the dictator slammed his fist on the table and shouted 'Impossible!' As far as he was concerned, 'The Army need only hit the Russian a few heavy blows ... Then you will see that the Russian colossus is standing on feet of clay.'

Now, leaning back in his chair in his cavernous Chancellery office, Hitler could be forgiven for smiling as he tapped the leather-bound cover of Gehlen's report; he'd been right all along, Stalin's Red Army was a busted flush and the German Army's own intelligence had proved it. There would be no contrary views or dissenting voices, after all, there was no-one left in any position of authority to challenge him. Walther von Brauchitsch – hopelessly financially compromised by a bitter divorce even before his sacking – was now languishing in obscurity, while Wilhelm Keitel and Alfred Jodl, OKW Chief (*Oberkommando der Wehrmacht* – Armed Forces High Command) and Chief of OKW Operations Staff respectively, were yes-men. Only Franz Halder as Chief of Staff of the Army High Command (*Oberkommando des Heeres* – OKH) raised any sort of objection to Gehlen's report, remembering his own astonishment at the Red Army's incredible ability to regenerate after colossal losses, but he didn't press the point and instead let himself be silenced by Hitler's optimism, just as he had the previous summer.

A dark stain tarnished that optimism, however, and that stain had a name – oil – or rather Nazi Germany's lack of it. Back in 1917 the irascible French Prime Minister, Georges Clemenceau, had written to US President Woodrow Wilson exclaiming that in war gasoline was just as important as blood, and twenty-five years later Adolf Hitler held that view wholeheartedly. The problem was that the Third Reich only had a small domestic supply from a few Austrian wells, while the power of the British Royal Navy cut Germany off from world oil markets. Foreseeing the problem as far back as August 1936, Hitler had ordered Goering – as head of Nazi Germany's economic Four-Year Plan – to prepare the Reich for a war that would begin no earlier than 1940, and in which oil would be critical to victory.

Goering's strategy called for internal production to be ramped up to some one million tons annually, with the heavy lifting done by science and imports. The former was synthetic oil manufacture; a process of extracting oil from coal that Germany had pioneered, and although ruinously expensive was furnishing Berlin with 2.7 million tons by 1940. That number had grown again the following year and would reach an astonishing four million tons in 1942. However, with annual wartime consumption running at some 7.5 million tons,[2] it still wasn't enough.

The gap was plugged by imports. A fraction came from Hungary's small oil deposits, while almost 600,000 tons was shipped from the Soviet Union as part of the economic agreements signed alongside the Nazi-Soviet Non-Aggression Pact of 1939. The lion's share came from the Kingdom of Romania. The Romanian oil fields, centred on the southern city of Ploieşti, were the largest in Europe and in the early 1930s were supplying Germany with around half a million tons per year. This figure had tripled by 1941[3] and explained Hitler's paranoia about Soviet bombing raids from the Crimea and southern Russia against what was a vital resource. Indeed, a VVS attack on 13 July 1941 on Ploieşti's Orion refinery had set some seventeen storage tanks ablaze in a fire that took over twenty-four hours to be brought under control. The result was over 9,000 tons of precious oil lost. Berlin's response was to station large numbers of fighters in the region, specifically tasked with protecting oil installations. In four months, the assigned Luftwaffe pilots shot down 143 Soviet bombers over the area, decimating the VVS bomber fleet and shielding the industry.

The launch of *Barbarossa* of course cut off the imports from the Soviet Union, but the Germans replaced them by stealing the reserves of their newly conquered European empire. Across Scandinavia and western Europe, German teams surveyed the contents of oil depots and storage facilities, confiscating most and leaving the local populations increasingly reliant on bicycles and horses for transport and crippling already fragile economies. France was the biggest victim, stripped of her strategic reserves and left to subsist on just 8 per cent of her pre-war consumption.

In all, the Nazis stole 600,000 tons of oil from the French, Belgians, Dutch *et al*, but this was a one-off. By March 1941 Georg Thomas – a general and military economist heading up the War Economy and Armaments Office in Berlin – authored a report forecasting that the demands of the war effort would mean the Reich would be reduced to using its own carefully husbanded strategic oil reserves by late October that same year.[4] Those reserves were pretty meagre, and throughout the war never exceeded three million tons – less than six months' consumption.

Even more of a problem was the poor state of much of Romania's drilling capacity. Lack of investment in equipment and new well exploration meant Romanian production was actually declining at exactly the time the Nazi war machine was crying out for an increase, with total yield falling from 8.7 million tons in 1937 to 5.6 million in 1941. Impassioned Nazi exhortations to the Romanian military dictator, Ion Antonescu, only brought the reply that 'Romania has given the maximum which it is in her power to give, she can give no more.'[5] Antonescu wasn't exaggerating; to keep up exports to the Reich he had been forced to cut the amount of oil available for domestic use to just 20 per cent of peacetime levels, crippling the kingdom's infant industrial sector in particular. Germany had done much the same and had also requisitioned the majority of the country's civilian vehicle fleet for military use, and while this helped to cut demand, the lack of oil products seriously hampered armaments production.

Neither were Germany and Romania the only Axis nations suffering from lack of oil, as the Italian Fascist Foreign Minister, Count Galeazzo Ciano, wrote in his diary in the summer of 1941; 'There is only one dark spot – the lack of oil. Just now we have barely a hundred thousand tons...' In contrast to Axis scarcity, Britain imported ten million tons of oil from the United States in 1942, as well as additional amounts from the fields in Iran and Iraq in the Middle East – the lights were never in danger of going out over Great Britain.

In Hitler's mind the answer to the Reich's oil problem was simple – the Caucasus. The Soviet republics of the Caucasus were awash with oil. The Grozny and Maykop fields (the former in modern-day Chechnya and the latter in Russian Adygea) both produced around two million tons per annum, while far-off Baku in Soviet Azerbaijan churned out an eye-watering twenty-four million tons in 1942.[6] That oil was shipped by tanker to Astrakhan and then by barge north along the River Volga to the very heart of Soviet Russia.

As early as 31 July 1940, Hitler had proposed seizing the Caucasus oil fields at a war planning conference at the Berghof, his mountain retreat near Berchtesgaden in the Bavarian Alps. His plan envisaged a pincer movement, with one arm coming south from Russia and the other a northern drive by Rommel's African forces. Outrageous though this idea clearly was, it was one that was widely bought into by the men of the *Barbarossa* invasion host. On the eve of the attack the previous summer, the panzer crewman, Richard von Rosen, mused on what he and his fellow tankers were doing sitting in a Polish forest on the Soviet border: '...either the USSR would allow us free passage into Persia or Iraq ... or we were to relieve Rommel.' The Messerschmitt Bf 110 pilot Johannes Kaufmann believed 'We were part of a gigantic pincer movement designed to trap the British and Free French forces operating in the Middle East. The southern arm of the pincer was to be provided by the German and Italian troops in North Africa.' A young Otto Skorzeny also speculated that

> ...our objective would be the oil fields of the Persian Gulf. Russia would grant the German Army free passage and we would march across the Caucasus into Iran... Another rumour was that we would march via Turkey into Egypt and surround the English Near-East Army in a pincer action.

The would-be Waffen-SS commando packed a copy of T.E. Lawrence's *The Seven Pillars of Wisdom*, just in case.

Hitler wasn't alone in his obsession with oil as he pondered his next move in the spring of 1942. In response to a warning on the shortage of oil from the commander of the Wehrmacht Reserve Army and head of its armaments supply office, Friedrich Fromm,[7] Alfred Jodl's *Wehrmachtführungsstab* (Wfst – Armed Forces Operations Staff) penned a report that stated:

> The supply of crude oil will be one of the weakest spots in our defence capacity during the next year... The shortage of crude oil of all kinds has reached a level that restricts the operational freedom of the Army, the Luftwaffe and the Kriegsmarine, and hampers war production.

Georg Thomas was even more forthright, telling Goering and Keitel: 'One thing is now clear ... without Russian oil the German war machine must from now on become increasingly impotent.'

Back in early 1941 the response from the Reich's ineffective military intelligence branch – the *Abwehr* – was to form a unit of about one hundred men, including some anti-communist Georgian émigrés, to make a dash to the Caucasus oil fields the moment the Soviet Union began to disintegrate. There, they would secure the oil wells and bring them back into production as quickly as possible for the benefit of the Reich. When *Barbarossa* fell short, the unit was left sitting on its hands in its Romanian base, but with the possible seizure of the Caucasus fields climbing the Nazi agenda once more, it was given a new lease of life and greatly expanded to become the *Mineralöl Brigade Kaukasus* (Oil Brigade Caucasus).[8]

For Hitler, the stars seemed to be aligning. In his mind's eye he could see a rejuvenated and reinforced *Heeresgruppe Süd* striking east before cutting south into the Caucasus. With the fate of much of the Soviet Union's oil supply on the line, Moscow would have no choice but to despatch every available division it had to the region, only for the Germans to trap and destroy them in a series of encirclement battles, just as they had the previous year. Once victorious, *Heeresgruppe Süd* would seize its oil field objectives, leaving the rump of the Red Army to wither on the vine from lack of fuel. Moscow and Leningrad would then fall into the Nazis' lap with little effort, and the Soviet Union and its bolshevist system would be consigned to history. The die was cast.

Hitler announced his intentions at a leadership conference in March where he instructed Halder to prepare a suitable plan. He followed this up a few short weeks later by issuing *Führerbefehl Nr. 41* (Führer Directive No. 41) on 5 April 1942. The big news in the Directive was that *Heeresgruppe Mitte* – the fulcrum of the entire Nazi war effort in the East – was to make no moves toward Moscow and instead maintain a wholly defensive posture throughout the entire summer and autumn. To the north, *Heeresgruppe Nord*, now in the final stages of crushing the Red Army's over ambitious Volkov offensive, was to capture Leningrad and link up with the Finns but make no other advances east. This would leave *Heeresgruppe Süd* to launch *Fall Blau* – Case Blue – Nazi Germany's main military effort in 1942.

Of huge significance given later events, the capture of Stalingrad was specifically not listed as an objective for the offensive. In fact, in the entire Directive the city is only mentioned twice and then only in general terms: '...formations thrusting down the Don River can link up in the Stalingrad area [and] forces should finally establish contact with the armoured forces advancing on Stalingrad.' The Directive is very clear on what *Fall Blau* was designed to achieve, and it wasn't the capture of Stalingrad:

> The enemy has suffered severe losses in men and material ...
> during the winter he has expended the bulk of his reserves
> intended for future operations... Our aim is to wipe out the
> entire defence potential remaining to the Soviets.

One senior officer was very clear in his understanding of the plan: 'The capture of Stalingrad was subsidiary to the main aim... Stalingrad was no more than a name on a map to us.' Reinhard Gehlen's controversial assessment of the parlous state of the Red Army had become the prime motivator for yet another throw of the dice from the gambler in the Reich Chancellery. Those dice would land in quicksand.

For Halder and his planners, many of the same problems *Barbarossa* faced were replicated with *Fall Blau*. First was the issue of distance. From the German's main logistics base at Kharkov (modern-day Kharkiv) to Baku on the shores of the Caspian Sea is around one thousand miles, far beyond what the Germans had been able to cover the previous year during *Barbarossa*. That vast distance encompassed huge swathes of sun-scorched steppe, numerous rivers both large and small, and some of the Soviet Union's great cities such as Voronezh and Rostov-on-Don. Beyond that lay the jagged peaks of the Caucasus mountains, snow-topped for much of the year, the interior accessible only by a small number of narrow passes. Amidst the tumble of peaks towers Elbrus, the highest mountain in Europe, 18,510 feet at the summit. To cover such enormous distances, and fight and win battles in such varied terrain, would require a huge force with a multiplicity of skills and equipment.

Secondly, writ large to anyone with a map, was the vulnerability of a northern flank for the offensive that would only get bigger as the Germans advanced. Guderian's *Panzergruppe* 2 had gotten away with a similar – though smaller – exposure during the Kiev operation back in August, but only just.

Well aware of the problems, Halder's team devised one of the most complex plans of the war, with the offensive broken down into no fewer than four separate phases. First, the Germans would advance east, defeating the bulk of the Soviet forces facing them, and reach the River Volga. Once there a mass of forces would form a hard shoulder as it were, while the majority of the offensive's mobile and armoured formations would break off and head south into the Caucasus and seize the oil fields.

The generalship required to pull off such an astonishingly complicated operation would be truly breathtaking, and to deliver it Hitler turned to Fedor von Bock – a man the dictator had relieved of his command the preceding year. To be fair, Bock wasn't Hitler's first choice, which had been Walter von Reichenau, one of Nazi Germany's most controversial general officers, and a man who inspired admiration and loathing in equal measure. If he had been English, Reichenau might have been called 'eccentric', and indeed like so many German officers of his generation he professed an affinity with his Anglo-Saxon cousins, insisting on wearing Saville Row suits when at home and indulging personally in all manner of English public school sports, including boxing. He had been an early supporter of Hitler and the Nazis, though more from opportunism than ideology, and had led 6. *Armee* during the *Barbarossa* campaign. Vain and ambitious, he desperately wanted to reach the very pinnacle of command and had been slated to replace Brauchitsch until a host of other senior officers made plain to Hitler they would refuse to serve under a man who made no secret of his willingness to clamber over anyone and everyone to reach the top. Elevated to army group command when his boss Gerd von Rundstedt had been sacked, the monocled Reichenau had gone on one of his habitual cross-country runs in sub-zero temperatures in mid-January, only to collapse from a massive heart attack an hour or so later after a light lunch. Five days later he had not regained consciousness and was close to death. The decision was made to fly him to a specialist facility in Leipzig and a medical team were put on standby. Strapped into an armchair for safety, the unconscious *feldmarschall* was carried aboard a transport aircraft at Poltava and flown west, only for the plane to crash en route. His body was found among the wreckage, his bejewelled *feldmarschall's* baton lying beside him, snapped in two.

Full of contradictions – he supported German Jewish First World War veterans against Nazi attacks while originating his so-called 'Severity Order', which helped pave the way for the mass murder of Soviet Jews during *Barbarossa* – Reichenau's conduct of the planned campaign would without doubt have been radically different from Bock's, but instead *Fall Blau* was left to 'the holy fire of Küstrin', as the tall and vainglorious Bock was known throughout the Army. Universally described as capable but not brilliant, Bock was unpopular personally, distant from his men and discordant with subordinates and peers alike – he and Guderian couldn't stand each other and Leeb and Rundstedt had little good to say about him, Leeb in particular thought him a martinet. His failure to successfully prosecute *Taifun* and capture Moscow had been his undoing in 1941, but fate had now handed him an opportunity for redemption if he could lead *Heeresgruppe Süd* to victory in 1942.

Just as with *Taifun* back in October, Bock was once more in command of the most powerful of Nazi Germany's groupings on the Eastern Front, a force whose organisation and composition would to a large extent dictate the campaign that would follow.

2

ARMY GROUP SOUTH – GERMANY'S HOPE

The *Barbarossa* invasion force had been a true leviathan. The Nazis 1935 *National Defence Regulations,* and the accompanying rearmament programme, combined to produce an ever-growing trio of armed services, while a series of short and successful campaigns from 1939 onwards gave those same services an invaluable bedrock of experience. By invasion day, some three and a half million Germans stood massed on the border, alongside almost half a million allied soldiers, boasting three and a half thousand panzers and supported by over seven thousand guns and nigh on three thousand aircraft.

As it turned out, lack of mobility soon became a major problem for the invaders, their 600,000 motorised vehicles and equivalent number of horses simply not enough to sustain the advance. Tenacious Soviet resistance and the dire state of the country's transport infrastructure hobbled *Barbarossa*, the *Ostheer* losing one in six of its vehicles by the end of 1941 including 41,000 precious trucks – the work horses of the German logistics system. Of the actual horses, half were dead, some 180,000 lost in the winter months alone. Ammunition stocks were down to just a third of their June 1941 levels, and fuel supplies were much the same. The panzer fleet had suffered terribly having lost 3,252 tanks by early January, and only having received 1,138 replacements, many of them plundered Czech models.[1] Taking into account serious serviceability issues, the sixteen panzer divisions on the Eastern Front at the beginning of 1942 could only muster around 140 operational tanks in total – less than a single division's roster at the same time the previous year.

The human toll had been even more devastating, with just under one million men listed as killed, wounded or missing. Losses were concentrated in the fighting formations and in their frontline companies, with the minority of mobile formations hardest hit. Swathes of trained specialists – drivers, panzer crew, gunners, signallers and combat engineers (*pioniere*) – were gone, along with almost thirty thousand officers, mainly at platoon, company and battalion level. The atrocious winter weather had wreaked havoc, with over 100,000 cases of frostbite, 14,000 of those requiring an amputation of some kind: fingers, toes, nose or ears.[2] The panzer crewman Gustav Winter lost the little fingers on each of his hands, 'also the tip of my nose, and my toes were damaged as well.' Little wonder the Nazis' Minister for Propaganda, Joseph Goebbels, wrote in his diary that Hitler 'became quite grey ... merely talking about the cares of the winter makes him seem to have aged very much'. Back home in the Reich the term 'Russian Front' had become synonymous with a near death sentence. Draftees warned off for service in the East found themselves treated as condemned men by friends and relatives alike, with pity at their fate an almost universal reaction. Having been stunned by the staggeringly long casualty lists from the failure of *Barbarossa* and *Taifun*, for the very first time in the war members of the Wehrmacht began to try and engineer postings in the safety of occupied Europe, even preferring the wilds of Yugoslavia to the dreaded vastness of Russia.

An OKH report prepared for Halder in March 1942, as Hitler contemplated the summer campaign, assessed that of the 162 *Ostheer* divisions, only eight were at that time able to mount offensive operations, another three could do so after a short period of rest, while forty-seven were capable of limited attacks – all the others were only deemed suitable for defence.[3]

If the Germans had been bled white in 1941, what of her allies, what of the other Axis forces who had taken part in the failed invasion? If anything, they were in an even worse state than their Teutonic comrades. The Romanians had made the largest contribution to *Barbarossa* – two entire armies – but having taken 100,000 casualties capturing the port city of Odessa on the Black Sea, their formations were hollowed out. The Slovaks had restructured their poorly equipped Slovak Army Corps into two far smaller divisions, one for frontline action and the other for rear area security duties, with the rest of the troops sent home. The Hungarian's grandiosely titled Carpathian Group had marched and looted its way across Ukraine, suffering heavy losses while having to be kept separate from the Romanians, whom the Magyars detested far more than they did the Soviets.

As for the three divisions of the Italian *CSIR* (*Corpo di Spedizione Italiano in Russia* – Italian Expeditionary Corps in Russia) they had limped ever eastwards in boots 'flimsier than ballerina shoes', armed with First World War vintage rifles and carrying grenades that were just as likely to kill the thrower as the intended target. In all, Germany's allies had sent twenty divisions and thirteen brigades into the Soviet Union, plus over two hundred aircraft, and their reward had been lengthy casualty lists and disgruntled populations bemoaning what many viewed as Germany's war and not theirs.

In truth, the *Barbarossa* invasion force had died in 1941. Both in personnel and in every equipment category imaginable, it had suffered harrowing losses with little or no requisite replenishment from the homeland, and it was still losing men, panzers and guns in the fighting on the Volkhov in the north. The numbers made for grim reading for the staff officers in Berlin's Bendlerblock.[4] There were officially only 500,000 recruits in the Reich's 1942 age class, but the *Ostheer* alone was short of its establishment by 625,000 and the Wehrmacht's planners had scheduled an overall growth in the nation's armed forces from five million men to 5.8 million to cope with the growing strains of the war. Key equipment categories were in much the same position as the manpower graph; in 1939 German industry was building just 62 panzers a month, this had risen to 182 by the end of 1941, and to 356 by 1942, but this barely kept up with ongoing losses and would mean almost an entire year's production would be needed to replenish the *Ostheer* fully. Clearly, there was no chance of a renewal of the three-pronged offensive that had been *Barbarossa*'s signature – there simply weren't the men and machines for that – so the Reich would gird its loins for a single, all-powerful thrust in the summer of 1942, a thrust Hitler fervently believed would bring the attainment of the objectives set by his Directive; and one which would be delivered by *Heeresgruppe Süd*.

This would mean making some difficult decisions in the spring of '42, but with *Blau* given top priority, Nazi Germany set about preparing *Heeresgruppe Süd* the best it could. First on the list was a rebuild of the backbone of the *Ostheer*, its infantry divisions. Cut to around half their establishment by the bitter fighting over the previous eight or so months, all fully trained infantry replacements from the Reich's training depots were sent to Bock's army group. One such recruit was Günter Koschorrek from north-western Germany near the Danish border. Rumbling into southern Russia on a troop train he noted in his diary: 'We were about 300 freshly trained, 18-year-old recruits ... rushed through preliminary training at the Stablak centre in East Prussia.' Yet to experience the horror of combat, Koschorrek thought he and his compatriots had 'a first-rate attitude ... and we felt extremely proud to have finally passed out and be considered fully fledged frontline soldiers.' Among them were 'Hans Weichert, who is always hungry ... a tall fellow called Warias... Then there is Küpper, a muscular guy with fair hair ... quiet, sensible Grommel... Heinz Kurat who plays the harmonica and Otto Wilke who uses every free moment to play cards.' They all remembered the six months of 'harsh training' but with heads full of youthful idealism they were now looking forward to 'a new era, a new adventure, a great future'.[5] Russia would soon disabuse them of all those notions.

Men like Koschorrek and his comrades were the products of a highly militarised society, having been through time in the *Hitlerjugend* (HJ – Hitler Youth), followed by service in the paramilitary *Reichsarbeitsdienst* (RAD – compulsory Reich Labour

Service), then full army training. Many would also carry out a stint in a *Marschbataillon* in occupied territory before joining a regular *Feldeinheit* (field unit) controlled by the eighteen new *Reserve-Divisionen*, which had replaced the previous training formations, where they carried out anti-partisan and local security tasks to accustom them to combat. At that point they would then finally go forward to take their place in the line. By no means would all draftees follow this process step by step, but even if some of the latter elements were skipped, the result was still a fit and capable individual used to the strictures of military life and suitably trained and qualified for his designated role.

Ideally, in preparation for the forthcoming offensive, Berlin hoped to rotate divisions out of the line and back to designated rehabilitation areas where they could rest, marry up with their reinforcements, replenish their arsenals and carry out work-up training. For Bock's men their assigned zone behind the line centred on Dnepropetrovsk (modern-day Dnipro in Ukraine), an industrial city chosen for its still usable pre-war Red Army facilities. For the men of *Heeresgruppe Süd*, the rehabilitation programme brought blessed relief as division after division boarded the transport that took them to the suddenly busy barracks on the banks of the River Dnieper. The tired and filthy veterans of the *Barbarossa* campaign were then de-loused, and many had their old uniforms burnt and new ones issued.

Those new uniforms were a sign of the times. Gone was all the fancy pleating and extraneous piping of the previously ubiquitous *M41 feldbluse* (field jacket), replaced instead by the far plainer *M42* made using more synthetic and recycled material. Changed too was that totemic symbol of the German soldier, the jackboot, the *Marschstiefel* to give it its proper name, or *knobelbecher* ('dice shakers') as the men themselves nicknamed them. All-leather, expensive and time-consuming to manufacture, the new jackboot was reduced in height from 41cm down to 29cm and restricted for issue to combat infantrymen only, but even then there weren't enough to go round, so far cheaper ankle boots and gaiters swiftly became the norm. The infantryman's boots and jacket were not the only pieces of personal equipment to get a makeover, out went the old style *M35* helmet and in came a new, cut-down version with the rolled edges removed, a cheaper paint finish and simplified inner lining. The Germans were cutting their cloth accordingly.

The opportunity for a good sleep and some proper food away from the dangers of the front was welcomed, but not all aspects of the rehabilitation centres found favour with the *landsers*. Helmut Paulus and his comrades in Otto Röttig's *198. Infanterie-Division* had been fighting since day one of the invasion when they had crossed the River Prut on the Romanian border in inflatable dinghies. Now, taken out of the line on the River Mius to prepare for *Blau*, they found themselves having to take part in extensive training exercises, often with live ammunition, which resulted in what they considered to be completely avoidable casualties. After another day sweating on a long route march, his *kompanie* were able to relax and watch the screening of a comedy film, *The Merry Vagabonds*, although 'laughter has become rare amongst us ... if you think that pretty much every one of us has at least ten dead Russians on his conscience.'

 · Paulus, very close to his family and the apple of his mother's eye, was also worried about the news from home that food was getting scarcer, particularly potatoes, and that despite his strenuous objections his mother still insisted on sending him her tiny chocolate ration.[6] He also noted that his division received some fresh faces – around a thousand of them – all looking very young and very nervous. They were the promised reinforcements for all the rehabilitated formations, although the not so good news was that some of them had only received a few months training, and a few just eight weeks.

A lack of fully trained men wasn't an issue in Hans Heinz Rehfeldt's *Grossdeutschland*, the Army's premier motorised infantry division. An all-volunteer formation, the *Grossdeutschland* could take its pick of the litter to fill the ranks. 'Our *kompanie* has received reinforcements and we are fully up to strength ... our workshops haven't been idle either and all our trucks and cars have been repaired as much as possible.' Unlike Helmut Paulus and his comrades, Rehfeldt didn't mind the training exercises: 'The steep banks of the Dnieper are perfect for training ... memories of our recruit time came flooding back, and in the afternoons we played sports in glorious weather.'

While the *Grossdeutschland*'s surfeit of replacements was the envy of the army group, all the other infantry divisions were forced to make compromises to fill their regiments. Under instruction from OKH, divisional commands restructured their supply sub-units into four smaller columns, releasing spare men – drivers, cooks and signallers – to be drafted into the line. One such 'volunteer' was Gustav Kaminski. Kaminski was a highly trained signaller in Friedrich-Georg Eberhardt's superb *60. Infanterie-Division (mot.)* who found himself on parade with the rest of his comrades to hear the '*kompanie* commander announce that everyone who was not essential was being transferred to the infantry. A total of fourteen of us had to hand in our surplus equipment...we were given a short course as machine-gunners.' Another NCO in a veteran infantry division remembered:

Division issued a new order: supply, the workshops, administration and so on had to prune their staffs for anybody able to use a weapon and send them to the fighting units ... we received twenty men, amongst them five *unteroffiziere* from the *feldgendarmerie* [field police] and a veterinary *leutnant*.

This process, known as 'combing out', was unsurprisingly very unpopular with the men affected, who now found themselves among grizzled *frontschwein* ('front swine', as veterans called themselves) who took every opportunity to remind their new comrades of the deadly dangers they would soon face.

As for *Heeresgruppen Mitte* and *Nord*, they were not immune to the needs of their southern neighbour and were under strict orders from Berlin to make sacrifices for the proposed offensive. Both were forced to give up cadres of experienced veterans and send them south to reinforce Bock, and much of their equipment went with them. All *Mitte* and *Nord* received in return were 200,000 raw recruits fresh from their *Wehrkreise* (German administrative recruit areas) with barely a few weeks basic training behind them. It would be down to *Mitte* and *Nord* to train them in the field. Needless to say, this crop of newbies wasn't nearly enough either to fill the gaps left by the winter battles or compensate for the reassigned veterans, so a good number of the two army groups' infantry divisions had no option but to disband their third rifle regiment – if they were still lucky enough to have one – and stick to a two regiment-strength, relying on their artillery to keep the Soviets at bay.

At least *Heeresgruppe Mitte*'s units were able to rotate out of the line to their designated rehabilitation centres set up near Orsha, Minsk, Gomel and Bryansk, unlike *Heeresgruppe Nord*'s *landsers*, who weren't as fortunate and instead had to stay in the line and refit there. Neither army group was placated by a signal from OKH referencing future replacement numbers. OKH forecast that some 60,000 trained men would be available for the month of August with 14,000 allocated to *Heeresgruppe Mitte* and just 8,000 for *Nord*. Northern Finland would get an additional 4,000 and even Rommel would receive 10,000 for Africa. The largest contingent – some 24,000 men – would go to reinforce *Blau*, but even for Bock this was meagre fare when expected losses were taken into consideration.

For Bock, manpower wasn't his only issue, equally critical was transport. *Barbarossa* had amply demonstrated the need for the Germans to keep moving in order to succeed. Given the huge distances his men would have to cover to reach their objectives, motor vehicles were vital. The problem was that German industry had still not adapted to this most pressing of needs and the flow of trucks, half-tracks and prime movers was anaemic. The most Georg Thomas – he of the oil memorandum – could promise 'the holy fire of Küstrin' was enough to half fill the establishment of his infantry units and a shade more for his motorised formations. For a standard Type 1939 infantry division that meant around four hundred vehicles of all kinds, mostly two-wheel drive trucks. A precious commodity, the trucks would be used to carry bulk supplies such as ammunition and fuel, the men themselves would be expected to march, just as they had the previous year. As ever, the fallback for the lack of motorised vehicles would be the horse.

The infantry divisions that made up the bulk of the army group still relied overwhelmingly on draught horses to pull carts filled with everything from ammunition, spare parts, food and field kitchens, but most importantly they moved the cannons and howitzers with each division, requiring no fewer than 229 horse-drawn vehicles for that task alone. In the First World War the Imperial German Army had displayed a lack of care for its animals that had seen huge numbers perish and necessitated constant fresh arrivals, and it was clear that the German Army of this new war had not learned from those mistakes. Too many horses had not been habituated to military conditions and were all too often put in the untrained hands of young men with no experience of horses. The results were predictable with thousands going lame, becoming diseased and eventually dying. *Barbarossa* had been exceptionally hard on the *Ostheer*'s equine cohort with tens of thousands dying from cold, exposure and hunger, alongside those killed by Soviet fire.

To plug the gaps, the call went out to the Reich and some 109,000 new mounts were procured from farms and fields across Germany, but that was nowhere near enough. Never an institution to shy away from plundering, the Wehrmacht scoured the occupied lands and requisitioned an additional 118,000 horses and shipped them east. Incredibly, even this wasn't enough and almost every division in *Heeresgruppe Süd* would be short of its complement of horses that summer. Improvisation was the order of the day and just as their brethren had done in occupied Western Europe so those in the occupied East now confiscated locally bred steppe ponies to pull the eponymous *panje* carts. Most *landsers* preferred the steppe ponies anyway as they'd proven themselves far hardier and easier to look after than the heavier and more 'refined' western breeds. Rudolf Oehus, a farmer's boy from Lower Saxony, had served throughout *Barbarossa* in an artillery battery, which was now being brought back up to strength

> We'd only been in our quarters two days when 15 of us were sent back around 60 kilometres to fetch new horses. It took us three days to get back. Today at noon six of us are going

away again to collect more horses. We've already got 90 so in a short time we should have our old complement again… Otherwise the situation is the same here, it's all very quiet. I'm no longer pulling a signals wagon, now I'm pulling a gun![7]

With most of the divisions earmarked for the forthcoming offensive still short on manpower, the Germans turned to firepower to help fill the gap. The individual German infantry *gruppe* (an eight to ten man-strong section), which was the foundation stone of all their formations, had been built around the MG34, the world's first true light machine-gun, able to be carried by one man, operated by two and provide a weight of fire of around 800 to 900 rounds a minute. Game changing as the MG34 was, it was also expensive to manufacture and difficult to maintain. Its successor was the MG42. Less costly to produce (250 *reichsmarks* against the MG34's 327) it used welding and riveting of stamped parts for ease of manufacture and was far more reliable in field conditions. However, its biggest advantage was its rate of fire, which could reach an astonishing 2,000 rounds a minute, although doing so would quickly exhaust the ammunition supply and melt the barrel, so a figure closer to around one thousand was more usual. Rehfeldt remembered the gun's arrival in his unit; 'We heard for the first time the rattle of the new MG42 and its terrific rate of fire … the Russians call it the 'Hitler saw' and also the 'electric machine-gun." Like its predecessor it could be carried by one man and operated by two, although given its prodigious appetite for ammunition it wasn't unusual for a further two, three or even four men to be detailed with the job of keeping it supplied with ammo belts.

Just as important to *Blau*'s success as men, trucks, horses and machine-guns, was heavy weaponry, and above all that meant panzers. *Barbarossa* had proved the Wehrmacht's mastery of armoured operations. The four hard-hitting and fast moving *panzergruppen* (panzer groups) had streaked ahead of their pedestrian infantry comrades and caught the Red Army in a whole series of enormous pockets that had taken millions of prisoners of war and more or less destroyed the entire pre-war Red Army. But the price had been high. Forced to man the picket lines around their trapped foes, losses among the panzer crews and their motorised infantry had been appalling. Only when the slower moving infantry had arrived could the panzer forces leave the line, and only then to resume their advance rather than rest and recover. At crucial points in the invasion the fast-charging armoured formations were ordered to hold fast and allow the infantry to catch up, much to the frustration of panzer generals like Erich von Manstein and Heinz Guderian, but the halts were seen as essential by the conservatively minded majority on Germany's general staff and Hitler himself, who feared his prize units would be cut off and annihilated in the depths of Russia.

The question then was how to avoid the *panzergruppen* from having to play a game of hurry up and wait, during which they were exposed to destruction before the bulk of the infantry caught up with them. The obvious answer was to motorise the entire army, but that was a task far beyond the Reich's capability, so the solution adopted was a reorganisation of the *panzergruppen* into *panzerarmeen* (panzer armies) containing far more infantry and far fewer panzers. For example, Erich Hoepner's old *Panzergruppe* 4 which had been instrumental in conquering the Baltic states and almost taking Leningrad, had transferred south after *Taifun* and was now renamed 4. *Panzerarmee*. Previously armour-heavy, with three panzer and three motorised infantry divisions, it was forced to give up two panzer formations and one motorised, and in their place received two foot-borne infantry divisions.

As an idea to solve a very real problem it was patent nonsense. The net result was the shackling of the Wehrmacht's precious panzer divisions, reducing them to the pace of their incumbent foot sloggers. This robbed the Germans of their most effective weapon – speed – and meant the Soviets would have the time to react to German operations in a way they couldn't the previous summer.

The panzer divisions themselves were also overhauled, their reconnaissance and motorcycle battalions merged, mainly due to horrific losses in the latter, and wholesale changes were made to try and combat the threat of the dreaded T-34 tank. At first believing the Red Army's tank fleet to be composed of obsolete light tanks such as the T-26 and BT series, or useless behemoths like the twin-turreted T-100, the invading Germans had been stunned by the appearance on the battlefield of the T-34 and accompanying KV heavy tank series. Rugged, reliable and with bigger and more powerful guns than the panzers, the new tanks also had superb cross-country capability, but most shocking of all, their armour – sloped in the case of the T-34 and tremendously thick for the KVs - proved impervious to all but the heaviest German guns. Unwilling to admit that Slav *untermenschen* (sub-humans) could design and build tanks far superior to their own, the Wehrmacht had no option but to adapt.

First to go was the standard German Army anti-tank gun, the ubiquitous 3.7cm Pak 36. More than adequate against soft vehicles, armoured cars and light tanks, it had failed miserably against the new kings of the battlefield. Disparagingly nicknamed the *Panzeranklopfgerät* (tank doorknocker) by the *landsers* due to its inability to destroy the T-34 or KVs, it was immediately retired and replaced by the bigger 5cm Pak 38, and the excellent 7.5cm Pak 40.

Of even bigger import were the changes wrought among the serried ranks of the panzers themselves. Previously, the *panzerwaffe* had operated on the basis that a tank's main asset was its mobility. By using speed and agility, tanks could dislocate and then shatter an enemy's ability to resist, but with almost every gun the Germans had proving unable to stop a T-34, let alone a KV-1 or 2, the young panzer officer Helmut Ritgen realised a sea change had occurred:

[The new Soviet tanks] changed the character of tank warfare ... no weapon in the Division was able to penetrate their armour. Rounds simply bounced off the Soviet tanks... In the face of the assault some infantry panicked... German panzers had hitherto been intended mainly to fight enemy infantry and their supporting arms. From now on the main threat was the enemy tank itself, and the need to kill it at as great a range as possible led to the design of longer-barrelled guns of larger calibres.

The all-too brief age of mobility was being superseded by a new era of firepower.

This was easier said than done, with production lines back in the Reich geared to manufacture lightly armed *Panzerkampfwagen* IIs and IIIs (*PzKpfw*) with their 2cm and 3.7cm guns. Indeed, by the time production of the PzKpfw II was halted in July 1942, some 256 had already been built since the new year, along with 195 light PzKpfw 38(t)s that had rolled out of the factories of occupied Czechoslovakia. Death traps in tank versus tank actions against T-34s and KVs, both types were still useful for reconnaissance tasks and were sent east. Their stable mate the PzKpfw III was the most common model in the *panzerwaffe* with almost a thousand in the ranks, with just over a third having the newer, more powerful 5cm cannon. Regardless, they were still at a huge disadvantage against the T-34 as one of their crewmen, Ewald Klapdor, acknowledged:

> The frontal armour of our panzers wasn't able to stop the larger calibres of the enemy's anti-tank guns and tank cannon, like the T-34 ... in the field we reinforced our frontal armour by bolting spare track onto the panzer's front, and as the side armour was the weakest point it forced us to change the way we advanced so only the vehicle's front was exposed to the enemy if at all possible .... our main gun allowed us maximum ranges of about 500 metres, while the T-34 was dangerous to us at 1,500 to 2,000 metres.[8]

The new long-barrelled *PzKpfw IV* was the only tank the Germans possessed in 1942 that could possibly stand toe to toe with the T-34 and hope to win out, but production was only just beginning to step up, and by the time *Blau* was launched only 133 of the Mark IV had reached the frontline. There they would take their place in an armada of 1,495 panzers in total, with Bock's panzer divisions averaging anywhere between 120 and 140 tanks each, and the motorised divisions between 40 and 50 apiece. The poor old panzer formations in *Heeresgruppen Nord* and *Mitte* were not only starved of replacement panzers but were ordered to send some of their best south, leaving them with an average of 40 to 60 per division if they were lucky.[9] It wasn't just the machines that went to *Heeresgruppe Süd* either, it was the men who crewed them. 'The best NCOs were ex-Reichswehr, they were always more knowledgeable and knew the form [but] we were always short of good, veteran officers, because so many had fallen already.' As the older officers were lost so their place was taken by younger, inexperienced men, *frei-geschossen* or 'shot free' as they were nicknamed.[10]

The Germans also tried to beef up the *panzerwaffe* with the introduction of large numbers of self-propelled guns, able to provide firepower support for assaulting infantry or take on Soviet tanks. The first models combined captured former French Army *Lorraine 37L* artillery tractors chassis[11] with similarly captured Soviet 76mm F-22 field guns or 76.2mm anti-tank cannon, the barrels of which had been re-chambered to fire German 7.5cm ammunition. Christened the *Marder I* (Marten I) by the Germans, a second model was soon produced, the *Marder II*, which used the same concept but utilised former PzKpfw II and PzKpfw 38(t) chassis. Cheaper, quicker, and easier to build than a panzer with its complicated rotating turret, the numbers of these squat, workaday vehicles would grow dramatically as the war went on, and *Blau* would prove their usefulness.

Although the core of Bock's strike force would be German, *Heeresgruppe Süd* had always been a joint enterprise where Nazi Germany's Axis allies could demonstrate their commitment to the anti-Bolshevik crusade. The army group's first commander, the venerable Prussian warhorse Gerd von Rundstedt, had described his polyglot force as an 'absolute League of Nations army'. The Romanian officers and NCOs were 'beyond description', the Italians were 'terrible people' and the Hungarians 'only wanted to get home quickly'. Rundstedt's dismissive views were not universally shared by his soldiers and subordinates, but it's fair to say the prevailing view among the ranks of the Wehrmacht towards their allies was one of casual disdain. The panzer driver Henry Metelmann and his crew often referred to the Romanians as 'silly goats' and thought them jumpy in the line and all too ready to believe any noise in the night was a Soviet attack, but generally found them acceptable.

Regardless of Rundstedt's views, pragmatism won out, as it was abundantly clear that even with the lion's share of Nazi Germany's dwindling manpower heading south there simply weren't enough bodies to guarantee success for the upcoming offensive. Berlin's answer was to dispatch an envoy around the capitals of Germany's eastern European allies to sweet talk them into sending fresh forces to support the campaign. The envoy chosen was none other than Wilhelm Keitel, undoubtedly senior enough to flatter his Axis hosts, but an odd choice given his dislike of all foreigners and well-deserved reputation for arrogant pomposity. Amazingly, Keitel's mission was an unqualified triumph. Hitherto a reluctant contributor at best, Admiral Miklós Horthy's Hungarian government not only agreed to keep its existing forces in-country, but to increase them five-fold.

A slew of formations was dispatched at the beginning of April, creating the *Második Magyar Hadsereg* (Second Hungarian Army), composed of ten divisions numbering some 209,000 men in all. Astonishing though this was, the bald numbers hid how poorly equipped Budapest's troops were. Indeed, Hungary had not recognised the need to modernise its army until the 1930s, when it belatedly instituted a series of military reforms. However, lacking advanced heavy industry, the formations of the Second Hungarian Army were still woefully ill-equipped, as the Hungarian priest Dr Stephen Ritli saw for himself on joining his regiment en route to southern Russia: 'There was barely a rifle for each man. There were no tanks, no proper artillery, no motorised vehicles and few provisions.' The lack of any suitable transport would prove a fatal flaw for the Hungarians on the open steppes of Russia; 'In our regiment only two officers – the colonel and myself – had any sort of transport and that was a horse.'[12]

At least the Hungarians did have some armour in the form of Lajos Veress's 1st Hungarian Armoured Field Division. Having nowhere near the potency of a German panzer division, Ritli recalled the unit having 'a few tanks which were Italian and of poor quality, we called them "matchboxes."' István Balogh was a corporal in Veress's division, and he wrote in his diary of an impending sense of dread:

> In the name of God we are leaving for the blood-soaked land of Russia, and we ask him to return us safe and sound and bring us final victory! Mother of God guarding over Hungary, pray for us and defend us from all sins and disasters! Saint Stephen, raise your miraculous right hand over us and plead for your orphan people. Amen.

Having secured major reinforcements from Hungary, Keitel was keen to repeat the trick in neighbouring Romania. The Romanian military dictator, Ion Antonescu, had already committed half the country's pre-war army to *Barbarossa*, and now felt honour-bound to continue the struggle, even after the appalling losses incurred in capturing the Black Sea port city of Odessa the previous autumn. Troop trains rattled east from Bucharest at the same time as István Balogh was reluctantly leaving Budapest central station, carrying fresh troops to the *Armata a 3-a Română* and *Armata a 4-a Română* – the 3rd and 4th Romanian Armies. The former would soon boast over 150,000 men, but the latter would only muster half that number.

Zagreb was Keitel's final destination, although with Josip Broz Tito's communist partisans engaged in open warfare with the fascist Ustaše government, he could consider himself lucky to get the Croat Light Transport Brigade to supplement the in-country *Verstärktes (kroatisches) Infanterie-Regiment 369* (Reinforced (Croatian) Infantry Regiment 369).

As it turned out, the largest Axis reinforcement contingent came not from eastern Europe but from the balmy shores of the Mediterranean, as Benito Mussolini saw an opportunity to reap the fruits of future victory in the Soviet Union. In truth, Berlin did not even approach the Italians for additional troops. Hitler would much have preferred his fellow dictator to send any spare men he possessed to North Africa or even Yugoslavia, and thereby relieve the need for German divisions to be committed to those theatres. But as ever with *Il Duce*, straightforward military logic was never the priority. So, having already sent three divisions to take part in *Barbarossa*, he now doubled down and committed a further seven including three from Italy's rightly famed *Alpini* mountain Corps. The new force was upgraded from its old CSIR title and now became the far grander *Armata Italiana in Russia* (*ARMIR* – Italian Army in Russia), commonly called the Italian Eighth Army. Giovanni Messe retained command and felt compelled to describe the situation on the ground to his over-optimistic boss:

> Our meagre, antiquated armaments, the absolute lack of suitable armoured vehicles, the insufficient number of trucks, the grave problems of transport and supply, made more difficult by the lack of understanding and unyielding selfishness of the Germans, will create problems for the Army that are really insoluble.

As ever, Mussolini brushed away an awkward reality with typical bombast: 'Dear Messe, at the table of peace the 200,000 men of the ARMIR will weigh a lot more than the sixty thousand of the CSIR. The decision has been made.' When Messe persisted in pointing out the folly of sending an entirely ill-equipped army to Russia, Rome had had enough and he was quietly replaced by the far more compliant Italo Gariboldi. Not a natural choice – having been sacked from his post in North Africa the previous year for his inability to work with Rommel – Gariboldi was 63 years old and had shown little flair for command during his progression through the ranks, his main selling point to his superiors being a willingness to carry out whatever orders he was given and not rock the boat. In Russia he would prove himself a downright liability.

Nevertheless, with the additional Italian divisions en route there would be well over thirty allied Axis divisions committed to *Blau*, and it all made for a colourful spectacle in the rehabilitation area of Dnepropetrovsk, as one Italian observer noted:

The khaki uniforms of General Antonescu's Romanians with their large moustaches rivalled the blue of the Luftwaffe, the red of the Cossacks [collaborationist anti-communist cavalry units], the grey-green of the Italian and German infantry, the yellow of the party leaders and the green and brown of the gendarmerie. The Italian carabinieri [paramilitary Italian police] had on their marvellous three-cornered hats ... the rectangular pointed hats worn by the French soldiers [collaborationist Regiment 638] and the light caps of the seamen from the Black Sea were no match for them. The troops of the Croatian Legion, with their little shields on their right sleeves, were few compared to those of other armies, but they also contributed something with their Balkan personality, as did the French, Slovak, Dutch and Hungarian contingents.

Hans Heinz Rehfeldt remembered seeing 'Slovak and Hungarian troops ... their infantry wear yellowish brown uniforms and high puttees' and drinking pilfered schnapps with a 'Slovak corporal [who] fetched out his mandolin and we stayed until evening listening to Slovak folk tunes.'

It wasn't all bonhomie, though, particularly between the Romanians and Hungarians who nursed a deep-seated hatred of one another, as Stephen Ritli knew only too well: 'The Germans had to put the Italians between us and the Romanians because they knew if they didn't we would be fighting each other instead of the Russians.'

On paper, by the beginning of June, Bock could look down an inventory detailing almost one million German soldiers and over 600,000 Axis allies. A number of his sixty-eight German divisions were new and fresh from the training depots, while half of the rest had been rehabilitated and rebuilt. He had some fifteen hundred panzers and self-propelled guns concentrated in nine panzer and five motorised infantry formations, but transport complements were still not back up to strength and neither were numbers in the frontline infantry companies. To help make up for these deficiencies, the Germans would need to look to the skies and the might of the Luftwaffe.

That was easier said than done. Having not had a period of recuperation after the Western campaign back in 1940, the Luftwaffe then found itself still fighting the RAF over the English Channel, and increasingly stretched in North Africa as it battled the Desert Air Force in support of Erwin Rommel and his men. It had suffered around one thousand pilots killed, wounded or missing during *Barbarossa*, and aircraft production back in the Reich was struggling to replace monthly losses, never mind build up significant reserves. The biggest cause for concern however was the fuel situation. Aircraft require high octane aviation spirit, but the difficulty of its production was always a major headache for Nazi Germany's overtaxed refining capabilities. The result was that even though the Luftwaffe in the East could only muster 1,591 aircraft at the beginning of 1942, *Oberkommando der Luftwaffe* (OKL – Luftwaffe High Command) was forced to cut fuel allocation to flight training schools by half and institute a number of austerity measures across the Russian Front, including ordering ground attack units to carry out their own pre-operation reconnaissance flights and removing the guarantee to provide fighter escort for bombing missions. Unsurprisingly, losses began to rise, but Berlin had little choice given the circumstances. New pilots were now arriving at their frontline *staffeln* (German equivalent of a British squadron but smaller) with between 220 to 270 flying hours, a drop of a third from the previous year, and consequently the accident rate climbed sharply with new pilots twice as likely to be killed or wounded in an accident than in combat.

The picture wasn't all bleak. With the winter over, the Luftwaffe in the East experienced an increase in numbers up to between 2,600 and 2,750 aircraft in the frontline *staffeln* by early June,[13] with perhaps another 3-400 in allied squadrons, although the equipment and training of the latter were often indifferent or downright poor. Friedrich Lang, a Stuka pilot at the time, described how he and his comrades dreaded being supported by Italian fighter escorts for their missions as they were prone to leave the Stukas unprotected when VVS fighters showed up. Lang said the Italians' performance was 'most disappointing'.

Heeresgruppe Süd would be supported by Alexander Löhr's *Luftflotte 4* during *Blau*. Löhr was an experienced air commander and was ably supported by his two chief subordinates, Kurt Pflugbeil and Wolfram von Richthofen, in charge of *Fliegerkorps* (Air Corps) IV and VIII respectively. Richthofen was especially capable, the Red Baron's cousin and a former First World War fighter pilot himself, he had turned his command into an incredibly effective strike force, arguably the finest close support formation in the Luftwaffe. With units ruthlessly stripped from covering *Heeresgruppen Nord* and *Mitte*, leaving them with fewer than a thousand aircraft combined, the OKL was able to assemble between 1,500 and 1,600 aircraft under Löhr's command[14] for the big assault in the south. This was a third less than had been available for *Barbarossa*, which was a third less than had taken part in the Battle of Britain – Nazi Germany's air force was shrinking as the war went on. However, among the German *staffeln* were some of the best combat pilots in the world. With no concept of tour rotation away from the front – as was common practice in the Anglo-American air forces – the pilots of the Luftwaffe were left to battle it out with the VVS and rack up three, four even five hundred operational sorties apiece, as long as they could survive the terrible attrition. The German pilots, benefiting from better machines and training and let loose on *freie Jagd* (free hunting) missions over Soviet lines, were able to amass huge scores that will never be beaten in aerial warfare. Johannes 'Macky' Steinhoff remembered 'we had a profound feeling of superiority over the Russian airmen during those days' while another thought 'the standards of the Soviet pilots varied from very good to extremely poor. In fact, some of their pilots were hardly able to control their aircraft at all.' Steinhoff would reach 100 kills on 31 August that year, becoming the 18th German pilot to achieve that distinction.

With the destruction of the pre-war VVS the previous year, the Soviets were still in survival mode to a certain extent, throwing masses of ill-trained pilots into the air in often obsolete aircraft types that were easy pickings for Steinhoff and the like – the Soviets themselves admitted to losing a staggering 1,644 aircraft in July that year against Luftwaffe losses of just 264. But Soviet production was beginning to ramp up with 1,835 planes built that same month, increasing to just under 2,300 in November.

Those numbers also included newer and better models such as the Yak-1 and LaGG-3 fighters and the Pe-2 light bomber, and, of course, the Il-2 Shturmovik, nicknamed the *Schlächter* (Slaughterer) by the German ground troops who were its main target. Large numbers of American and British aircraft also began to appear in the ranks of the VVS as Lend-Lease stepped up. *Jagdflieger* (fighter pilot) Adolf Dickfeld recalled seeing 'rows and rows of brand new Airacobra [American] fighters, lined up as if on parade ... painted frog green with huge red Soviet stars on the wings.'

The Germans, too, were being supplied with new models, the Bf 109 G (Gustav) fighter model increasingly taking its place in frontline *staffeln*. Hermann Graf was 'wild with enthusiasm' over his new *Gustav*, but not every pilot was so enamoured, with more than one describing the newer aircraft as *'Scheissbocke'* – shit buckets – and the air ace Günther Rall insisting on having his newly fitted 2cm underslung gondola wing cannons removed, as they 'often jammed and made the aircraft very clumsy and difficult to fly, especially in air-to-air combat'.

Overall, Bock probably had about as powerful a force for *Blau* as the Wehrmacht and its Axis allies could muster at that stage of the war. Its weaknesses were fearful though. Just as with *Barbarossa*, the new offensive would be launched without any strategic reserves of men or *matériel*, while asking the assault divisions to advance huge distances and remain battleworthy at the end of ever-extending supply lines. Fuel and ammunition stockpiles were already low and with no mass transport fleet available to ferry supplies forward, logistical failures could once again stymie the German plan. Bock's hope was that he could eliminate the bulk of Red Army forces in front of him in a series of swift encirclement battles and cause a widespread collapse, whereupon his men could then advance to their far-off objectives at their leisure. It was a tall order.

3

FIRST BLOOD

During the headlong advances of *Barbarossa* the previous year, Walter von Reichenau had found himself personally leading his troops in combat after all the officers in one of his regiments had been killed or wounded. Recounting the tale to his old friend Alfred Jodl at OKH, Reichenau said 'I led the assault for three kilometres, while literally not only with the first wave, but as the leading man in it.' Jodl didn't doubt his fellow general. Back in September 1939 he'd swum across the River Vistula to become the first German soldier to cross into Poland at the very beginning of the invasion, and even at the age of fifty-six was known to relish taking part in boxing bouts. The force that followed him across the Vistula in 1939 and into the Soviet Union two years later was one of the Wehrmacht's most powerful field formations; *6. Armee.* Originally numbered as *10. Armee,* it was redesignated for the Western campaign and fought in the Battle of Belgium, before taking a leading role in breaking through the French defences around Paris. It ended the battle for France in the lush fields of Normandy. Earmarked to take part in *Barbarossa*, it was sent east to form part of Gerd von Rundstedt's *Heeresgruppe Süd.*

There, it received four new divisions: *168, 297, 298* and *299. Infanterie-Divisionen.* The first was composed of existing replacement units and the others were full of men from the 1940 draft class. Most of the existing seven divisions in the Army had been raised in the 1939 *Welle* 2 (Wave 2)[1] from men classed as *Reserve I*,[2] although one, Siegmund Freiherr von Schleinitz's 9. *Infanterie-Division*, had been established back in 1935, while Friedrich Siebert's 44. *Infanterie-Division* was an expanded version of Austria's famous *Hoch und Deutschmeister* Regiment. All seven had taken part in the Western campaign and were seasoned units, full of trained and experienced officers and men, equipped with the very latest weaponry the Third Reich could offer. Brought up to full strength of around 17,000 men each, Reichenau's 6. *Armee* was a formidable beast that acted as the spearhead for the army group as it blazed a path across Ukraine. Its greatest moment came when it formed the anvil at Kiev upon which the hammers of Kleist and Guderian's *panzergruppen* smashed the mass of Soviet forces on the southern front, leading to the biggest encirclement battle ever fought.

It then withstood the winter fighting and as 1942 dawned its reputation in the Wehrmacht was sky high. It had taken heavy losses in men and equipment during *Barbarossa* but had proven itself a crack formation, able to beat pretty much anything the Red Army could field against it. On Tuesday 20 January, its world changed. The man who had commanded it since its inception was gone, elevated to army group command before dying in a plane crash. On his promotion Reichenau had personally recommended his replacement – Friedrich Wilhelm Ernst Paulus.

The 51-year-old Paulus had been born in the small central German town of Guxhagen to a solid middle-class family. He had served in the infantry during the First World War, although pretty quickly his superiors realised his talents lay in staff work rather than field command and he finished the war as a *hauptmann* in the *Alpenkorps*. He stayed in uniform after the Armistice, being chosen as one of only 4,000 officers in Weimar Germany's Versailles-reduced 100,000-man army and was a company commander in the same regiment as Erwin Rommel. One of many *Reichswehr* officers sent to the Soviet Union as part of the secret military protocols between the two pariah states, Paulus had guest-lectured in Moscow and knew the country and its army well, knowledge he would later use to help plan *Barbarossa* as a senior member of the OKH. Returning to Germany, he briefly commanded one of the new motorised infantry battalions in what proved to be his highest and last direct command appointment. Thereafter, he achieved a steady rise through the ranks by excelling in a variety of staff positions, including serving under Heinz Guderian, one of the fathers of Germany's *panzerwaffe*. Guderian described him as 'brilliantly clever, conscientious, hard-working, original and talented'. But he also considered that he lacked decisiveness and was slow, 'inclined to spend too much time on his appreciation before issuing his orders'. Another officer said of him that he was 'a meticulous desk worker, with a passion for wargames and formulating plans on the map board or sand table. At this he displays considerable talent...'

Clearly a very able staff officer, he nevertheless failed to shake off the sense of personal inadequacy he felt due to his modest family background, in what was still a very class-conscious institution. In Germany's army having a *von*, *freiherr* or *ritter* in your name brought a distinct advantage. His peer Rommel had the same relatively humble origins but overcame them through an overweening self-confidence and belief in his own abilities; Paulus had neither trait. Indeed, he had developed an unfortunate tic on the left side of his face which was most pronounced when he was under stress. Under the bullish and domineering Reichenau, Paulus's flaws were more than compensated for, but now his mentor was dead, and he was left alone to bear the crushing responsibility of high office.

He made an immediate impression on his new command, quietly dropping Reichenau's Severity Order which had seen elements of 6. *Armee* indulge in wholesale atrocities and pogroms and downgrading the enforcement of the infamous Commissar Order that had already cost the lives of thousands of captured Communist Party functionaries. Not that he was any sort of saint, rather he believed the killing of civilians and PoWs had an adverse impact on discipline.

It soon became clear that all was not well in 6. *Armee*. Whereas Reichenau had been adored by his soldiers as a man of action who understood their lot, Paulus by contrast was not popular, lacking the common touch and feeling little empathy for the trials and tribulations of the soldiery. As for his subordinate corps and divisional commanders, relations with them were somewhat cool and reserved. Most viewed him as a planner rather than a leader and privately criticised his lack of combat experience. Tall and ascetic, a heavy smoker and constant coffee drinker, he was most at home hunched over a map table and seemed out of place on campaign, habitually wearing gloves as he hated getting dirt under his fingernails and insisting on a bath and changing into a fresh uniform twice a day. Little wonder he was sarcastically nicknamed 'Our Most Elegant Gentleman' and 'der Lord' behind his back.

The Army he took over was also undergoing fundamental change throughout its structure. No fewer than eight of its *Barbarossa* divisions were transferred out to other formations – some even to *Heeresgruppe Mitte* – and were replaced by a host of new units, reflecting the hybrid organisation 6. *Armee* would now become. Its heart remained its infantry; nine divisions split into three corps, with one composed of three of its *Barbarossa* units, while the other six were all new. Two of them, 79 and 294. *Infanterie-Divisionen*, were veteran formations that had fought across France, the Balkans and southern Russia already, but the others; 113, 305, 376 and 389. *Infanterie-Divisionen*, had yet to see any action having originally been raised to carry out garrison duties in western Europe. They were joined by something entirely new for 6. *Armee*, a motorised corps of four divisions, two of which were panzer and one motorised infantry with an integral tank battalion.

The cream of the crop was Hermann Breith's 3. *Panzerdivision*. One of the original three panzer divisions in the German Army, the '*Bär*' (Bear) division as it was known had fought in the Western campaign before excelling during *Barbarossa*, its then commander Walter Model leading it to success after success, including the madcap charge that sealed the Kiev pocket the previous autumn.

Its fellow armoured division was Hans von Boineburg-Lengsfeld's 23. *Panzerdivision*, one of a number created in 1940 and 1941 to expand the *panzerwaffe* and initially equipped with captured French tanks before swapping them for more favoured German models. Alongside them were the Thuringians of beak-nosed Max Fremery's '*Falke*' (Falcon) 29. *Infanterie-Division (mot.)*. An outstanding unit, it had covered itself with glory during the Smolensk and Bialystok-Minsk battles and would provide 6. *Armee* with mobility and strike power. Last, and definitely least, in what was a very powerful corps, was 336. *Infanterie-Division*. Led by the artilleryman Walter Lucht, the 336. *ID* was newly raised and originally intended to join its sister 3-series formations in nothing more taxing than carrying out occupation duties in France and the Low Countries. However, the huge losses of the winter had forced OKH to order its transfer east and now it found itself at the cutting edge of the Wehrmacht's summer offensive, where its inadequacies would be cruelly laid bare. Paulus was also given a reserve, the 100. *Leichte Infanterie Division*. Far smaller than a standard infantry division, Werner Sanne's light infantry command was bolstered by the veteran volunteers of Ivan Babić's Croat regiment.

On paper, 6. *Armee* was an incredibly powerful force. Well over 200,000-strong with more than 300 panzers and self-propelled guns and an abundance of artillery, heavy cannon and howitzers. But appearances can be deceiving. Whereas the old 6. *Armee* was a tried and proven formation, almost half the new 6. *Armee* hadn't seen any combat, with large chunks recruited and trained as garrison troops, not frontline infantry. The inclusion of armour and motorised infantry in what was still essentially a foot and horse-drawn force was an untried experiment. To top it all it had a new commander whom Wolfram von Richthofen – who would work hand in glove with Paulus during *Blau* – described as 'worthy but uninspiring'.

Whatever 6. *Armee*'s shortcomings and potential flaws, it would have little time to overcome them as Moscow looked to spoil German plans. The previous summer Stalin had been caught completely by surprise by the German attack and had compounded his mistake by believing the Wehrmacht's main thrust would be in the south, to capture Ukraine and the mineral wealth of the Donets basin. This basic error, and a refusal to follow Russia's traditional invasion strategy of trading space for time, had led to a disastrous series of battles where vast numbers of Red Army troops had been encircled and annihilated. German exhaustion and logistical failure had helped come to Moscow's rescue and, allied with an incredible national effort and ferocious resistance by ordinary Soviet soldiers, had turned the tide with a series of counter-offensives that had checked and then pushed back the depleted *Ostheer*.

Though chastened, Stalin still had not learned by this stage to leave generalship to the generals and once again looked to dabble in the field of battle. In truth, hubris had seized the Soviet dictator, who now believed that with the Germans reeling in disarray a new series of assaults would not only drive the *Ostheer* further back but would deliver the initiative to the Red Army and potentially lead to Nazi Germany's total defeat in 1942.

Having bet on black when it came up red in 1941, Stalin did the same again at the beginning of '42 and repeated the mistake by this time predicting Moscow would once more be the *Ostheer*'s main target and that the Germans would use their salient at Rzhev as the launch pad for a renewed attack on the Soviet capital. To frustrate this anticipated assault, Stalin ordered the Red Army to maintain an offensive posture and launch spoiling attacks in the north on the River Volkhov, against the trapped German forces in the Demyansk pocket, and most significantly for *Blau*, in the Izyum bridgehead near the city of Kharkov. As the Soviets prepared to attack out of the Izyum salient, the Germans – clueless as to Soviet intentions – prioritised capturing the Kerch peninsula in eastern Crimea. Spearheaded by the assault divisions of Erich von Manstein's superb *11. Armee, Unternehmen Trappenjagd* (Operation Bustard Hunt) began on 8 May supported by massive air power.

'Terrible! Corpse-strewn fields from earlier attacks... I have seen nothing like it so far in this war.' Never a squeamish commander, nonetheless Wolfram von Richthofen felt physically sick at what he saw during the Kerch fighting: 'Dreadfully many dead horses and Russians lay strewn all over and stinking accordingly.' His *Fliegerkorps VIII* had pounded the enemy day after day and the stench of death was like a pall hanging over the battlefield. The 11-day battle was a tactical triumph for German arms. Manstein showed his mastery of the battlefield:

> ...around 170,000 prisoners, 1,133 guns and 258 tanks fell into our hands. Five German infantry divisions and one panzer division, as well as two Romanian infantry divisions and a cavalry brigade, had destroyed two full Armies and the greater part of a third, comprising 26 major formations.

Manstein lost just 7,388 men killed, wounded or missing. But even as his German and Romanian troops were celebrating their victory, the Red Army launched its own attack more than 300 miles to the north at Izyum.

At Stalin's urging, Semyon Timoshenko launched the 640,000 men and 1,200 tanks of his South-Western Front straight into the heart of *Heeresgruppe Süd*, only to hit a brick wall of German resistance. It was Friedrich Paulus's first battle as 6. *Armee* commander and he handled his troops well, using massed artillery and waves of medium bombers first to halt the Soviet offensive before counterattacking. Refused permission by Stalin to withdraw – just as in summer 1941 – the major portion of Timoshenko's Front was cut off and isolated. Hubert Lanz, commander of the mountaineers of *1. Gebirgs-Division*, witnessed the desperate Soviet attempts to escape the pocket:

> The Russian columns struck the German lines in the light of thousands of white flares. Orders bellowed by officers and commissars fired up the battalions. The Red Army soldiers stormed forward with arms linked, their hoarse shouts of 'Urrah!' resounded terribly through the night. The first waves fell, then the earth-brown columns turned away to the north.

Despite suffering dreadful losses, in scenes reminiscent of the previous year, the Soviets refused to give up and once more turned into the German guns:

> But there they ran into the barricades manned by the gebirgsjäger [mountain troops], they now reeled back and charged into the front without regard to losses. They slew and stabbed everything in their path, advanced another few hundred metres and then collapsed in the flanking machine-gun fire. Those who weren't killed, staggered, crawled or stumbled back to the ravines of the Bereka river.

Lanz – who had experienced first-hand the horrors of the First World War – was appalled and exasperated by what he saw; 'The scene was repeated the next evening … some of the masses advancing arm in arm were under the influence of vodka, where else could the fellows have found the courage to charge to certain death shouting 'Urrah!"

In six days of ferocious fighting some twenty-two Soviet rifle and seven cavalry divisions, along with no fewer than fifteen tank brigades, were destroyed. Seventy-five thousand Soviet soldiers were killed, including Timoshenko's own deputy, Fyodor Kostenko, and another quarter of a million went into captivity. Timoshenko lost all his 1,200 tanks plus 2,000 guns and 542 aircraft.[3] Once more, endless columns of Soviet PoWs found themselves trudging back towards an uncertain fate at the hands of their German conquerors. The Italian filmmaker, writer and sometime war correspondent Curzio Malaparte had been with *Heeresgruppe Süd* since the launch of *Barbarossa* the previous summer and was used to seeing the massed prisoner columns: 'Most of them are wounded. They wear no bandages, their faces are caked with blood and dust, their uniforms are in rags, their hands blackened. They walk slowly, supporting one another.' Fritz Pabst, serving in a 6. *Armee* construction battalion charged with bridge building, wasn't nearly as compassionate as Malaparte and watched the trail of human misery without a trace of sympathy. 'You really have to see the Asiatic prisoners and the like, if they'd have come to our Fatherland there'd have been such an enormous killing, because they aren't human ... they are wild beasts.' Hitler - elated at what he thought was a huge triumph – remarked to Franz Halder that 'The Russian is finished.' To which the savagely crewcut general conceded, 'I must admit it looks like it.'

Izyum – also called the Second Battle of Kharkov – had been another stunning German success, and a huge feather in Paulus's cap as he and his new army claimed the glory. In gratitude, Hitler awarded Paulus the much-coveted Knight's Cross – 'curing his throat ache',[4] in Wehrmacht slang. However, 6. *Armee* had lost 20,000 men and around one hundred panzers during the fighting, and while a relative drop in the ocean compared to Moscow's losses, it was a painful blow to an Army still in the process of coming together as a cohesive unit. Perhaps even more worrying was the inexperience shown during the battle by Paulus's untried divisions. Unlike the veterans of *Barbarossa* who were used to such things, an NCO in Erwin Jaenecke's *389. Infanterie-Division* was dumbfounded when faced with female Red Army soldiers, whose fighting '...showed itself in treacherous and dangerous ways. They lie concealed in heaps of straw and shoot us in the back when we pass by.'

Heeresgruppe Süd had now fought two pitched battles in three weeks while trying to prepare for a major offensive. Surely now was the time to consolidate and focus exclusively on preparing for *Blau*, but instead, in typical Nazi fashion, a further battle was fought for reasons born more out of the desire for headlines than military necessity. This was Sevastopol.

Lauded as one of the strongest fortresses in the world on the advent of war, Sevastopol was less a fortification and more an armed city ringed with huge concrete emplacements and bunker complexes. Miles of trenches connected artillery and anti-tank gun batteries with machine-gun nests, troop concentration areas and supply and ammunition dumps. First attacked during the previous year's near conquest of Crimea, it had held out, the Soviet amphibious landing on the Kerch peninsula finally halting

German attacks in December. Now, with the Kerch bridgehead extinguished, Manstein was ordered to finish Sevastopol off once and for all. Again supported by Richthofen's ground attack armada, *11. Armee* went into the assault, only this time there was no room for manoeuvre and only a constant grind of head-on attacks to subdue strongpoint after strongpoint. The German air commander noted that 'the infantry suffered heavy losses as it struggled to gain a single kilometre' and his diary entry for 7 June read that 'Russian artillery and armoured fortifications spring to life everywhere... The whole horizon is one tremendous gun-flash.' One of his own Stuka pilots; *Hauptmann* Herbert Paber, said that the defending Russians 'were bombed again and again, one explosion next to another, like poisonous mushrooms ... one can only stand amazed at such resilience – it is unbelievable in the truest sense of the word ... the whole country had to be literally ploughed over by bombs before they yielded anything.'

Paber wasn't exaggerating. To try and break the bloody stalemate Manstein brought up a trio of heavy gun types that exemplified Nazi Germany's taste for the weird and wonderful at the expense of practicality. First up was the *Gamma-Gerät*, a hangover from the trench warfare of the First World War. Weighing 150 metric tons it was almost immobile as it fired its 923-kilogram shells at a rate of around eight an hour. Even larger was the *Karl-Gerät* cannon, three of which were utilised at Sevastopol, firing shells weighing up to 2,170 kilograms each. The battery exhausted its entire stock of ammunition in just two days with limited effect. Last, and most extraordinary, was the railway gun the *Schwerer Gustav* – also known as the *Dora*. The largest and heaviest artillery gun ever built, it needed 4,000 men and five weeks just to get it into position. It fired 47 rounds over five days, by which time its barrel was worn out.

Sevastopol – the home base of the Soviet Black Sea fleet – finally fell on 4 July. The combined German-Romanian *11. Armee* had lost 36,000 men killed, wounded and missing taking it, and perhaps just as importantly had used almost 70,000 tons of munitions. OKW's plan to use Manstein's force as the *Ostheer*'s strategic reserve had to be abandoned as the Army's nine German and three Romanian divisions were burnt out and 11. *Armee* was disbanded thereafter. Its two signal successes at Kerch and Sevastopol were truly pyrrhic victories, fought in a theatre of no strategic value, costing thousands of German and Romanian lives and expending vast amounts of already scarce bullets, bombs and shells.

The three early battles of Kerch, Izyum and Sevastopol had indeed been terrible blows for the Red Army, which lost some 600,000 men in total, but just as in the previous year the ruthlessness of the Soviet state could deal with such horrendous casualties, this time by turning to its vast *gulag* prison population and releasing upwards of a million men out of the camps for service at the front. Poorly trained and equipped they might have been, but they were still there and served to fill the Red Army's ranks once more.

4

BLAU BEGINS!

Even as Manstein's precious assault regiments were being bled white under the blazing Crimean sun, frenzied preparations continued for the launch of *Blau*. Wolfram von Richthofen was constantly in the air in his personal Fieseler Storch visiting his airfields and seeing the front for himself. On Thursday 25 June he was up in the skies once more, binoculars glued to his eyes as he strove to see what was happening on the ground. His pilot knew what his boss wanted and took the tiny aircraft as low as he dared. Overflying the German lines, the Storch found itself above Arno Jahr's *387. Infanterie-Division*. The inexperienced Bavarians and Austrians of the former policeman's *Rheingold Division* were spooked by the sudden appearance of the unfamiliar aircraft and let fly with small-arms fire. Richthofen's pilot was hit and the fuel tank was punctured, but the Luftwaffe general showed his cool head and skill by landing the stricken plane safely on the open steppe. The wounded pilot survived, and on returning to his headquarters Richthofen sent Jahr a short letter thanking him for his men's alertness; 'While it's a delight to see the fighting spirit of the German ground troops against aircraft, may I request that these troops direct that fighting spirit against the Red Air Force.' Writing in his diary he was far less gracious: 'Damn dogs! They don't fire at the Russians but at my Storch!'

Richthofen should have counted his blessings. A few short days before his almost fatal encounter with the men of the *Rheingold*, *Major* Joachim Reichel, chief operations officer for 23. *Panzer-Division*, had been in another Storch flying to one of the final planning missions of the new offensive when Soviet ground fire had brought him and his aircraft down over Red Army lines. What made the incident doubly worse was that contrary to all standing orders Reichel was carrying a complete set of operational orders for *Blau*. A large German patrol – a reinforced *kompanie* from 336. *Infanterie-Division* – was sent out to try and recover both the plans and the bodies and succeeded in finding the downed light aircraft in a small valley. The Storch had a single bullet hole in its fuel tank and there was no sign of fire. A search of the nearby area yielded up two fresh graves some thirty yards from the plane. Digging up the bodies it was difficult to make any identification as the Soviets had taken their papers and ID discs and the corpses were badly disfigured, but it was clear it was Reichel and his pilot. The upshot was that Moscow now had its hands on the entire offensive blueprint.

On being informed of what was a huge breach of security, Hitler flew into a rage and Reichel's boss; *Generalmajor* Hans von Boineburg-Lengsfeld, was immediately sacked and replaced by Erwin Mack. The decision was made to continue on as planned nevertheless, and final preparations for the offensive were made.

Although nowhere near as powerful as the horde massed for *Barbarossa* the previous summer, the *Blau* attack force was still impressive given the *Ostheer*'s considerable limitations. Ewald von Kleist's *1. Panzerarmee* was its largest formation at over 220,000 men with some 480 panzers and self-propelled assault guns, while Paulus's 6. *Armee* wasn't far behind with 200,000 men and 300 panzers. Hoth's 4. *Panzerarmee* had the same number of panzers and only 20,000 fewer men, while 17. *Armee* would put 150,000 troops and 180 tanks into the battle. Hans von Salmuth's 2. *Armee* would largely carry out a flank protection role but would still contribute 95,000 men to the offensive. That meant over three-quarters of a million German troops with 1,440 panzers and self-propelled guns would be committed, including no fewer than 125 Panzer Mark IVs with the new long barrelled 7.5cm cannon. On top of that would be the 200,000 men each of Italy's Eighth Army and Hungary's Second, and they would soon be joined by the 230,000 men of Romania's 3rd and 4th Armies. They would each bring their own armour and air support as well, albeit they were pretty thin gruel in comparison to both their German and Soviet counterparts. The Luftwaffe would put almost 2,700 aircraft into the sky at first, although this figure wasn't sustainable for more than a few weeks at best.

Finally, on Sunday 28 June 1942 – a week later than *Barbarossa* had begun the previous year – Nazi Germany's renewed attempt to defeat the Soviet Union and win the war began as *Heeresgruppe Süd* began its march east. To mark the occasion Wilhelm Keitel – with his usual dreadful sense of timing and obsequiousness to his master – sent a signal to all the senior commanders about to be involved stating that 'Fleeing prisoners of war are to be shot without a preliminary warning to stop. Any and all resistance by PoWs, even passive, must be entirely eliminated by the use of arms.' The officially sanctioned murder of PoWs that had been such a facet of *Barbarossa* was to be continued with *Blau*.

Even as Keitel's message was being digested, the guns boomed. Hans Heinz Rehfeldt was awed by the spectacle:

> Our artillery and Nebelwerfer [literally 'smoke mortars', multi-barrelled rocket launchers] fired from all barrels. Fountains of earth, dust and smoke rose up on Ivan's side from the impact ... in the midst of this deafening racket, panzers, assault guns and tank destroyers came up ... and headed for the Russian positions... High above us appeared formations of the Luftwaffe; He 111s to bomb the rear areas, Ju 87 Stukas to circle the advanced trenches and then ... fall almost vertically to attack with 'Jericho sirens' howling.

The assault was a complete success. 'We reached the forward Russian line unopposed. Everything was bombed to rubble ... we saw their many dead, destroyed machine-gun posts, mortar pits – all ruined. We had broken through!'

Salmuth's 2. *Armee* and Hermann Hoth's 4. *Panzerarmee* moved off across the steppe towards the city of Voronezh, the men full of confidence. 'As far as the eye can see our German forces were advancing. Panzers, assault guns, light armoured personnel carriers, half-tracks, twin-barrelled flak … all pushing forward … we never expected success on this scale and we all now believed we would be victorious in the East in a short time.'[1] Another *landser*, Hans-Albert Giese, was also in good spirits: 'I saw with my own eyes how our panzers shot the Russian colossi to pieces. The German soldier is just better in every department. I also think that it'll be wrapped up here this year.'[2] His comrade Gustav Böker was less optimistic when he wrote home to his parents just before the attack started.

> A year ago we drove into Russia. I can tell you it was a long day back then. At 9 o'clock we crossed over the frontier and now we have been in the workers' paradise for one year. Who thought that back then? Like many others, I guessed it would be about four weeks of war, and how differently everything turned out. Nobody had expected Russia to be so strong a military power. I think if someone would have said back then: 'You will still be in Russia in a year,' we would have thought them crazy. Yet here we are, still in Russia, and who knows for how much longer.[3]

In the wide-open spaces of the south, air power was crucial as Heinz Ludwig, a rear gunner in a ground attack *staffel*, knew only too well: 'The main jobs for our Me 110 … were quite simply everything; pin-point bombing of all sorts of targets – tanks, trains, supply columns, airfields, plus strafing runs in support of our ground troops and also aerial combat with enemy fighters and Il-2 ground attack aircraft.' Ludwig remembered one mission in particular:

> …we attacked enemy tank columns … and in pulling up to re-join our comrades we found ourselves in the middle of a

number of MiG-5s [more likely to be La-5s]. My *Kutscher* [literally 'coachman' i.e. pilot] had one about 100m in front of him in our defensive circle ... and I had another 30-50m behind the tail and flying somewhat lower, so I couldn't hit him without hitting our tail. I kept seeing the face of the Russian pilot appearing in my view but couldn't shoot. I called to my *katschmarek* [wingman] that he should catch up as I had an 'indian' behind me – he must have had jammed guns or he would have shot him down ... for several minutes we flew together in our circle and my backside was twitching. Then my wingman's aircraft appeared ... but he couldn't shoot without hitting us too. I suggested to my pilot that he take some evasive action so I could open fire at him but it didn't come to that as at that point the MiG in front of us tried to leave the circle with a tight right turn and Bruno [pilot *Unteroffizier* Bruno Baumeister]) opened up with all his guns and hit the MiG full on, and all I could see was a fireball ... it was a lovely feeling of waggling our wings to signify our victory when we returned to base.[4]

Another of Ludwig's fellow heavy fighter comrades – Hermann Buchner – was involved in the same attacks. 'We dropped our bombs on our targets and then finished off by flying low-level attacks on any enemy positions we could see, concentrating particularly on breaking up vehicle convoys and destroying as many vehicles as we could. As we pressed home our attacks everything lit up spectacularly ... when we hit munitions dumps.'[5] The air crews' efforts were greatly appreciated by the men on the ground; 'Our planes are now hard at work, it's really fun when you see them flying overhead in droves all heavily laden with bombs ... they never leave Ivan in peace, flying back and forth non-stop.'[6] It was far from being a walkover though, as Horst Ramstetter explained:

When our advance began ... everyone said 'great, we're moving, marching, everything's fine'.... some of the pilots were just 18 and had never flown a mission, they'd had their heads filled with 'Führer, Volk and Vaterland' [Leader, People, Fatherland]. 'We'll storm onwards, we heroes will win the war!'... they came back crying their eyes out. They were ready to drop, they hadn't been prepared for an enemy as ferocious as the Russians. The raw reality dragged them back down to earth.

Just how ferocious the Soviets were was soon demonstrated to the young fliers as some of their opponents turned to a tactic they had used during *Barbarossa* – the *taran*. *Leutnant* Herbert Kuntz saw it for himself. 'A Soviet fighter flies straight into the He 111 [medium bomber] that was flying behind us ... the two aircraft intermingled with each other, and whirled down vertically, no parachutes! The wings are separated from the fuselage and disappear into the clouds below – still no parachutes!'[7] This wasn't the only suicide attack. A day later Lieutenant Vasily Kolesnichenko was killed ramming a Bf 110 fighter.

Shocking though the *taran* tactic was, it failed to hide the fact that the VVS had still not recovered from its near destruction the previous year. Soviet flight academies were churning out masses of ill-trained young pilots who were easy meat for the hugely experienced Luftwaffe *Experten*, as their flying aces were called. 'At 0850hrs ... I took off with Major Herbert Ihlefeld to find an appropriate place for our new airfield. Above the most advanced panzer columns we were suddenly attacked by seven to ten MiG-1s at 2,000 metres altitude... Major Ihlefeld shot down a MiG-1.' Viktor Petermann then had his own opportunity: 'I pursued another one and I fired while banking left, and my burst was so devastating that his left wing was torn off. The aircraft went into a spin ... the pilot saved himself by bailing out.'

Just as in the previous summer, Luftwaffe pilots were scoring freely and their kill numbers once more began to climb dramatically, but their Soviet opponents kept on coming – much to the *jagdfliegers'* consternation. 'Sometimes half their aircraft were shot down, but the Ivans still kept coming.' The Soviet willingness to take terrible casualties and keep on fighting was once again wearing down their enemy, as Heinrich Setz acknowledged in his diary: 'Day after day we hurl ourselves against masses of Russian aircraft... I'm left alone with my few aircraft in an area where the devil himself is let loose...'[8]

On the ground, it seemed the good times were back for the Germans. After the horrors of the winter fighting, once more 'as far as the eye can see armoured vehicles and half-tracks are rolling forward over the steppe. Pennants float in the shimmering afternoon air.'[9] The mass of *landsers* followed in their wake, marching east in the baking summer heat. There was an enforced delay, 'waiting for fresh horses and people too'. Rudolf Oehus declared: 'The offensive has begun! Troops are constantly marching past, the Russian seems to be able to run well again ... we will probably have to march a long time before we catch up with the Russian, he makes a quick escape... We'll only march at night, it's unbearable during the day, it's incredibly hot here.'

Oehus would not be involved in the advance for long. He was kicked in the head by one of the new horses as he went to put him in his traces and would spend weeks in a field hospital recovering before re-joining his gun battery.

As for the rest of his comrades in the army group, they trudged on, marvelling at the enormity of the country as Wilhelm Hoffmann – a *landser* in Georg Pfeiffer's 94. *Infanterie-Division* – described in his diary; 'What great spaces the Soviets occupy, what rich fields there are to be had here after the war's over!' As ever, the roads Hoffmann and his fellow *landsers* were advancing on were just dirt tracks and they threw up clouds of choking dust as one young officer told his brother in a letter home. 'The roads are shrouded in a single thick cloud of dust through which man and beast make their way; it's troublesome for the eyes. The dust often swirls up in thick pillars that blow along the columns making it impossible to see anything for minutes at a time.'[10]

Those same dust clouds were thrown up by Soviet columns, too, and made tempting targets for the likes of Johannes Kaufmann and his *staffel* of Bf 110s: '...the weather was on our side. Day after day the midsummer sun blazed down out of a clear blue sky … this baked the countryside hard … any significant troop or convoy movements were easily spotted by the clouds of dust they threw up.' As soon as the enemy was spotted, the German aircraft 'were ordered to first dive bomb enemy artillery positions and then carry out ground strafing in support of our troops. As usual the pre-op briefing offered very few details…we had to be very careful not to hit our own troops.' Soviet anti-aircraft fire was heavy and accurate. Then Kaufmann was attacked by 'a group of about 15 to 20 I-153s [old-fashioned biplanes] … our Bf 110s were simply too sluggish to indulge in dogfighting.' However, he did manage to shoot one down:

> …to be perfectly honest it was more a matter of luck than skill. My opponent popped up out of nowhere right on front of my nose, he was so close I almost rammed him, and it was sheer reflex that made me jab the gun button. At that range I couldn't miss and the I-153 tipped over and went down shedding pieces.

The tempo of operations was high, and amidst the rolling steppe the German fliers often struggled to identify friend from foe. German troops used so-called *fliegertücher* (flying cloths) – usually a large red, black and white swastika flag – to show the pilots they were friendlies, but the Soviets soon cottoned on and started using them too. Forward units also used white flares as markers, but again, the Soviets copied them, although Kaufmann noticed that 'unlike ours the Russian flares weren't pure white but had a faint yellowish tinge to them, [but] this wasn't always easy to see in the heat of battle, especially in bright sunlight.'

The German advance was rapid. Having positioned the bulk of Red Army reserves to the north for the anticipated German thrust on Moscow, the Soviet supreme military council, the STAVKA, scrambled to send reinforcements south. *6. Armee* had begun its part in the offensive two days after *Blau* had been launched, striking southeast and heading towards the River Don. Its armoured and motorised formations made a big impression on one young *landser* from 389. *Infanterie-Division*: 'You can't imagine the speed of our dear motorised comrades.' He was also impressed with the support the Luftwaffe was providing; 'What a feeling of security we get when our pilots are above us, because you never see any Russian aircraft.' The rapidity of the advance brought problems too, as one of the supporting fighter pilots, Hermann Wolf, detailed;

> We were seldom accommodated on proper airfields ... mostly we occupied poorly prepared meadows or even just fallow land, often directly behind the advancing panzer columns and in front of the infantry ... in the first few days only the most necessary ground crew were with us, by the time the main body of support personnel caught up with us we were often already at the next advanced field base. Our quarters were in tents or in a farmer's hut if a village was nearby. We slept on air mattresses in sleeping bags. We only very seldom came near any populated towns or cities.[11]

Wolf was no fan of living rough on the steppe, but not all the Luftwaffe pilots felt the same. Johannes Kaufmann for one rather enjoyed it; 'We were back under canvas, there was the same healthy spirit of unity and comradeship ... there was no sense of apathy among us ... we all had surprisingly hearty appetites and we were very well fed. We suffered few illnesses as our medical officer kept a close check on us, and we were given regular injections against a variety of diseases...and at the end of a day's labours we all slept soundly.'[12]

While the Luftwaffe's logistics system seemed to be working well, the same could not be said of the Army's. With motorised transport at a premium, feeding the troops was left to the horse-drawn *Gulaschkanone* (goulash cannon), complete with its 200-litre cooking pot, 90-litre coffee kettle, and crew of cooks and bottle-washers. Envied by many of its opponents for its ability to prepare hot, fresh food for its soldiers, the German system was severely hampered by its reliance on horsepower and the need to source ingredients locally. Buying already scarce food from reluctant farmers wasn't easy in western Europe, but in the Soviet Union it was altogether harder from people who had barely enough to feed themselves. One German officer wrote in his diary that his men's hunger was so bad that 'The *landsers* go to vegetable gardens and take everything.' A war correspondent attached to 6. *Armee* for the advance saw how troops 'jump down from panzers and half-tracks. Suddenly a great execution is carried out. The poultry, with bloody ruffs and beating their wings in a paroxysm, were carried back to the vehicles. The men jumped back on board, the tracks ground the soil and the vehicles moved on again.' The theft of what little food the local people had was entirely predictable, given the Germans unwillingness to stockpile enough rations to feed their troops, as one officer remarked: 'It's a scandal. Severe prohibitions are published, but the ordinary soldier hardly restrains himself. He is forced into such conduct by hunger.' Not all the advancing troops had the same experience. Remarkably, one officer said, 'I've never eaten so much as here. We eat honey with spoons until we're sick, and in the evening we eat boiled ham.'

The Germans weren't the only Axis soldiers looting as they went. On Paulus's left flank were the Hungarians of Gusztáv Jány's Second Army, and they lost no time in stealing whatever they wanted from the terrified locals as one of their NCOs noted: 'Our lads have stolen three jugs of milk. The women had taken the milk down to the basement when our lads appeared with grenades and pretended to throw them. The women were scared and ran away, and our lads took the milk.' Hurrying to join Jány's force was István Balogh. Sitting on a troop train he saw

...the sites of the great battles of 1941. Everywhere destroyed Russian tanks can be seen. We look at them and fear the idea of this Red hell moving against Hungary ... we are firmly confident that we shall smash the Red threat to Europe... It is frightful to think how many people sacrificed themselves, how many of our heroic German comrades gave their lives here.

Getting closer to the front, his early confidence began to waver:

> Artillery fire can be heard. We are likely to enter battle soon. Everywhere the remains of burnt-out German vehicles can be seen. Are the Germans starting to lose their military luck? The graves of German and Hungarian soldiers can be seen... Everywhere there are corpses, field guns, vehicles and scattered weapons.

Before long, he and his comrades were faced with the threat of partisans, who were almost certainly Red Army soldiers stranded behind the German lines as the advance swept over them. 'We were again attacked by partisans. One of our men was wounded. At seven o'clock we set off to sweep the district. We killed five Russian soldiers. Two more were taken for interrogation and shot afterwards.'

With the Germans and their allies pressing forward, Stalin then did something new and startling – he sanctioned a strategic withdrawal by the Red Army. Hitler believed – as did Bock incidentally – that the Red Army was unable to learn from the mistakes it had made during *Barbarossa*, and that swift German action would enable *Heeresgruppe Süd* to trap the remaining mass of Soviet formations against the Don. Hitlerian logic then decreed that with little or no reserves to speak of, the Soviets would collapse in the south, allowing 6. *Armee* to reach and cut the Volga as a supply route north, and then the Caucasus would fall like a ripe plum into the Reich's lap. The lynchpin to this thinking was that the Soviets would stand and fight where they were, enabling the far nimbler Germans to encircle them in a series of pockets. The Red Army withdrawing in good order was not part of the plan. In the face of this new strategy, Bock was unable to recreate the success of Bialystok-Minsk, Bryansk or Vyazma, and even though the advance was capturing vast new territories for the Reich, it was failing to achieve a decisive victory. Thousands of Soviet soldiers did indeed become captives, but the numbers were nowhere near what the Germans expected.

Most of the men involved in the offensive itself didn't appreciate the reality, as all they saw were columns of prisoners and daily advances. Franz Wertheim was serving in a military hospital behind the advancing troops: 'With a powerful thrust the newly gathered troops threw themselves on the enemy and pressed him back in mighty battles. Now endless trains of prisoners began to pass our hospital again, and the majority of our patients came from the other side.' The overt racism that had characterised *Barbarossa* surfaced once more and Wertheim seemed to forget his Hippocratic oath:

> Unbelievably primitive people they were now who came under my knife! We had to economise in the use of anaesthetics which we saved for our troops. But these near-animal creatures dumbly submitted to our operations without speaking and almost without wincing. I felt more like a vet than a doctor, and the primitive conditions under which we worked as we followed our advancing troops seemed less incongruous than they would have if I had been working on ordinary civilised and sensate beings.[13]

'Primitive' as he thought the Russians were, that didn't stop him from taking one as a mistress. 'Olga was wonderfully built and enveloped me with the warmth of her charms.'

Back at the front, the same old pattern as the previous year reappeared with the panzers racing ahead and the infantry marching in their wake struggling to keep up. Driving forward under the night stars, a young panzer officer recalled that 'if we wanted to capture the bridges over the River Kalitva intact we had to reach Rossosh by dawn ... we roared unrecognised past advancing Russian artillery and infantry units.' Reaching the town's outskirts by 0300hrs, the panzers spotted a newly built military bridge and without hesitating charged across. Timoshenko himself was almost captured as the town fell, only escaping at the last minute. A great success though Rossosh's capture was, there were ominous signs for the Germans as the same panzer officer admitted, 'All contact with the enemy had to be avoided due to the shortages of ammunition and fuel.' The much-lauded *Grossdeutschland* was in the same position. 'We ground to a halt in open fields, out of fuel, and had enforced rest waiting for Ju 52s to bring us more up in barrels.'[14] Another panzer crewman bemoaned the fact that 'the orders came to form a hedgehog and wait for fuel and the infantry to catch up.' The offensive was barely a week old and lack of supplies was already a problem.

Behind the panzers the footsore *landsers* continued to march into the tinder-dry vastness that is southern Russia in the summer. A newly fledged recruit experiencing his first campaign wrote that they were always so tired:

> At night we made camp in the fields and each man had to dig his own bed with an entrenching tool ... we stopped and simply fell asleep where we were, suddenly a general appeared and bawled us out as the rifles had to be stacked properly ... we marched day and night.

German commanders, like the panzer officer Erhard Raus, understood just how difficult the advance was for the ordinary *landser*:

> Each village in southern Russia has one or two wells, but during summer their water is scant and warm ... many wells dry up, and such water as there is must be boiled before drinking... German troops fighting between the Don and the Volga had practically no local water supply.'[15]

One *landser* put it more succinctly; 'On this endless steppe there are no forests to give protection from aircraft, and, above all, no water for the men and horses.' Helmut Wegmann agreed with his nameless comrade: 'The terrain here is simply featureless; a huge steppe of sand. It cannot be any worse in Africa.'

5

THE CAUCASUS – THERE AND BACK AGAIN!

Adolf Hitler was not a patient man. Neither was he a man prepared to accept what he saw as failure from his subordinates. As far as he was concerned, he had been extremely generous in giving Bock a second chance after the disaster in front of Moscow the previous winter, and now Bock was failing him again by not finishing off the Red Army in the south. He wasn't the only one underperforming either. The 'Little Emperor', as Alexander Löhr was called behind his back, was hitting the VVS hard and in two weeks his fighters had destroyed almost 500 Soviet aircraft, but he hadn't landed the hammer blows Hitler expected of him. Running out of patience, Hitler had him shuffled off to command *12. Armee* in the Balkans, while his aggressive subordinate, von Richthofen, was promoted to take his place and lead *Luftflotte 4*. Richthofen in turn handed his corps to Martin Fiebig, who would now head up the most potent aerial weapon the Reich possessed at that point. However, it was the changes made on the ground that had the biggest impact on *Blau* – now rechristened *Braunschweig* as of 30 June – and the entire future of the campaign.

Immensely irritated at what he saw as Bock's overcaution, the dictator decided to radically alter the very basis of the offensive. The original plan called for the Germans to reach the Volga, cut it as a supply route and form a hard shoulder along the River Don away to the northwest. Then – and only then – would the bulk of their forces begin the advance south to reach the Caucasus and take the oil fields. Now Hitler effectively threw that plan in the bin. Instead, he would split *Heeresgruppe Süd* into two, with one part heading east to the Volga and the second heading south at the same time. Neither would be able to support the other, their objectives would be hundreds of miles apart, and German resources, already creaking under the strain, would have to support two completely separate assaults. Senior officers, led by Bock himself, were horrified.

When Hitler flew to Bock's headquarters at Poltava in Ukraine on 13 July – the very site of Tsar Peter the Great's decisive victory over the Swedish king Charles XII in 1709 – the ramrod-backed Prussian *feldmarschall* came the closest he ever did to openly arguing with his leader, telling him that the new plan was folly and that in his view the Soviets were 'gradually getting smart'. Halder – forever at his master's shoulder – agreed with Bock, only for Hitler to wave away their arguments. 'Nonsense. The Russians are in full flight, they're finished, they are reeling from the blows we have dealt them during the past few months.' Hitler was wilfully misinterpreting Moscow's new willingness to retreat in front of the *Ostheer* and avoid becoming encircled to prove beyond question that he was right and the Red Army was close to collapse. When Bock continued to disagree, he sealed his own fate and was sacked four days later, ostensibly for health reasons, although the news wasn't made public, and Bock continued to be featured in the newsreels back in the Reich for weeks afterwards.[1]

Hitler then did something he almost never did during the war and moved his headquarters out of Germany and closer to the front. The day before he dismissed Bock the Führer's entire staff were taken to an airfield and greeted by 'an imposing sight – with the great aircraft lined up ready to take off, their engines turning over, and the air filled with the deep roar of vibrating wings and wires,' whereupon typists, cooks, drivers and the entire paraphernalia of the dictator and his entourage filed aboard sixteen waiting aircraft and 'one after another they rolled down the runway and lifted into the air.'

Three hours later they had all landed safely at Vinnytsia in Ukraine. There, in a nearby triangular-shaped forest, was a brand-new complex camouflaged under the tall pine trees. Built by the paramilitary construction gangs of the *Organization Todt* (OT) the new headquarters – codenamed *Werwolf* – comprised a collection of wooden huts and two reinforced concrete bunkers in case of air attack. The site was not well chosen, being plagued by damp, stifling humidity and swarms of mosquitoes. The staff hated it, and Hitler, far more appreciative of the freshness of the mountain air at his beloved *Berghof*, was even more irritable and bad-tempered than usual under the blazing sun of a Ukrainian summer. The three and a half months they would spend in the Ukrainian forest were remembered as some of the most miserable of the war by surviving members of the *Führerhauptquartier Werwolf* staff. Now, believing himself close to the action – in fact Vinnytsia is over 600 miles from Stalingrad – Hitler began to routinely interfere in the minutiae of operational detail. As Halder said, 'What had been comparatively infrequent in previous campaigns now became a daily occurrence.'

Nevertheless, one week after arriving at *Werwolf* Hitler issued *Führerbefehl Nr. 45* (Führer Directive No. 45), which formally split Bock's former command into *Heeresgruppen A* and *B*. *Heeresgruppe A* would primarily be a German affair, with Ewald von Kleist's *1. Panzerarmee* and Richard Ruoff's *17. Armee*, bolstered by some nine Romanian and Italian divisions. Its task was to head south, take Rostov-on-Don and then advance into the Caucasus. It would be led by Siegmund Wilhelm List, a man the contemporary Nazi writer Paul Carrell described as 'clever, cool … not an impulsive charger at closed doors, but a man who believed in sound military planning and detested all military gambles.' Little wonder then that Hitler disliked him and was only persuaded to appoint him by Alfred Jodl's entreaties.

As for *Heeresgruppe B*, it would comprise Hans Salmuth's *2. Armee*, Hermann Hoth's *4. Panzerarmee* and Paulus's *6. Armee*. Its objective was the Volga, and for the first time the city of Stalingrad was mooted as an area of focus. Given the enormously long frontage it would then have to hold while the Caucasus was plundered for oil, all four allied Axis armies were pencilled in to join it once the river had been reached. Command of the army group was given to Maximilian von Weichs, a Catholic Bavarian aristocrat whose wire-rimmed glasses and tall, slightly stooped frame reminded those who met him more of a university professor than a field general. He was, however, quite highly rated, with even Guderian – notorious for being scathing about his fellow officers – saying he was 'as clever as he was upstanding and valiant'.

With the decision made to divide *Heeresgruppe Süd*, a major regrouping exercise followed with several corps and divisions reassigned. The most important of these for Paulus and 6. *Armee* was the loss of *3. Panzer* and *23. Panzerdivision*, both sent to bolster Kleist's *1. Panzerarmee*. The idea was that Hoth's armour would more than make up for their exclusion. However, the real problem for the new plan lay in the allocation of air power and logistics support, neither of which was in abundance. In the air, Fiebig's corps would remain in the north with Weichs, and would even receive some units that would otherwise have expected to head into the Caucasus. It was considered by Vinnytsia that the major threat from the VVS would be in the Volga area, while the Caucasus would be starved of Soviet aerial units who would find it nigh on impossible to operate in the mountains and semi-deserts of the region, hence the balance of German Luftwaffe *staffeln* being kept up north.

Logistics was an even bigger headache for the Germans. There simply wasn't the fuel and ammunition to properly supply both offensives – one would have to take priority over the other. Hitler though, was unwilling to make that decision, so opted for the worst of all worlds and insisted both army groups would have to try and get by on what they were given. So began what the *landsers* ironically nicknamed the *Kaukasus hin und zurück* (Caucasus there and back) offensive, as the Germans advanced out of Europe and into Asia.

For Helmut Paulus and his comrades from Albert Buck's *198. Infanterie-Division* the offensive began with them crossing the

River Mius in inflatable dinghies in a re-run of their *Barbarossa* operation the previous year. That river crossing had been followed by a terrifying few days being bombed, shelled and shot at by the Red Army until relieved. He prayed this time would be different. When Paulus and his comrades reached the far bank of the Mius with only sporadic fire greeting them, a huge sense of relief gripped the young *landser* and his comrades.

Forming up, his regiment headed east and for almost a fortnight they marched on, constantly having to deploy and fight the Soviet rear guards left behind to slow them up. Soon the *landsers* realised that something had changed from the battles of '41. No longer were large Red Army formations sitting almost immobile and allowing themselves to be cut off by the advancing Germans, now they retreated in an orderly fashion – and even worse, they did so in the backs of American-made trucks. As one of them noted 'Some Russian tank units were equipped entirely with Shermans, Ami [German slang for American] Dodge trucks and jeeps. Even the uniforms the Russian soldiers wore … were of Ami origin, and so were the rations we pulled out of the containers on knocked-out vehicles. The only thing left of Russian origin was the soldier himself.' The Lend-Lease program was proving its worth for the Red Army.

Stumbling ever onwards, Paulus found himself 'completely exhausted and over-strained, eyes burning for sleep, nerves totally overstrung'.[2] He wasn't alone. Ewald Klapdor, still a panzer crewman in *SS-Division Wiking*, noted that 'within a single regiment of *73. Infanterie-Division* forty men were lost to heat exhaustion within a very short period.' Not surprising given that 'the weather was sunny and hot. The almost unbearable heat demanded the utmost from the infantry.'[3] While Hans Heinz Rehfeldt remembered that 'the sun was beating down and the sweat stung our eyes. After a short while the dust caked our faces like a mask.'

Riding alongside Klapdor and his fellow Waffen-SS troopers was the south Tyrolean Josef 'Sepp' de Giampietro, a special operations soldier in *Bau-Lehr-Bataillon z.b.V. 800 (800th Special*

Duties Construction Training Battalion, better known as the *Brandenburgers*). Initially without transport, de Giampietro remembered:

> We marched beneath the boiling hot sun, the sweltering summer heat was unbearable. Our thoughts went out to those poor bastards in the infantry who had to go through this hell on a daily basis ... sweat poured down our bodies in rivulets, our feet were burning and our tongues were stuck to the roofs of our mouths ... after several hours we arrived at a fountain and literally raced up to it!'[4]

Finally allocated a few trucks, the Brandenburgers rolled forward through the countryside. 'There wasn't a bush in sight, no houses, no hills, nothing but clouds of dust and dirt as our travel companions ... enormous fields brimming with sunflowers bordered the road. People greeted us and were friendly, the children had blond hair and sparkling light-blue eyes.' The advance became a nightmare of heat and dirt. 'We inched forward enveloped by a huge cloud of smoke and dust, driving past units marching alongside us, those poor devils having no choice but to soldier on under the oppressive heat ... the sky was blue, there was no breeze, no relief, full of envy their red-rimmed eyes looked up at us sitting in our trucks, smoking.'

One of those infantrymen sullenly looking up at de Giampietro and his fellow passengers was Helmut Paulus. Choking on the clouds of dust that settled on clothes, faces and lips, their only relief came when they captured a Soviet village and plundered it for food, 'eggs, milk, butter and first-rate white bread, which tasted wonderful.' A handful of Red Army stragglers put up their hands and surrendered. They were immediately pressed into service as ammunition carriers, and the advance went on.

The next major objective was the great city of Rostov-on-Don – the gateway to the Caucasus. Captured late the previous year, it had been given up as indefensible by Reichenau in his first act as commander of *Heeresgruppe Süd*. Now, eight months later, the Germans would once again try and take the city. Richthofen ordered all available air assets to attack: 'The bridges have been destroyed ... our aircraft drop their bombs into massed concentrations of enemy troops.' Lying as it does across the Don estuary, the key to the city was a huge dam topped by a causeway and railway line connecting Rostov to neighbouring Bataysk some fifteen kilometres away, and most especially the last section of the causeway, which was a bridge. Capturing that bridge was a job for the Brandenburgers. Specially trained and selected, with many of them being ethnic Germans – *volksdeutsche* – who had lived abroad and spoke an array of languages, the Brandenburgers had proved their worth during the Western campaign and *Barbarossa*, seizing vital bridges before the enemy could blow them up. Often, they would wear enemy uniforms and appear in captured trucks, creating chaos and confusion and giving themselves the edge they needed for success against the odds.

Approaching the city from the west, de Giampietro watched fascinated as 'a Russian plane cruised above us ... tracer bullets caught up with him and with a cloud of smoke trailing behind, he came swirling down, smashing to smithereens as he hit the ground.' Working their way through the city's outskirts, the Brandenburgers made common cause with SS grenadiers from the *Wiking*:

> Right from the word go, and without having to say much, we got along famously. They provided us with covering fire while we moved forwards, and vice versa. Alternating our movement, we systematically cleared street after street, garden after garden, and house after house.

Lying up for a couple of hours near the target, *Leutnant* Siegfried Grabert finally gave the orders for the assault: 'We are attacking at 0230 ... listen up, you're to run for your lives. You've got to get across before Ivan realizes he's being attacked. When the first shot is fired our covering fire starts... Don't worry a damn about the

Ivans at the bridge, we'll take care of them – just push ahead.' It was the very early hours of Saturday 25 July when the commandos went into action.

> As was our practice we stormed the enemy without uttering a sound … we didn't shout 'Hurrah!' as the infantry did, we Brandenburgers never did that sort of thing … our panting was drowned out by the firing around us … we stumbled across dead bodies, were they Russians or ours? There was no time to check … hand grenades were thrown, shooting from the hip and swinging a spade we penetrated the Russian posts and wiped out their crews. We threw out the dead Soviets from their holes and jumped in ourselves.

With the bridge in their hands the Brandenburgers then had to sit and wait for the follow-on troops to arrive and relieve them. Knowing full well just how important the bridge was, the Soviets soon overcame their initial shock and threw everything they had at the German commandos. When one of his men went down wounded, de Giampietro called for volunteers to help go get him; 'I'll dash out and pull him in – who'll join me? "Me, me, me" came the responses – everyone volunteered to help our friend.' Under a smattering of covering fire the rescuers sprang forward. 'We fired our machine-guns and in a few short strides were by our injured comrade's side. He didn't move … was he dead already? We pulled him up, that's when Krüger screamed and collapsed; "I'm hit in the knee!" We were swept by gunfire, bullets ploughing into the mud around us.' Grabbing Krüger, de Giampietro pulled him towards a ditch; 'Head-first we flung ourselves into cover. Machine-gunner Nr. 1, Linhart, who was covering us got hit in the head and tumbled backwards. Another shot literally tore Grabert's cap into shreds, another comrade cried out "Help! Help!"'[5]

Lack of numbers and the sheer weight of Soviet fire soon began to tell and left the Brandenburgers hanging on by their fingertips, but they were saved.

They came straight at us … a heaving steamroller with sparks spraying in all directions … each of us was fully aware we would lose the fight if Ivan succeeded in penetrating our hedgehog position. We wouldn't stand a chance if it came to close combat fighting… Our Stukas appeared, roaring and dropping bombs right into the midst of the attacking Russian lines … they had come late … very late, but not too late.

The Brandenburgers had won out, but the price was heavy indeed. 'The first half-company was completely wiped out … we'd suffered 30 losses, four were still missing, probably drowned in the brown waters of the Don, and there were 36 injured, some of them seriously.' *Leutnant* Grabert had lost half a finger to a stray bullet at the beginning of the assault and had then – in accordance with *landser* lore – believed himself invulnerable and on his way home. It was not to be. Hit again, this time by machine-gun fire, de Giampietro recorded that '*Leutnant* Grabert died of his wounds.'

Despite the Brandenburgers losses, the capture of Rostov was a stunning success that filled the headlines back in the Reich. Thousands of Soviets fell into German hands as Ewald Klapdor saw for himself: 'Russian prisoners with bread bags in their hands or blankets half slung over their shoulders … the local people looked on seemingly apathetically. I thought 'why didn't they offer their fellow countrymen something?' but I'd been told that they believed the prisoners were traitors who hadn't fulfilled their obligation to fight to the end.'[6]

With Rostov in his hands, Wilhelm List contemplated the next stage of his offensive. It was more than 700 miles from the city to the oil Mecca of Baku. With 4. *Panzerarmee* supporting Weichs's drive for the Volga, List could count on just 400 panzers to spearhead his own advance, and many of those were in need of maintenance after already covering close on 300 miles since the start of *Blau*. The terrain he had to cross was a military planners' nightmare, with the open steppe waterless and almost desert in the main, but also cut by several large rivers which would need fording. He couldn't rely on the Luftwaffe to smooth his path either, as despite the VVS having lost almost 800 aircraft since the start of the campaign, a steady stream of reinforcements meant that the Soviets now outnumbered the Germans in the air. The situation wasn't helped by that old Luftwaffe bugbear of serviceability, with one of List's key fighter wings – Günther Lützow's *Jagdgeschwader 3 Udet* – struggling to keep half its aircraft able to fly. Lützow's men had passed the 2,000-kill mark earlier in the year but were now increasingly thinly spread. As a pilot, Johannes Kaufmann saw just how difficult it all was: 'Our ground crews came under even greater pressure … in addition to keeping our aircraft serviceable they were also responsible for our many moves forward.' There were five different temporary airfields in one month for Kaufmann's *staffel*.

The main issue, though, was the lack of fuel. There wasn't enough aviation fuel for the Luftwaffe, or gasoline for the panzers and other motorised transport, and as Kurt von Tippelskirch noted, 'Supply routes had become so long that the supply columns used up virtually all the fuel they could carry just to cover the long distances.' The situation led to some novel measures. 'Finally, the paradoxical situation came about that camel caravans had to be pressed into service for the transportation of fuel supplies.' An SS trooper seeing those same caravans wrote in his diary, 'We saw actual camels for the first time, which meant Asia was coming in sight. It is unbelievably hot here.'

Regardless, the advance ploughed on with the panzers taking the lead. 'Like the iron tip of a long-shafted spear, our armoured group drove on into the slowly withdrawing columns of Russians which, nevertheless, continued to escape complete envelopment… No-one took an interest in taking prisoners, our motto was Forward!' That initial optimism soon dampened. 'Several panzer commanders got shot in the head [and] we became more cautious.' For most of List's men the renewed advance meant trudging forward on foot, covering up to thirty miles a day at what the Luftwaffe general Hermann Plocher called 'an incredibly fast pace'. Exhausted though the infantry were, they still found time to appreciate the efforts of their Luftwaffe comrades: 'Everywhere there were traces of German air attacks. On the roads there were overturned vehicles and heavy weapons. Freight trains were still burning on open stretches of tracks.' Another *landser* remarked that 'If we looked up we saw our aircraft, *staffel* after *staffel*, in endless aerial fighting ... it was a proud feeling for us to be supported so well from the air.'

Gerd Schindler was a *jagdflieger* supporting the offensive and described how he and his fellow fighter pilots adapted to the conditions they faced.

In the Caucasus the fighter activity had its own character ... tactics against Russian aircraft differed as per type, so for fighters we tried to surprise them from altitude, from out of the sun or from behind, or in dogfights we shot at them with deflection using machine-guns or 2cm cannons ... we flew in well-defined *Rotte* [Pack – pair of aircraft] and *Schwarm* [four aircraft in two *Rotte*] formations and could see the Russian fighters from a long way off. They typically flew in large beehive formations of 20-30 aircraft – in bullet-shaped masses. We tried to burst through them or to pick off one flying on the edge of their formations. Their ground attack IL-2s were still flying without rear gunners in those days ... the aircraft were flown by women sometimes ... when attacked they formed a defensive circle and protected each other's tails or flew stubbornly on to their targets. They relied on their thick armour as our rounds bounced off these cumbersome aircraft. We soon found out that to be successful we needed to hit the oil coolers in their bellies, or fire right into the cockpit during a dogfight ... bombers we attacked from behind trying first to eliminate the rear gunners and then either hit the wing tanks or engines and set the aircraft on fire. Our machine-gun belts were loaded with different types of ammo such as explosive rounds, AP [armour piercing], incendiary and tracer. Boston bombers [the American designed and made Douglas A-20 Havoc medium bomber] stubbornly flew onto their targets, either alone or in formations of up to ten aircraft. Parachute escapes from shot-up Russian aircraft were seldom seen, it being rumoured that either they weren't allowed to jump or they didn't have chutes.[7]

The likes of Schindler and Kaufmann couldn't be everywhere at once though, and the VVS soon became a real threat, as a Finnish SS grenadier recalled:

> They were constantly above our marching columns and caused confusion … direct losses were limited but they had a significant effect on our fighting spirit … our men became very frightened when they came diving towards the columns. If the vehicles didn't stop fast enough the soldiers simply jumped out at full speed.

Even the panzers weren't immune as Ewald Klapdor witnessed at first-hand: 'We were suddenly attacked by Russian fighters whose machine-gun fire pelted the quickly closed hatches and the rear decks like hail. They could tell we were helpless and wouldn't leave us alone.'

The advance went on towards an endless horizon. 'The great wide openness, which seemed to go on without end to the south and east, swallowed us up … our column appeared to get ever smaller … there was only enemy in front of us, who appeared to be withdrawing in an orderly fashion.' The élite Grossdeutschland was at the forefront: 'The sun beats down, often up to 41 degrees Celsius, the columns whip up clouds of dust, often hiding the following vehicle from sight. We wear green rubber goggles against it, but the dust and sweat sticks and you get grit between your teeth.' Another *landser* wrote:

> There are harvested fields as far as the eye can see. We start off singing, but slowly and surely this dies away … during the afternoon the sun really beats down. We carry on past nightfall … we collapse to the ground in a hollow in the steppe … that night we sleep like the dead.

Roused at 0500hrs the exhausted *landsers* were given 'hot coffee, half a loaf of Army bread per man and a piece of hard-cured sausage' and headed east once more. The heavy weapons and supplies – mortars, infantry cannon, howitzers, extra ammunition and so on – went on the *kompanie's* horse-drawn wagons, but even so every man was burdened with a mountain of equipment.

> Full kit with blanket and ground sheet, steel helmet... We have a full ammo pouch on our belt, on our backs the kitbag with a field canteen, and on the other side the folded entrenching tool. A gas mask is slung around our necks ... and the heavy rifle swings back and forth from its strap around our necks. Lastly, a ditty bag is carried in one hand, filled with clean socks, underwear and similar items. The whole lot weighs about 40lbs.

Unsurprisingly, even among these young, fit men, Russia's endless miles took their toll, the sun flaying the *landsers* as they marched ever on. 'Men regularly fall to the ground shattered. After a while they stand up again and struggle on ... they are completely exhausted.'

Senior officers were not immune to the immensity of the trackless steppe either, with Kleist writing in his diary: 'These vast spaces depress me. And these vast hordes of people! We're lost if we don't win them over!' The panzer general wasn't alone in thinking the key to final German success was to use the peoples of the Soviet Union themselves to defeat Stalin and the communists, but in the Nazis' twisted world there was never any real chance of the population being seen as anything other than something to be abused, exploited and murdered. The previous year, this poison had helped create an atmosphere in the *Barbarossa* invasion force that had left the conquerors' path strewn with the bodies of hundreds of thousands of unarmed Red Army PoWs, innocent civilians, and Soviet Jews. With the German advance now going beyond the major areas of Jewish settlement, the SS and police murder squads and their local militia helpers were concentrating on the surviving Jewish populations in the occupied territories. The Nazis were also evolving their murder machine and the infamous Wannsee Conference held six months previously on 20 January had paved the way for a move away from mass shooting to the use of gas chambers and the killing centres of Treblinka, Sobibor, Belzec and Auschwitz-Birkenau.

For Red Army PoWs, the outlook wasn't that much better. The German military hierarchy still had little or no interest in their survival, and large numbers were killed as soon as they surrendered. 'Many Russians were hidden in the cornfields. We shot five of them dead for refusing our order to drop their weapons ... another fired at one of our men, hitting him in the stomach. This Russian was beaten to death with rifle butts.'[8] Just as during *Barbarossa*, a great many ordinary German soldiers saw continued Soviet resistance not as courage in the face of an invader but as fanaticism on the part of uncivilised savages, and therefore felt it acceptable to commit atrocities, as Eberhard Kehrle described: 'We were with 1. *Gebirgs-Division* and when one of us had been killed, no *leutnant* needed to give any orders. It was pistols drawn, and women, children, everything we saw.'[9] It wasn't just the Germans who showed themselves prone to fits of barbarity, as one Russian *babushka* (grandmother) remembered: 'The Romanians were terrible, they wouldn't leave the women alone. There was a lot of rape in the town. I didn't hear of anybody being shot, but maybe 30 or 50 people were taken away...' as for the Germans, 'They just thought we were their slaves.'

By now the German supply lines were ridiculously long and food in particular became scarcer, with predictable consequences. 'Faces gradually became narrower, uniforms became more and more loose fitting ... the food became more monotonous; boiled chicken, eggs and cucumbers were the standard meal.' As ever in the fighting in the East, the idea of a solid frontline was an illusion. Large numbers of Red Army troops were either cut off behind the advance or deliberately biding their time for an opportunity to attack. Those attacks fell on soft targets such as single vehicles and supply columns, as despatch rider Wilhelm Eising witnessed:

A large supply convoy had been attacked during the night by the Russians and destroyed. The lorry drivers had been shot where they sat; the co-drivers who had attempted to flee lay stabbed or clubbed to death near the vehicles. We found neither wounded nor survivors. The vehicles had been plundered and the dead had been relieved of their effects. The body strippers had been!

When the Red Army did stand and fight, the battles were vicious; 'Direct hit! There was a flash right in front of me on the gun mantel. A shot of flame, a terrible crack. I could move all my limbs but the flash didn't go out, it was burning inside our fighting compartment, "Bail out!"'[10]

Henk Kistemaker, a Dutchman serving in the *SS-Wiking*, vividly recalled those days:

The temperatures were blisteringly hot … the Russians on the other side of the river expected our attack … suddenly we heard a scream from the next-door machine-gun post – someone had been hit – again by a Russian sniper… It turned out to be a Belgian guy … a nice guy but I thought he was a little careless about his cover and this had now cost him dear … he was bleeding like a slaughtered pig. The bullet had entered his head by his right cheekbone just below his eye, went straight through part of his head and exited at the left side of his neck. The shot went through his tongue but not his windpipe.

Kistemaker and another comrade took him to a medical station. 'The nurse offered us a cup of chocolate milk.' The Belgian boy had some too, but 'he poured it into his mouth and it ran out through the hole in his neck!'[11]

Beyond the plains were the Caucasus mountains themselves, crowned by the giant Mount Elbrus. On 21 August, a 23-strong party of *gebirgsjäger* (mountaineers) led by *Hauptmann*'s Heinz Groth and Max Gämmerler planted the swastika flag on the mountain's summit and celebrated with a glass of ice-cold schnapps. A week earlier, the first of the trio of oilfield objectives was reached when Maykop in the Kuban region fell to Traugott Herr's *13. Panzerdivision*, only for the panzer crews to find the huge oil storage tanks ablaze, the oilfields stripped of equipment, and the wells themselves capped with tons of concrete poured in by Red Army demolition teams.

Despite the capture of the oilfields being the raison d'etre for the entire offensive in the first place, the Germans were ill-prepared to reap the benefits of taking Maykop and discovered that the necessary equipment needed to reopen the wells was snarled up far to the west somewhere in the rail network. A group of drilling engineers did indeed arrive, only to be targeted by Soviet partisans who mounted a night attack on their barracks, killing and wounding several. The Germans then struggled to make headway in putting the facilities back into production and never succeeded in extracting more than a minuscule seventy barrels a day from what should have been an oil bonanza.

Helmut Paulus was marching in the wake of the panzers and wrote home about seeing the Caucasus foothills for the first time: 'I could almost imagine being back at home. The place resembles the edge of the Black Forest so much.' He was wounded for the first time the next day. His comrades were shocked as they regarded him as charmed, given he had survived *Barbarossa* and the subsequent winter fighting without so much as a scratch. 'At first I didn't realise that I was wounded at all. I saw the hole in my trousers but there was no blood, then I saw my underwear turn red and so knew what was up.' Shot clean through the left thigh, he hobbled back to a first aid station and was evacuated by handcart.[12]

6

EAST TO THE VOLGA!

With *Heeresgruppe A* embarking on its long march to the south, the bespectacled Max von Weichs gave the order to his own troops to carry on rolling east – and in the lead was Friedrich Paulus's *6. Armee*. Still bathed in the glory of their victory at Izyum, Paulus's men pushed forward – 'We're advancing towards Stalingrad along the railway line' – but just as was happening in the south, the Soviets refused to let themselves be encircled and annihilated, instead retreating in good order across the steppe. The only success achieved of any note was at Millerovo on 17 July, but even then, the bag was a miserly 14,000 prisoners, a fraction of the huge totals of the 1941 battles. Just as worryingly, the success at Millerovo was only achieved by the Luftwaffe airlifting forward 200 tons of fuel to panzers stranded on the steppe from lack of gasoline. Improvised airlifts were only ever going to be a stopgap, and sure enough, by the end of the month *6. Armee* was forced to halt while still over a hundred miles from its next objective, the bridge over the River Don at Kalach-na-Donu. Franz Halder was infuriated at the situation, and even with supplies airlifted forward it wasn't nearly enough. Paulus was now 'bogged down'.

An entire week was lost while adequate fuel was brought up, and then, finally, Paulus could advance once more, his goal now being the destruction of the remaining Red Army formations west of the Don. Kirill Moskalenko's 1st Tank Army – created just a couple of weeks previously and only partially equipped – was the main opposition and it was badly hit, as was the Soviet 62nd Army. The fighting was hard:

> A dozen flares lit up the air over the hill and Russian fire shook them [the attacking landsers]. Grenades were falling all around them ... the number two machine gunner groaned, He was hit ... they spat fire at the Russians and behind came the roar of the German infantry. The Russians were attempting a defence but from every side German soldiers were pouring through the barbed wire, breaking over the trenches. Ahead and to the right the artillery was bombarding a town, spirals of smoke rolled along the ground from the fires the shells had started.

German panzers joined the attack, which proved almost as dangerous to the *landsers* as to the Red Army:

> One panzer went by the *gruppe's* [German infantry section or squad] hillock, crossed the trench that was now overflowing with Russian bodies, and plunged on. A second and then a third followed, ploughing through the bloody paste of the trench... The infantry had to get out of the way. Any wounded who couldn't move just had bad luck. One panzer came by so close it nearly hit them ... one *landser* lay there watching the treads inches from his nose.

A soldier who was involved in the grisly battle remembered

> ...nothing ... except indistinct memories which flash into my mind with sudden brutality. The cries of the wounded, or the agonizingly dying, shrieking as they stare at a part of their body reduced to pulp ... guts splattered across the rubble and sprayed from one dying man onto another, tightly riveted machines ripped like the belly of a cow which has just been sliced open, flaming and groaning.

The Germans won through, and 'all resistance was overwhelmed and once again everything was either German or dead.' Flying over the battlefield in its aftermath, Wolfram von Richthofen described 'extraordinarily many knocked-out tanks and dead [Russians]'. He used the phrase *'Blut gerührt!'* – 'Blood flowed!'

Not that everything went the way of the attacking Germans. Just as in *Barbarossa* the previous year, the German panzer commanders found many of their armoured chargers still under-gunned in comparison to the far better T-34 and KV models. 'They [the Soviet tank guns] had a longer range. We couldn't attack them across open steppe, so, like ships at sea, I pulled my panzers right back out of sight, made a wide detour and attacked them from behind.' Even then the Soviets often got the drop on their enemy, as the war correspondent Clemens Graf von Podewils noted caustically in his diary: 'Not an encouraging sight … vehicles of every sort chaotically trying to overtake each other as fast as they could to get away!' Still shaken by the Red Army ambush, Podewils sought sanctuary with the divisional commander, the one-armed Hans Hube, who told him; 'You'd better go up to the front line, it's safer there.' Unconvinced, the 36-year-old Podewils nevertheless complied.

It was still a German victory, but not on the scale of many earlier encirclement battles. The Soviets lost some 50,000 men killed or missing, along with 270 tanks and 600 guns, although much of 62nd Army in particular managed to escape the trap, hampered as the Germans were once more by lack of fuel. The situation was worsened by the VVS specifically targeting already scarce German fuel supplies, including a successful raid on a big fuel dump north of Morozovsk on 15 July by Soviet Pe-2 bombers. An OKL report at the time read:

The enemy appears in large numbers in the air on 6. *Armee's* front. Our fighters are able to score heavily. The commander … reports a considerable drop in the quality of the Russian airmen … our fighter pilots encounter no serious opposition in air combat, it is only a matter of catching the enemy …

our fighters are able to shoot down large numbers of Russian aircraft. Obviously the enemy still has large quantities of material, but is hampered by the low training qualities of the personnel.

Two pilots who would agree with that statement were Walter Tödt and Johannes Wiese. Flying a sortie on 27 July, Tödt

> ...spotted two MiGs below and diving out of the sun we managed to catch them by surprise. Dzal [Lieutenant-Colonel Franjo Dzal, a Croat pilot] flew ahead of me and was first to attack ... while Dzal's victim had already fallen in flames, my Russian simply dove into the ground. A victory without a single shot being fired!

As for Wiese, he recalled 'climbing behind the smoking plane with my bullets hitting it with such an impact that I even brought home some parts of the aircraft. It sloped down gently, leaving a thick trail of smoke.'[1]

At the same time as Wiese's easy victory, one of the most famous rivalries in the Luftwaffe's war was playing out between two of its own *jagdflieger* as they battled over the advancing troops and in the process kept the VVS at bay – Hermann Graf and Gordon Gollob. Both men were pilots in the superb *Jagdgeschwader 52*, although Gollob had been drafted in from *JG. 77*. A former amateur footballer, the tall and slim Graf was easy-going, popular with his peers and subordinates and had been the seventh *Experte* to achieve 100 victories, shooting down a remarkable 47 aircraft in just 17 days after the launch of *Blau*.

Gollob by contrast was a difficult man to get along with. An Austrian by birth, he had a chip on his shoulder about it and felt looked down on by his German superiors despite his impressive record. He could be curt to the point of rudeness with peers and many of his fellow pilots trod carefully around him to avoid a lashing from his acerbic tongue. Superb pilots both, they disliked each other immensely and each was determined to outshine the other. They channelled that sense of competition into a veritable aerial slaughter of their opposition. By 14 August, each had achieved 120 victories, whereupon Gollob piled the pressure on his rival by claiming an additional thirty kills over the next fortnight, becoming the first fighter pilot to reach 150 enemy aircraft destroyed. He was awarded the Knight's Cross with Oak Leaves, Swords and Diamonds as a result – Nazi Germany's highest decoration at the time. Graf was not far behind him.

The two *Experten*'s success and continued survival couldn't hide the fact that they were the exception rather than the rule among the dwindling numbers of Luftwaffe pilots. The Stuka pilot Hermann Buchner remarked that 'Each mission becomes increasingly dangerous as resistance gets tougher ... stronger anti-aircraft fire and aerial battles becoming increasingly common as we are intercepted by enemy fighters.' In an attempt to cover the increasing gaps in the air, the Germans began to rob Peter to pay Paul, and Johannes Kaufmann found himself and his unit recalled from the Caucasus: 'We were given orders to return ... our destination was Frolov, an airfield almost in the centre of the great Don bend and just 150 kilometres from our new area of operations – Stalingrad.' Conditions for the newly arrived pilots and crew were not salubrious: 'There were no permanent buildings ... the heat was stultifying. Frolov consisted of nothing more than a large flat expanse of very hard, sun-baked steppe ... drinking water had to be brought in by horse-drawn tanker.' Even sleep wasn't easy to come by for the hard-pressed Luftwaffe men. 'As well as being almost unbearably hot, the atmosphere proved to be very tense at times, particularly during the hours of darkness when the Red Air Force sent light aircraft to carry out harassment raids.'[2] The night-time harassment tactic wasn't new, in fact the VVS had deployed it with great success during *Barbarossa*, and now it was again proving its value as another German flier attested: 'The night disturbance aircraft known as 'sewing machines' due to their tinny engines dropped small, unaimed bombs – it was said they dropped them by hand! They came after dark almost every night, for hours, hit very little but robbed us of sleep and that was also their purpose!'

By now the Luftwaffe had stopped expecting to achieve air superiority and merely hoped to maintain air parity – the numbers were against them and the likes of Graf and Gollob were simply masking that unpalatable truth.

On the ground, having finally taken Kalach-na-Donu, 6. *Armee* was now just 40-odd miles from the Volga. There, exhausted after the battle with the 1st Tank and 62nd Armies and once again short of fuel, it halted and gathered itself for a final push to the river despite its losses. 'Kalach cost lives. Our *kompanien* were mostly now only 30 to 50 in number, and our main frontline had gaps in it.' The shortest and most obvious route to the river from Kalach-na-Donu was now due east to the city of Stalingrad. Having recovered from being kicked in the head by one of his gun's horses, Rudolf Oehus, the farmer's boy from Saxony, was back with his battery and wrote to his parents. The young 21-year-old seemed in two minds as to the future course of the fighting:

> I got back to the battery on Monday, and now we're in action, we're about 30 kilometres from Stalingrad. We haven't moved all day, it's pretty cheerful … there's a lot of artillery here, and our pilots are at work all day – they are mostly ground attack or destroyer aircraft as they are called, they assist the infantry in their assaults… It won't be long then Stalingrad will have fallen … it still doesn't look like the war will be over soon. But when Stalingrad is taken we will probably be left here. Dear mother, to be on the safe side, send gloves and head protection in good time, because parcels can get blocked again from time to time. I don't think we'll still be here this winter, but it's better to be safe than sorry.[3]

Wilhelm Hoffmann was in no doubt as to the eventual outcome of the fighting: 'The *kompanie* commander told us that if our future operations are successful we'll soon reach the Volga, take Stalingrad and then the war will inevitably be over. Perhaps we'll be home by Christmas.' Another wrote in the same vein: 'The Russian troops are completely broken, to reach the Volga and take Stalingrad is not so difficult for us. Victory is not far away.' Yet another was even more optimistic when he wrote to his sweetheart Else: 'Our *kompanie* is tearing ahead ... all of us feel that the end – final victory – is near.' However, some – like *Gefreiter* Werner Halle – sounded a note of caution:

> Nr. 10. *Kompanie* was down to platoon size. We rarely knew our *kompanie* and platoon commanders. We had many long casualty lists, for us not a good sign. Every one of us – it sounds harsh but it was true – was now thinking, which of us is next?

With gasoline at a premium, and his men tired and worn down after fighting a number of battles and having marched well over two hundred miles already from their jumping off points, Paulus now set his sights on a city that had rated barely a mention in his original orders, a city whose name would come to represent the horror of the Russian Front in all its magnitude and become a turning point in the war itself.

Stalingrad was a strange city with a somewhat odd shape to it. An industrial hub – it was the third largest industrial city in the entire Soviet Union – it hugged the western bank of the Volga, but whereas other river-based cities like Moscow on the Moskva and Leningrad on the Neva were roughly circular, with the river acting as a massive artery dividing the cities in two, Stalingrad was a straggly affair that barely touched the eastern bank; in fact, the only significant settlement on the far bank was Krasnaya Sloboda, ironically an old Volga German plantation centre. Instead, it stretched some thirty miles from north to south but barely reached two and a half miles at its widest. Home to some 525,000 people when the blood and fire of *Barbarossa* was unleashed on their country, the city's inhabitants toiled away in its many factories and workshops producing heavy machinery, chemicals, and vehicles. With the country under attack, it was a relatively simple process to swap production over to weaponry, so that the Dzerzhinsky tractor works, for example, had become the leading manufacturer of the Red Army's superb T-34 tank by the beginning of June 1942. It would only lose this accolade in September as German aerial bombing took its toll and the huge new Ural-Kirov Tank Factory in Chelyabinsk began production.

Originally founded as a fortress town in 1589 as part of Russia's defences against the nomadic Turkic-speaking peoples to the south, the city had been fought over many times during its long history and had been badly damaged in the Russian Civil War, particularly during the battle in which Stalin himself had been heavily involved and hence why it had been renamed in his honour in April 1925. Thereafter, it had been earmarked as one of a handful of Soviet 'garden cities' created to act as models for the future of Soviet society. Centrally planned – of course – the concept was to build a series of state-of-the-art factory complexes located alongside living quarters for their workforces; dormitories for the single men and women and detached wooden houses for those with families. Those houses would have flower gardens and vegetable plots with picket fences and latched gates. A civic and governmental district would be built in Stalin's favoured modernist concrete gingerbread fashion, all overlaid with broad, tree-lined boulevards and acres of public parks and open spaces. In essence the new city was intended to stand in stark contrast to the old, overcrowded urban centres of Moscow, Kharkov and elsewhere. The workers would in theory finish their shift in the new factories and make their way home to their freshly painted wooden houses or dazzlingly white apartment blocks past huge government buildings clustered around the almost 12-mile-long city centre.

That centre was – and still is – dominated by the massif of the Mamayev Kurgan – Russian for the 'tumulus of Mamai'. An ancient Sarmatian burial mound named after a warlord of the Mongol Golden Horde, Mamayev Kurgan stands 102 metres high, and so would inevitably be called Hill 102 by the military of both sides. The hill provides a superb view of the city centre but covers little of the south and north. Converted into a park by the authorities, the Kurgan was laced with paths and walkways along which starry-eyed couples and proletarian families would stroll in the summer sun, looking for a shady spot for a picnic or simply somewhere quiet to sit and relax and while away the few hours of rest they were granted.

Those same couples and families might even find the time – and the money – to wander over to the *Univermag* department store and browse its endless shelves laden with the kinds of consumer goods that the Soviet Union struggled to produce. An alluring veneer was added, with beauty parlours and dance halls and, of course, a huge opera house for public concerts. Mobile soda fountains toured the city during the hot summers with thirsty citizens lapping up the cool drinks in between shifts in the city's industrial heartland.

Born again in the 1930s, the city was originally called Tsaritsyn, not in any reference to the Tsar but rather as a corruption of its local Tatar name of *Sary Su* meaning 'Yellow River' for the colour of the Volga itself, which is yellowish from the clay soil. Those wide waters would ebb and flow round numerous islands, large and small, with the western bank especially harbouring a multitude of beaches and sandy banks that were as popular with the city's inhabitants as the Kurgan.

As well as being a haven of tranquillity for Stalingrad's thousands of workers, the Kurgan also effectively split the city into two parts. To the north were four huge heavy industry hubs; the *Krasny Oktyabr* (Red October) metal works, the *Barrikady* (Barricade) gun factory, the *Dzerzhinsky* (named after the Cheka secret police chief Felix Dzerzhinsky – sometimes also called the *Stalingradsky*) tractor factory and the Lazur chemical works. Each was well over a kilometre long, up to a hundred metres wide and all ran parallel with the river. Modern and built to last – the Dzerzhinsky for example was built in 1930 as part of the first Five-Year Plan – the factories had glazed ceilings and were all connected to one another by tunnels with power and telephone lines running underground. Each factory site was self-contained, not only with its workers domiciles but also its own schools, shops and parks.

To the south of the Kurgan was the old city, *Dar Gova* – a bit of a misnomer as all the 'old' architecture was long gone and replaced by acres of concrete and red brick buildings, including the main railway station, the pillared *Univermag*, the Square of the Fallen Fighters (renamed Red Square by the Germans), the Gorky theatre, a number of grain storage silos and a towering grain elevator complex. The latter were built as part of the city's function as a collection centre for the south's wheat, with the grain then shipped north via the river to hungry Russian mouths. Citizen workers lived here too, their white painted wooden bungalows stretching for several miles out into the open steppe.

But it was the river that dominated the city – the mighty Volga, a tangle of tributaries and midstream islands with the waters reaching a kilometre wide in some places. Along its much higher western bank, ravines – called *mechetkas* – ran down to its shores, dotted with caves and gullies amid thick undergrowth. The Volga holds a special place in the heart and soul of the Russian people. Long considered the country's national river, it flows at the centre of myriad folk tales and songs and is often affectionately referred to as *Volga-Matushka* – Mother Volga. It is easy to scoff at such romanticism, but with a people as sentimentally inclined as the Russians, the Volga is an incredibly powerful symbol of their history, traditions and, indeed, their very existence as a nation. In all states, symbols are important, and doubly so in totalitarian ones, which made a clash between the two most powerful dictators in the world over a city named after one of them – that also sat on a revered river – not inevitable, but more likely than not.

Stranded for five days yet again while waiting for more fuel to be brought forward, Paulus was now considering his options. His partial victory at Kalach-na-Donu had forced Moscow to disband its battered 1st Tank Army, but the surviving units had been absorbed into 62nd Army, which had successfully escaped the trap and withdrawn in good order into Stalingrad. This wasn't a disaster for the Germans as far as Paulus was concerned. His main goal was to reach the Volga and cut it as a supply route, once that was done, in all likelihood 62nd Army – not a hugely powerful force anyway – would look to save itself by retreating across the Volga to its eastern bank, thus abandoning the city to be occupied by the Germans. That would leave Weichs free to move up the rest of the army group and position them along the Don, so fulfilling his mission to form a hard shoulder to cover *Heeresgruppe A*'s continuing advance into the Caucasus.

Paulus decided his first priority was to neutralise 62nd Army's ability to interfere with his march to the Volga and so turned to Wolfram von Richthofen and *Luftflotte 4*. The air fleet commander demanded a maximum effort from his crews and somehow managed to put a thousand aircraft in the sky on Sunday 23 August. As the panzers rolled forward below them, *Macky* Steinhoff remembered:

> We flew low above the roads on which our troops were advancing ... or rather the tracks on the steppe leading towards Stalingrad. Everywhere the soldiers on the ground acted crazy with joy. The summer was dry and as we flew over the spearheads the dust clouds from the panzers reached high above them into the clear sky.

Johannes Kaufmann was also in the action. 'At 0525hrs on 23 August we took off from Frolov for our first mission against Stalingrad. We had been briefed to attack any rail traffic we found around the city ... the landscape was alien, almost sinister ... the ground in front of Stalingrad resembled the wrinkled hide of an elephant.' Kaufmann and his comrades were now carrying huge 1,000kg bombs for the first time and the weight made them wary: 'We approached our first take-offs very cautiously indeed, no-one knew if the undercarriages would take the extra weight ... under no circumstances did we want to lift off too early and risk hitting the ground again.'[4]

Werner Thaler – a war correspondent with the Luftwaffe's *Der Adler (The Eagle)* magazine hitched a ride in a Stuka:

> We fly with the sun at our back... I can see a hellish activity emerge in the seemingly tranquil group of trees below. Camouflage nets are pulled away from anti-aircraft guns and the quiet ground is abruptly changed into a fire-spitting inferno to an extent I had never previously seen. Multicoloured chains

of light from the quadruple machine-guns pass by between our diving aircraft.

Heavy though the anti-aircraft fire was, the city's defences were swamped by the sheer size of the German armada and the bombs rained down on 62nd Army and the hapless civilian population alike. Stuka pilot *Hauptmann* Herbert Pabst recalled:

> Since early morning we were constantly over the panzer spearheads, helping them forward with our bombs and machine-guns ... we landed, refuelled, loaded up with bombs and ammunition and immediately took off again. It was 'all go' and wonderful advances. As we took off, others landed. And so on it went.

The Heinkel 111 crewman, Michael Deiml, had flown in the Battle of Britain and was now in the air above Stalingrad; 'We took off at 0630, 1130 and 1515hrs and made high level bomb attacks on the city, particularly the railway station, usually under very heavy anti-aircraft fire...our orders were to drop our bombs on target ... we had to attack time and time again.'

The barrel-chested Soviet general Andrei Yeremenko said of the day:

> We'd been through a lot in the war up to that time, but what we saw in Stalingrad that day was like a nightmare ... huge sheets of flame stabbed the sky, deluging the ground with a sea of fire and acrid fumes. Torrents of burning oil and petrol flowed into the Volga until its surface was a river of fire.

A *landser* advancing on the city wrote in his diary; 'We can see the smoke of fires ... they say that the city is on fire; on the Führer's orders our Luftwaffe has sent it up in flames. That's what the Russians need, to stop them from resisting.' A report from a senior Red Army officer in the city back to headquarters simply said 'Everything is on fire...' It was impossible to accurately count the dead amid the rubble and burning buildings, but perhaps as many as 30,000 people died in the attack, certainly over 40,000 were killed during the first week of raids.

On the ground Hans-Valentin Hube's panzers were racing to the north of the city under the command of the aristocratic Hyazinth von Strachwitz, renowned throughout the *panzerwaffe* as *der Panzergraf* (the Panzer Count). 'We had started early in the morning on the Don, and then we were on the Volga' as one young officer recalled. Another, the Baltic German *Hauptmann* Bernd Freytag von Loringhoven, gazed in awe across the river. 'We looked at the immense, immense steppe towards Asia, and I was overwhelmed.' The Germans had finally reached the Volga at the northern suburb of Rynok. Wilhelm Hoffmann was elated: 'Splendid news – north of Stalingrad our troops have reached the Volga and captured part of the city.'

Now all that was needed was for the Germans to start working their way south down the riverbank and the Soviets would be forced to evacuate to the east – Paulus estimated he would take the city in two days, and Hoffmann agreed with him: 'The Russians have two alternatives, either to flee across the Volga or give themselves up.' So, at 0440hrs the following morning, *16. Panzerdivision* began an attack on the neighbouring suburb of Spartakovka. But there was a stone in Paulus's boot, and that stone was Anton Lopatin's 62nd Army.

Only formed in May, the 62nd Army was the usual Red Army mix of rifle divisions and brigades – about ten of the former and half a dozen of the latter – stiffened up with a tank corps and a dozen or so regiments of artillery and mortars. Some of the men were veterans of *Barbarossa* but the majority were conscripts with barely a few weeks training behind them. They'd already faced *6. Armee* at Kalach-na-Donu, where they'd come off second best, and would now fight them again in the city itself. As Hube's motorised infantry – now renamed as *'panzer grenadiers'* across the Wehrmacht as of 5 July – pushed south, the going proved harder than expected, not only due to stiff resistance but also a lack of fuel and ammunition.

In the skies above them their Luftwaffe comrades were up against different problems as *Leutnant* Johann Badum remarked: 'Even with the best of luck one is only able to come across Russian aircraft now and then.' The *jagdflieger*, accustomed to flocks of usually ill-trained Soviet pilots, were finding the lack of targets frustrating, however with not a little *schadenfreude*, the following day one of Badum's comrades, Werner Hohenberg, went up with 40-victory *Experte Oberleutnant* Otto Decker. 'Decker and I were out on a freie Jagd [free hunting] sortie northeast of Stalingrad, deep into Soviet territory. Suddenly I spotted a lone aircraft at a distance of more than a mile away. As we approached, we could see it was an Il-2.' Decker made several attacks on the heavily armoured ground attack plane. 'Large parts of the aircraft were torn away but it continued flying, suddenly I saw Decker turning away towards the northeast, I called him but he didn't reply.' Flying closer, Hohenberg saw 'his windscreen was covered in oil, he made a wide turn, went down and carried out a belly landing.' Seeing Decker climb out of his cockpit Hohenberg went into land and pick him up – common practice on the steppe – but 'lots of Russians surrounded the bellied-in Messerschmitt and I was met by a hail of rifle fire.' Hohenberg had no option but to abort and head home. 'That was the last time I ever saw Decker. He never returned from captivity. His family searched for him for many years after the war.'[5]

In truth, the VVS in the south was in trouble. It still had not recovered from its near destruction the previous year, and even though the number of modern machines rolling off the Siberian production lines and stevedored out of the belly of Lend-Lease ships was growing all the time, the men sitting in the cockpits were still too inexperienced and poorly trained to go toe to toe with the Luftwaffe and survive for long. Heinrich von Einsiedel saw it at first hand during a dogfight when he latched onto a Soviet opponent. 'Fear seemed to have crippled him. He raced ten feet above the ground in a straight line and didn't defend himself.' But war is war and Einsiedel – an honourable man and no cold-blooded killer – still did what was expected of him: 'My machine vibrated with the recoil of its guns. A streak of flame shot from the petrol tank of the Russian plane. It exploded and rolled over on the ground. A broad, long strip of scorched steppe was all that was left behind.'

OKL now faced a dilemma. For years it had glorified the cult of the *Experte*, with pilots and the public encouraged to judge success on the number of kills a flier achieved, but with suitable VVS targets in short supply the priority now was close support of the army. This was not a mission that bestowed much glamour, but OKL held its nose and instructed the frontline *staffeln* to concentrate on acting as flying artillery for the ground troops rather than increasing their victory tallies. Bypassing Richthofen – to his intense frustration – Luftwaffe high command issued an order to all units in the Stalingrad area of operations, and on 28 August it fell to Wolf-Dietrich Wilcke to read out said order to his pilots after they had successfully fought off a VVS attack on the new Luftwaffe base near Kalach-na-Donu. Wilcke, tall, blond, nicknamed *der Fürst* (the Prince) by his men on account of being something of a clothes horse, was also a veteran of the Condor Legion and *die Luftschlacht um England* (the Battle of Britain), and was obviously unimpressed by his instructions.

> Gentlemen, flying for fun and seeing who can shoot down the most enemy machines must stop. Every machine, every drop of fuel, every hour's flying is irreplaceable. The easy [!] ground life we are leading is completely irresponsible, in the air it is even more so. Every shot must go to support the infantry if there is no target in the air.[6]

The reaction from the assembled pilots after weeks of living hand to mouth out on the steppe can be imagined. In the end it made little difference as the former baker turned *16. Panzerdivision* artilleryman Karl Nünninghof explained to his parents back in Mühlheim an der Ruhr:

> There is not much to report. The same thing happens here every day and every night, Russian planes come, drop bombs and fire at us, then we take cover, they fly away again, a little dogfight develops between their fighters and ours, they fly

away again, then 20-25 of our bombers come and punch the Russians, and so it goes day after day and night after night.[7]

In fact, the practical young 22-year-old was far more interested in the 'four parcels with biscuits and a letter from Kathe [which had just arrived], which is not much, but at least it's better than nothing. I was very happy about the biscuits and thank you very much.' Of the confused state of the fighting, he wrote:

We had become encircled again and the Russians were all round us, which is not uncommon by the way, we have now fought our way back where ammunition, supplies and food can get to us ... yesterday our infantry were supplied with ammunition from the air. You can surely guess where our current battle zone is, precisely where the hardest fighting is going on.

By now the German summer offensive had been running for two months, and just as at the same point during *Barbarossa*, the men and machines were feeling the strain. Heinrich von Einsiedel remembered that 'Breakdowns [had] reached enormous proportions... A Gruppe of 42 machines seldom had more than ten operational.' For the pilots and ground crew their situation wasn't helped by the fact that 'The food was poor ... our requisition detachment mainly brought back melons.'[8] It all had a cumulative effect on the men who again and again had to drag themselves into the air, as Einsiedel discovered first-hand on a sortie with his boss, *Major* Wolfgang Ewald, when the pair spotted a Soviet fighter. 'He [Ewald] fired and a white trail behind the Russian showed that his engine had been hit, but Ewald was already behind a LaGG [Lavochkin-Gorbunov-Gudkov fighter] so I turned my machine to complete the job, when the Major yelled into the radio "Leave him to me, leave him to me!"' Ewald was an experienced flier, but it was obvious he was feeling the strain, and he wasn't the only one.

On the ground Paulus's two-day plan to capture the city had been and gone as Rudolf Oehus admitted to his parents:

We have been lying here in a suburb of Stalingrad for two days. The city is very fortified; it is only going slowly and very carefully. All service branches are being used here, you have to think that the Russians in the city must be gradually losing their minds because it is really hard to believe what is happening. The main role is played by our pilots, but the Russian has also used all sorts of planes here, watching a dogfight is nothing new to us anymore.

Ever the dutiful son, Oehus reassured his parents all was well. 'Our losses are only small, the battery has had three dead and five injured so far, so you don't need to worry too much about me.'[9] Another *landser* writing in his diary was less reassuring: 'the doomed [Soviet] divisions are continuing to resist bitterly. Fanaticism!'

Back on the River Don, near Uryv-Pokrovka, the Hungarian Second Army had been tasked with destroying a Red Army bridgehead on the western bank. István Balogh was in the middle of the fighting.

A continual artillery bombardment from 3 to 6am, the shells whistled over our heads. At home they must be preparing for holidays, but here death can find us at any moment. Stalin Organs [Katyusha multiple rocket-launchers] start speaking. Our hearts stopped beating. The village caught fire immediately and everyone ran away. The Russians destroyed an anti-tank gun. The fire has died down, but there is a mass of smoke. There are wounded. Those still at home cannot imagine what a struggle we have to have with ourselves to survive this battle.

With few heavy weapons and very little in terms of artillery support, the Magyars tried to force a way forward, but to no avail: 'We are back in our former positions because Russian troops have broken through again ... we've retreated... Russian shells hit the 6th Regiment's ammunition vehicles and they exploded one after another.'

Balogh was a member of Hungary's premier military formation, yet it was clear they were outgunned, ill-prepared and increasingly despondent.

> The ground is covered with corpses. We don't have a chance to carry the wounded away... There are just two NCOs left in the Company – me and a corporal who is the Company commander's assistant. We've been attacked again by bombers. Artillery and tanks are shelling us. It is like hell... The Russians are frighteningly brave. They are fighting to the last.

As Paulus and Richthofen prepared their next combined assault on Stalingrad's northern suburbs, the Hungarians were still 200 miles away and fighting for their lives. 'We were bombed through the night. Oh God how little human life is worth! The Russians are attacking again. We counted the losses in our Company: 20 dead, 94 wounded, and three missing... Morale is very low. All my friends are wounded.' Even the arrival of reinforcements could not lift the feeling of gloom among Balogh and his comrades: 'We spent the whole day redistributing the weapons of those who have been killed or wounded... If we have to go on our nerves will break.'

Repairing much-needed road bridges in the wake of Paulus's advance, Fritz Pabst wrote to his wife Hildegard at the end of August, 'I believe I'm not betraying a secret if I tell you that this city will be fiercely fought over.' At the same time Gordon Gollob, and his fellow *Experte* Günther Rall were having some tea with Major Yakov Antonov – a VVS flier just shot down and awaiting transport to a PoW camp. Sitting in a makeshift bunker, Antonov pointed to a map of the Soviet Union on the wall: 'Look at the map and you will see large areas of the USSR that you haven't captured. You will never be able to defeat the Soviet Union.'[10]

As for István Balogh, 'My rank of corporal was confirmed. I'm not very excited. I'd much rather go home.'

7

'HUG THEM TO DEATH!'

September started off well for Johannes Kaufmann. 'I was right behind a ground-hugging Shturmovik and a long burst from my 20mm nose cannon immediately sent him smashing into the baked earth. He couldn't have known what hit him.' As the young Bf 110 pilot chalked up another kill, as far as Vinnytsia was concerned all seemed well. The good weather of the summer was holding, Paulus's 6. *Armee* had reached the Volga at Rynok and the diminutive Hermann Hoth's 4. *Panzerarmee* was advancing from the south towards the city and crushing all opposition – 'We witnessed some incredible scenes as savage tank battles were fought at point blank range, gun muzzle to gun muzzle.' Back in Berlin the Reich Chief Press officer warned off journalists about the impending victory: 'Due to the successful course of our operations against Stalingrad, it's recommended that our newspapers now keep on hand material on the enormous economic and military importance of this bastion of communism and centre of Soviet industry.' Hitler meanwhile signalled to his commanders

Upon penetration into the city the entire male population must be eliminated since Stalingrad with its one million [the population was actually roughly half that] uniformly communist inhabitants is extremely dangerous.

He didn't specify what was to happen to the women and children. Soon, Stalingrad would be caught in a vice from north and south and the city would surely fall. However, there were some flies in that particular ointment.

Taking a Soviet city was nothing new for the *Ostheer*, they had captured dozens since the invasion began. The trick had been to make them indefensible. Most of the time that had meant isolating them, and then let lack of supplies and reinforcements do the work for them. That's how the likes of Kiev had fallen. The Germans had swept out far to the east and by the time they assaulted the city itself, the Soviet position was hopeless, and the fighting swiftly came to an end. Hyazinth von Strachwitz had advocated exactly that plan when his panzers had reached the Volga at Rynok. In his view that was the time to leap across the river, form a bridgehead on the eastern bank and then circle round behind the city, trapping not only the 62nd Army but the 64th and maybe even more in a *kesselschlacht* (cauldron battle). But where was the fuel for such a move?

Paulus's advance from the start of the offensive had been marked by its stop-start nature, and *der Panzergraf*'s vehicles had reached the river on fumes. There simply wasn't the gasoline to mount a grand encirclement. That meant the Red Army in the city itself was never truly cut off, and that in turn meant men and equipment could get across the Volga from its eastern bank and keep the fight going. Just as importantly, the defenders could call on artillery safely positioned on Soviet-held territory, and that soon added up to 300 guns, at first mostly of medium calibre, but then far larger when the STAVKA ordered forward massive 203mm B-4 howitzers from the Red Army's strategic reserve. Nicknamed 'Stalin's sledgehammer' by the *landsers*, the B-4 could hurl 100kg of high explosive over 11 miles, deluging any assaulting German units with fire and shot.

Perhaps even more telling in how the battle would be played out was the nature of the opposing forces and the men who led them. After his victory at Izyum, it seemed to Berlin that Paulus had proven himself an excellent choice to head a field army. Despite concerns over his prior lack of direct command experience he seemed to have adapted his planning expertise to suit his newly elevated position – but not all senior officers agreed. As early as 25 August Wolfram von Richthofen met with Paulus at his forward headquarters and been dismayed by what he found. Despite finding the time to don a fresh cotton collar for his tunic and keep himself assiduously clean, Paulus's nervous tic was now even more pronounced and the dysentery he frequently suffered from was raging, making him tired and listless as well as extremely irritable. In fact, so concerned was the Luftwaffe general that two days later he despatched *Oberst* Karl-Heinrich Schulz from his staff to meet with Goering and Jeschonnek (OKL Chief of the General Staff) to brief them on the continuing delays in Stalingrad and firmly lay the blame 'on the Army's weakness in nerves and leadership'. This was a coded attack on Paulus, and one not very well disguised.

The man Paulus would face across the city's rubble was his polar opposite. Vasily Ivanovich Chuikov was born into a peasant family where hunger had forced him to leave home and find work in the city as a factory worker from the age of 12, until the Russian Civil War had shown him his true calling as a soldier. Now 42 years old, he was nicknamed 'the stone' by his peers and subordinates alike, his shovel-flat face framed by thick, dark eyebrows and a piercing gaze that brooked no opposition. He had held field command in every rank and had all the leadership experience that Paulus lacked. Not that his career had all been plain sailing. As commander of the Soviet 9th Army during the disastrous Winter War against Finland back in 1940, he was adjudged to have failed against his outnumbered and outgunned foes and been sent packing to Chiang Kai-Shek's semi-imperial court in China as the Soviet Military Attaché. But with Soviet general officers being immolated and defeated by the truckload since the advent of *Barbarossa*, he had been given a second bite of the cherry.

Called to the front on 11 September to take over from the sacked Anton Lopatin as 62nd Army commander, when asked what he understood his mission to be, he replied it was to hold the city or die trying. Possessing a shrewd military mind, and as much a chain smoker as Paulus, he was a field soldier down to his boots.

Chuikov immediately realised the key to an unlikely Soviet victory was to force the Germans to fight a battle on Soviet terms and not theirs. That meant denying them their advantages of air power and manoeuvrability. One of his very first pronouncements to his men has gone down in history.

> We should reduce no-man's land as much as possible to the throw of a grenade … every German must be made to feel he lives under the muzzle of a Russian gun.

Making his headquarters on Mamayev Kurgan, he began his tenure in command by drawing a line in the city's sand; there would be no more retreats and deserters would be hunted down and executed. Those who disobeyed could expect no mercy:

> On the 14th [of September] I shot the commander and commissar of one regiment, and a short while later I shot two brigade commanders and their commissars. This caught everyone off guard. We made sure news of this got to the men, especially the officers.

Unsurprisingly, desertions tailed off as the soldiers in the line realised there was no safety to be had by trying to flee back east across the Volga.

The army those men were in was now nothing like the original 62nd Army, which in late July had been a relatively new and untried formation, but which, by early September, was a very different beast. It had gained in experience and been bolstered by the addition of some former 1st Tank Army units, and Soviet ruthlessness had also meant some 75,000 civilians from the city and its surrounding area had been drafted straight into its combat units as little more than cannon fodder. They were joined by 7,000 teenaged *Komsomol* members (the Soviet version of the Nazis' *Hitler Jugend*), 3,000 women and girls enrolled as telephone and radio operators, nurses and support staff, and some 50,000 additional civilians in the so-called People's Guard. Casualties among these volunteers and draftees would be massive, but Chuikov was prepared to sacrifice them to hold the city.

Now it was fighting in the city's streets, the limitations of 6. *Armee* were becoming more obvious. It was, of course, no longer the veteran formation that had been led by Walter von Reichenau, and the bulk of its infantry divisions were now being severely tested for the first time. Denied the ability to manoeuvre, the reservists and young draftees in its ranks found themselves battering away at the Soviet defences with little but unfounded optimism to fall back on. One soldier in the inexperienced *305. Infanterie-Division* wrote home saying 'According to what our officers tell us Stalingrad will certainly fall in the next few days.'[1]

Paulus's best formations were the panzer units reassigned to him from Hoth's 4. *Panzerarmee*, and, at first, they spearheaded the advance, but were robbed of their ability to manoeuvre effectively amidst the heaps of rubble and deep bomb craters. Forced to pick their way slowly through the rubble-strewn streets they became easy targets for Red Army anti-tank guns and even Molotov cocktail wielding infantrymen. Officers also noted sourly that when the lead panzer was put out of action, the accompanying infantry immediately went to ground and refused to go forward without further support.

With tank losses mounting, the Germans switched tactics and the infantry were now put in the lead, with the panzers holding back and acting as direct fire support. This reduced the numbers of tanks being put out of action but shifted the problem to the infantry, where casualties were mounting, and as usual were concentrated in the frontline companies, leading to Richthofen fuming over 'rigid Army formalism which tolerates only 1,000 men in the frontline out of a divisional ration strength of 12,000'. At the same time, 6. *Armee* headquarters was trumpeting that from the launch of its attack on 23 August up until the end of the first week of September it had taken 26,500 prisoners and destroyed 350 guns and 830 tanks.

With no quick victory in sight, Paulus's answer was to feed more divisions into the line. Wilhelm Hoffmann's 94. *Infanterie-Division* among them: 'Our regiment has been ordered to attack ... are the Russians really thinking of holding out in the city itself? We had no peace all night from the Russian artillery and aircraft.' Hoffmann's usual optimistic tone was beginning to desert him: 'Lots of wounded are being brought back. God protect me.' Increasingly frustrated, Paulus turned to shot and shell and his aerial artillery. The Stuka pilot, Herbert Pabst, recalled how 'The Russians throw in everything... Then we come, circle, search and dive. They camouflage their tanks brilliantly, digging them in to protect them from bombs, sparing no effort, but we find them and smash most of them.'[2] A *landser* in *389. ID* watched the armada flying above him; 'A mass of Stukas came over us and after their attack you couldn't believe a mouse would have been left alive.' But stay alive the Russians did, covered by their artillery on the eastern bank and sustained by a constant stream of reinforcements crossing the Volga – some 10,000 between 13 and 16 September. Pabst recorded his frustration: 'The Russians remain in their burning city and won't budge. There's hardly a house left, just an atrocious chaos of ruins and fire into which we drop our bombs ... but the Russians won't budge!'

The strain of such a concentrated effort on the Luftwaffe fliers was immense. On 15 September alone Pabst flew five separate sorties and was in the air for a total of seven hours. Paul-Werner Hozzel, commander of the famed *Immelmann* Stuka *geschwader*, was based some forty kilometres from the city and he and his men were flying even more missions than Pabst:

> For each sortie we needed a chock-to-chock time of no more than 45 minutes, which included taxiing to the start point, take-off, approach flight, the climb to an altitude of 4,000 metres, target pick-up, dive bombing attack, low-level flight departure, landing, taxiing to the apron. Each turnaround – a new loading, a short technical overhaul, checkout – took us another 15 minutes. We were consistently able with each aircraft to fly about eight sorties from sunrise to sunset.

Yet still the Soviets fought back, as Wilhelm Hoffmann noted: 'Two days of non-stop fighting. The Russians are defending themselves with insane stubbornness.' The VVS played its part, too, as the Stuka pilot Hermann Buchner, remarked: 'We encountered enemy fighter resistance from the very first sortie.' Pabst found the pressure hard to bear. 'Russian fighters suddenly turned up. For 20 minutes they attacked us, uninterrupted, from all sides, from above, from below. One can't describe it ... it took a heavy toll on our nerves.'

Night-time brought no respite for the Germans, either on the ground or in the air. The irritant of the VVS's night flying light bombers – the ever-present 'sewing machines' – robbed the German pilots of their precious sleep and played on their nerves:

During the night the Ivans were very busy. The tremendous noise woke me up. Sand fell from the walls of my sleeping pit. Again and again we heard the drone of incoming aircraft and pressed ourselves a little flatter against our straw mattresses, hoping to block out the noise of the falling bombs. [In the city] firing is going on all the time. Wherever you look is fire and flames... Russian cannon and machine-guns are firing out of the burning city. Fanatics.[3]

For the first time in the whole Soviet campaign cracks began to appear in the relationship between the Army and its flying artillery. Richthofen – as unsubtle as he was aggressive – remarked that 'With our Army being as feeble as it is there isn't much the Luftwaffe can do. Had there been more determination Stalingrad could have been taken in two days.' But on the ground Paulus's inexperienced divisions were taking terrible losses – especially among the ranks of their junior officers and NCOs – resulting in a lack of drive among the men as their leaders were killed or wounded; '*Leutnant* Kraus was killed yesterday and now there's no *kompanie* commander... the Russians are fighting desperately like wild beasts, and don't give themselves up but instead come up close and then throw grenades.'

Chuikov realised the increasing dependency of the German ground troops on aerial support and instructed his men to get as close to the Germans as possible to protect themselves from air attack. Hans-Ulrich Rudel saw the effect of this tactic:

> We have to drop our bombs with the greatest accuracy because only a few metres away, in another basement, or behind another remainder of a wall, are our own troops. On our photographic town maps every single house is marked. Each pilot receives his own specific target marked by a red arrow. We fly with this city map on our knees and no-one is allowed to drop any bomb before he has identified the exact position of our own troops.

There was no subtlety to Paulus's tactics, it was just ceaseless, remorseless hammering with men and machines. Bruno von Hauenschild's 24. *Panzer-Division* was fighting in the south of the city and among the ranks of the former Prussian cavalrymen was a young officer, *Leutnant* Reiner. More accustomed to fighting across the wide-open steppes on horseback or in the cupola of a panzer, Reiner described what German operations under Paulus were now reduced to: 'We have fought for 15 days for a single house, with mortars, machine-guns, grenades and bayonets. By the third day 54 German corpses are strewn in the cellars, on the landings and the staircases. The front is a corridor between burnt-out rooms, it is the thin ceiling between two floors.'[4] A Red Army soldier echoed the same view as his enemy. 'The first floor of a building is often occupied by Germans while we continue to hold the second and third floors. Floorboards are yanked up and gaps made in ceilings and walls. There is fighting in apartments and corridors.'

Gains were now measured by yards not miles, but still the Germans crawled forward, pushing the defending Soviets back from the outskirts of the city into its very heart. Gottfried von Bismarck was a young officer in 76. *Infanterie-Division* fighting his way forward: 'The struggle was man to man and house to house for every square metre ... the Russians had dug in and were clinging to a slope 300 metres wide which fell steeply down to the river. Because the area being fought over was so narrow there was no question of using heavy weapons.' That same river was a lifeline for the Soviets, as Bismarck appreciated. 'We never took that strip of land because we never managed to stop the Russians keeping it resupplied.' The result was a bloody stalemate: 'There was a house where the Germans were in the cellar and first floor and the Russians on the ground floor ... nobody wanted to give up the positions they held.' The fighting see-sawed back and forth, both sides alternating between attack and defence as the days passed. 'I reached the houses with only a handful of my comrades. Here we broke down the enemy resistance in close quarters fighting ... at the same time we made good our position and stood ready to defend it ... despite strong counterattacks we held our positions with only a few men.'

Increasingly, the fighting revolved around Stalingrad's major landmarks, and in the south that meant the imposing grain elevator and silo complex. Industrial in its construction, the grain elevator facility was designed like a modern-day fortress. Some ninety metres long, fifty metres wide and almost forty metres high, the building towered above its surroundings and held commanding views right down to the shores of the Volga. Made of reinforced concrete, it had multiple levels, a myriad of corridors and offices as well as a bucket elevator and conveyors to lift the grain from the ground into a huge array of silos where it was graded and stored ready for shipment onwards.

On 16 September Wilhelm Hoffmann got the word: 'Our battalion, plus panzers, is attacking the [grain storage] elevator from which smoke is pouring – the grain in it is burning.' The next six days would come to typify the Stalingrad struggle that autumn.

Initial infantry assaults were beaten back by strong Soviet defensive fire, as a German report of the time described: 'The elevator is heavily fortified, and in addition, an advance is impossible due to strong flanking fire from the east.' The *landsers* were undeterred and went in again, this time using 'individual and bundled grenades, with a concentrated charge, in the basement of the elevator', but even then 'it was not possible to break into it.' Once more the Germans turned to brute force with their corps commander, Werner Kempf, telling the Luftwaffe, 'Since we are talking about a gigantic stone structure, the heaviest bombs will be required.' Artillery, howitzers and cannons were brought forward to fire directly at the facility, but even the mighty 88mms could do little more than blast holes in the walls rather than bring it crumbling down. In the aftermath, Hoffmann and his comrades were sent in once more. 'Fighting is going on inside the elevator... If all the buildings of Stalingrad are defended like this then none of us soldiers will get back to Germany.' On the Soviet side a report was sent back from inside the elevator to Chuikov himself: 'Before, we occupied the upper part of the elevator and the Germans the lower part. Now we have driven them out of the lower part but German troops have penetrated upstairs and fighting is now going on in the upper part.'

Losses among the assault *kompanien* were rising steadily. In desperation the Germans tried to find reasons why the defenders continued to hold out. 'The *bataillon* commander says the Commissars have ordered those men to die in the elevator.' Hoffmann had another explanation: 'The Russians are not men, but some kind of cast-iron creatures.' By now the *landsers* were fearful of even showing themselves; 'The Russians are firing on all sides. We stay in our cellar, you can't go out into the street. *Oberfeldwebel* Nuschke was killed today running across a street. Poor fellow, he's got three children.' On 21 September, five days after the assault began, 'The Germans sent in envoys from the civilian population to try and persuade we soldiers who defended the elevator to lay down our arms and surrender. These envoys – after they refused to take up arms and fight with us against the Germans – we shot.'[5]

Finally, the following day, having exhausted their ammunition, the few surviving Soviet defenders decided to break out and try to reach their comrades down by the river. In the eerie silence that followed their departure, Hoffmann and the remainder of his *bataillon* took possession of the elevator. 'Russian resistance in the elevator has been broken.' According to the horrified *landser*, only forty dead Soviets were found in the ruins, 'half of them wearing naval uniform – sea devils'. Hoffmann's *bataillon* had been gutted.

In the skies above the city the story for the Luftwaffe was a variation on the same theme. The VVS was suffering breathtaking casualties and the *jagdflieger* were forced to fly further afield to find them, as one *geschwader*'s unit diary described. 'We are masters in the air over Stalingrad...the enemy's air activity is very limited. To achieve any victories, we position ourselves above the enemy's airfields east of the city in the hope of provoking some of them into the air.' The *Experten* still had the upper hand, with Hermann Graf shooting down an extraordinary sixty-two Soviet aircraft in the month of September – a monthly record that surely will never be beaten. But with few replacement pilots or aircraft coming forward, and serviceability rates plummeting, the physical and mental toll on the thinning German ranks was becoming unbearable and mistakes were being made, as Graf admitted in his diary: 'I failed to spot one of the enemy aircraft during combat. Suddenly bullets slammed into my cockpit.' His ground crew pointed out a how a Soviet cannon shell had only just missed his head. 'Ernst Süss [fellow *Experte* in JG. 52] urged me to take some leave before I end up a corpse.' Wilhelm Crinius was in an even worse state, constantly running a fever and losing weight; by mid-September he weighed just 118lbs. His friend, Alfred Grislawski, remembered that:

> He continued to fly, even though illness and exhaustion caused him to become sick to his stomach at the mere smell of gunpowder smoke from the cannon. In air combat he frequently threw up and had to keep his forage cap with him lined with paper so he could use it as a vomit bag.

Crinius achieved his 100th victory on 22 September and on reaching that milestone was straightaway sent on home leave. Graf refused to join him until he hit the magic 200-mark, but he was close to exhaustion. 'I had to take a day's rest... I just couldn't take it anymore.' His wingman, Heinrich Füllgrabe, achieved his 50th kill and then almost had a nervous breakdown.[6] As the ground attack pilot Horst Ramstetter said, 'Stalingrad was undoubtedly the most difficult mission … more than any other time in the whole Russian campaign.'[7] Perhaps there was an element of method in this seeming madness for the sorely tried *Experten*. Everyone knew a litany of stories of hitherto excellent pilots who had gone on leave only to return and instantly fall prey to the VVS or ground fire, and no pilot – always a breed sensitive to good luck charms – wanted to join that particular list.

The month had seemed to many to have started off with so much promise. But now in every objective sense it was clear Weichs's *Heeresgruppe B* was floundering. Hoth's 4. *Panzerarmee* was disjointed and spread out, losing the mass of fighting power so vital to an armoured formation. Indeed, it had been forced to cede some of its better formations to Paulus to keep up the pressure on the southern half of the city, leaving it with no identifiable centre of gravity. The four Axis allied armies that made up the bulk of Weichs's force were slowly moving into position along the Don, but the long trek across the parched steppe had put them under immense strain, and on arrival at the river they had been unable to destroy a number of deep Red Army bridgeheads on the western bank, at Uryv opposite the Hungarians and Kletskaya and Serafimovich in the Romanian sector. As for Paulus and 6. *Armee*, long gone were the dashing armoured thrusts across the wide-open steppe, searching out the enemy's weak points and lancing through them to create chaos and confusion and send the Soviets scuttling back. In their place was an infantry-dominated, close-quarter, urban battle of attrition; with gains measured in blood and yards.

The inexperience of pretty much half 6. *Armee* was now showing as division after division was bled white at the behest of a commander seemingly bereft of ideas, who rarely left his headquarters and increasingly relied on weight of fire and air power for any gains. That air power was a hostage to fortune as *Luftflotte* 4 itself was now irrevocably split covering both Stalingrad and *Heeresgruppe A* in the Caucasus. Just as worrying for the Germans was the perennial Achilles heel of *Ostheer* operations – logistics. Fuel was available in the supply chain, it just couldn't be brought forward quickly enough, but it was lack of ammunition that was keeping Weichs and his staff awake at night. In the month of September, 6. *Armee* alone expended 23,035,863 bullets, 752,747 mortar rounds, 575,828 anti-tank shells, 178,066 hand grenades, 116,932 infantry cannon shells and 14,932 mines.[8] At OKH on the Bendlerstrasse in Berlin the staff noted that at the front 'the size of ammunition stocks is critical.' On the ground black humour began to do the rounds with the *landsers*. 'There are a thousand artillery guns in the rear area, but each of them only has one shell!'

Over 600 miles west in Vinnytsia, Hitler – uninterested in trifles such as a lack of ammunition – was fuming at what he viewed as unnecessary delay in finishing the job at Stalingrad and securing the Caucasus oilfields. With Maykop reached, he expected List to charge onwards to Grozny and Baku, instead he was repeatedly told by his field commander that the forces available for the advance were insufficient for the task. Refusing to believe the word of his own *feldmarschall*, he despatched Jodl to see for himself and report back. On his return Jodl told the Führer that List's reasons for the delay were entirely correct and without reinforcements *Heeresgruppe A* was effectively stalled. The sharp-faced Jodl even had the temerity to quote some of Hitler's own words back at him to justify List's position. Shocked that the hitherto compliant Jodl had told him what he didn't want to hear, the dictator flew into a rage and set off a chain reaction of events that marked a turning point in his already fractious relationship with the senior command of the Wehrmacht.

The previous winter Hitler had personally turned a significant page. Having spent the first years of his dictatorship in fear of an Army coup that would oust him, he had always trodden carefully around his generals. But when they failed to deliver him an impossible victory over the Soviet Union Hitler in 1941, he had been emboldened to move against those he viewed as failures and dismiss them – and he had developed a taste for it. So now, he didn't hesitate and sacked List anyway. He then demanded that every word spoken at the daily situation conferences was from then on taken down by stenographers so he could not be 'misquoted' in the future. Furthermore, in a fit of petulance worthy of a spoilt child he stopped taking his meals with his generals and instead began to eat alone, although as this saved them from the inevitable historical diatribes Hitler insisted on delivering every time he sat down to eat, perhaps this went down rather well with his staff. He also refused to shake Jodl's hand for months and even considered replacing him with his deputy Walter Warlimont – not a prospect that filled the urbane Warlimont with joy, given he saw how his boss was treated.

In practical terms, List needed to be replaced, and Hitler's decision was simple – he would assume command. Who better to impose National Socialist will on the officers and men of the army group and lead them to victory? Hitler was now not only the commander-in-chief of the Army but one of his own subordinates. The ridiculousness of the situation seemed to escape the dictator. In the end it would make no difference, there simply weren't the men, machines or supplies to reach far-off Grozny, let alone Baku. One officer, Helmut Rohrbach, was exasperated: 'The Führer doesn't listen to our generals … one man can't be a politician, a statesman and a general at the same time, it's madness.'

A fortnight after List was shown the door and Jodl was put into cold storage, the biggest head of them all rolled: Franz Halder's.

> You and I have been suffering from nerves. Half my nervous exhaustion is down to you. It isn't worth it to go on. We need National Socialist ardour now, not professional ability. I cannot expect this from an officer of the old school like you.

With that the Army's Chief of Staff was gone, although in an attempt to help Halder save face, Hitler publicly said the reason was that 'General Halder … could not understand the spirit of my plans.' The man who had been a loyal supporter of Hitler since first meeting him back in 1937 went quietly into retirement. He would never hold a command position again. The officer Hitler chose to provide the 'National Socialist ardour' he so craved was Kurt Zeitzler. Eleven years younger than Halder, Zeitzler was relatively junior for the role and was a friend of the same Wilhelm List the Führer had just unceremoniously thrown aside, having been his Chief of Staff during the invasion of Poland. Somewhat perversely given the circumstances of his appointment, Zeitzler was also known for being a straightforward military man with expertise in logistics and planning rather than being an avid Nazi.

In the opinion of some of his contemporaries he lacked experience of – or indeed any gift for – handling large army groups, but Heinz Guderian for one hoped that Hitler would now listen to what he was being told 'Would Hitler now display more confidence in Zeitzler than he had in Brauchitsch and Halder? Would he now start paying attention to the advice of his experts? The destiny of Germany was dependent on the answer.' As usual Guderian was writing with one eye fixed firmly on posterity and his place in it, but you get the drift.

The omens, however, were not good, as Warlimont observed on seeing Hitler when he returned to his Ukrainian forest headquarters after a period of home leave:

His confidence has gone, he has realised that his deadly game is moving to its appointed end, that Soviet Russia is not going to be overthrown at the second attempt and that now the war on two fronts, which he has unleashed by his wanton arbitrary actions, will grind the Reich to powder. My thoughts ran on; that is why he can no longer bear to have around him the generals who have too often been witnesses to his faults, his errors, his illusions and his daydreams, that is why he wishes to get away from them, why he wishes to see people around him whom he feels have unlimited and unshakeable confidence in him.

As with Guderian's thoughts, there's more than a whiff of hindsight in the artilleryman's opinion, but also truth.

Back in Stalingrad, Rudolf Oehus found a moment to write home.

> We're still busy here in Stalingrad, it will take longer than we thought. The day before yesterday I was right in the city centre ... we were only about one kilometre from the Volga. But the city is completely destroyed, nothing remains intact, every house is a fortified position and is defended by the Russians to the last, and we're forced to destroy everything... Today Russian planes embarrassed themselves again, in an attack two of their bombers collided and crashed... Otherwise there's nothing new to say. I'm fine, don't worry too much about me. When Stalingrad falls we will probably be relieved, everyone is counting on that.[9]

Willi Eising, a motorcycle despatch rider at the divisional HQ of *16. Panzer-Division* up in the north of the city near Rynok, was less sanguine. 'Proven officers had fallen, *kompanie* strengths were shrinking ... we were short of fuel and ammunition – transport aircraft dropped bomb casings full of provisions – it wasn't possible to bring the wounded back from the collection point at the main dressing station, so they remained under enemy fire.'[10] Herbert Pabst recalled the sheer frustration that almost every German at the front now felt so strongly:

> We ploughed over the blazing fields of the Stalingrad battlefield all day long. It is incomprehensible to me how people can continue to live in that hell, but the Russians are firmly established in the wreckage, in ravines, cellars, and in a chaos of twisted steel skeletons of the factories.[11]

Right: 1. This is how the Nazis' international *Signal* magazine portrayed the German Army in the East on the eve of *Unternehmen Blau* – all-conquering soldiers of destiny. (Author's collection)

Below: 2. The Italian general Giovanni Messe (centre in cap) inspects soldiers of the ARMIR preparing to take part in *Blau*. (Author's collection)

3. The offensive begins – German armour drives east across the steppe. (Courtesy of 2 Bundesarchiv_Bild_101I-218-0510-22)

4. The backbone of the German Army - young German infantrymen march east in the stifling heat and dust. (Author's collection)

5. Friedrich Paulus (left) discusses the summer advance with Max Pfeffer, commander of the 297. *Infanterie-Division*. (Author's collection)

6. 6. *Armee* reaches the northern Stalingrad suburb of Rynok on 23 August 1942. In the half-track with glasses and peaked cap is Hans-Valentin Hube – commander 16. *Panzerdivision* – and Wolfram von Richthofen is beneath him with the field glasses. (Author's collection)

7. As 6. *Armee* reach Stalingrad, the rest of the army group sights the foothills of the Caucasus mountains. (Author's collection)

8. The exotic Orient. German *gebirgsjäger* mountain troops use Bactrian camels to help carry the load in the Caucasus. (Author's collection)

9. Stukas fly above a burning Stalingrad. (Author's collection)

10. Panzers from 24. *Panzerdivision* reach Stalingrad's suburbs. (Author's collection)

Left: 11. An NCO squad leader prepares to lead his men into action in the city. (Author's collection)

Below: 12. A Panzer Mark III from 24. *Panzerdivision* drives past one of Stalingrad's trams on its way into the city. (Author's collection)

13. *Signal* magazine trumpets 6. *Armee*'s success as its *landsers* advance on the River Volga. (*Signal* magazine)

14. The advance slows. German infantry wait for armoured support before advancing further into the city. (*Signal* magazine)

15. A half-track mounted flak gun provides covering fire for the 6. *Armee* advance into the workers' settlements in the north of the city. (Author's collection)

16. A German MG34 machine-gun crew amid the mud and rubble in Stalingrad. (Author's collection)

Right: 17. The highly decorated *Hauptmann* Friedrich Winkler of *305. Infanterie-Division* oversees yet another attempt to reach the Volga. (Author's collection)

Below: 18. Aerial view of the grain elevator and storage complex in the south of the city. The photo clearly shows how it dominates the area. (Author's collection)

Above: 19. Soldiers
from the *94.*
Infanterie-Division
prepare to attack
the grain elevator
complex once again
on 19 September
1942. (Author's
collection)

Left: 20. The
war reporter –
Leutnant Bruno
Wundshammer –
takes an aerial photo
of another Luftwaffe
raid on Stalingrad,
this time hitting oil
storage tanks and
factory complexes
near the river. (*Signal*
magazine)

21. Success at last! On 27 September 1942 the swastika was raised over the former Communist Party headquarters in the newly renamed Red Square. (Author's collection)

22. Stalingrad is still not captured. An infantry squad takes cover before going into yet another assault. (Author's collection)

23. October 1942 and *Hauptmann* Wilhelm Traub – commander of *Pionier-Bataillon 305* – sits amid the ruins of the Barrikady factory. He is armed with a Soviet PPsH-41 submachine-gun. (Author's collection)

24. The real face of the fighting in Stalingrad. An exhausted *panzergrenadier* from *16. Panzerdivision* after another failed attack. (Author's collection)

25. A German infantry officer points the way forward for his men. The weather is getting colder and he wears a greatcoat against the gathering chill. (Author's collection)

26. *Leutnant* Joachim Stempel. His father was a divisional commander in 6. *Armee* and young Joachim led a combat group that almost broke through to the Volga before being forced back by Soviet counter-attacks. (Author's collection)

27. The 1936 Berlin Olympics. The winners of the men's shotput stand should to shoulder. From left to right: gold medallist Hans-Otto Woellke, Finnish silver medallist Sulo Bärlund and bronze medallist Gerhard Stöck, liaison officer with the Romanian IV Corps when *Uranus* was launched. (Author's collection)

28. A German Army field bakery bakes fresh loaves of *kommissbrot* for the *landsers*. Without food like this 6. *Armee* was destined to starve. (Author's collection)

29. A Junker Ju52 comes in to land at Pitomnik airfield in January 1943. The Luftwaffe never had anywhere near enough lift capacity to supply 6. *Armee* and the airlift was a disaster. (Author's collection)

Left: 30. The corpses of German soldiers frozen in death amid the ruins of Stalingrad. (Author's collection)

Below: 31. Herbert Kuntz – Heinkel He 111 bomber pilot and the last flier to drop supplies to the remnants of 6. *Armee* as it trudged into captivity. (Author's collection)

8

RATTENKRIEG – RATS' WAR

'In the blocks captured two days ago Russian soldiers appeared from somewhere or other and fighting has flared up with fresh vigour. Our men are being killed not only in the frontline but in the rear, in buildings we've already occupied... Stalingrad is hell.' Willi Hoffmann's earlier optimism had evaporated, burnt away in Stalingrad's smouldering ruins, but at least he and the men in the other worn-out divisions in the southern half of the city had something to show for their blood-letting. 'In three and a half weeks we have taken about five and a half square miles. The commander has congratulated us on our victory.' The grain elevator complex was finally theirs, as was Red Square, the main railway station and most of the housing settlements.

Even Mamayev Kurgan was no longer safe for the Soviets when the Germans and Croats of Werner Sanne's *100. Jäger Division* received orders to take the hill. Trained and equipped specifically for fighting in difficult terrain – including urban warfare – the *jägers* and their Croat allies were a good choice for an exceedingly tough objective. The Croats especially were upbeat, having been visited a few days previously by their *Poglavnik* (Leader), the genocidal lawyer Anté Pavelic, who used the occasion to present numerous medals and awards and praised their valuable contribution to the Axis cause.

Among the attackers was the former private soldier and now *kompanie* commander Josef Goblirsch. 'At 0300hrs on

27 September preparations began and at 0500hrs our artillery was unleashed.' The Soviets refused to simply sit in their trenches and brought down their own fire with a 'Stalin Organ salvo landing in a gully killing 15 *jägers* and wounding another hundred'. After ninety minutes of intense shelling 'Our regiment attacked… [Mamayev Kurgan] had been ploughed over by bombs and shells and richly soaked in blood. We knew we would be up against the stiffest resistance.' Regardless, Goblirsch was taken back by the ferocity of the defence. 'Incessant mortar fire kept our heads down … after heavy losses we only advanced 200 metres.' With casualties mounting, Goblirsch received orders to dig in. 'Cowering in the shell craters and shelter-trenches abandoned by the Russians … we awaited the approaching darkness with longing.' Pulled out to rest and recover after nightfall, Goblirsch saw with horror that the 'wheeled vehicle *zug* [platoon] had been shrivelled to ten exhausted men'. Heavily supported by massed artillery and Stukas, Goblirsch and his division kept on attacking, even receiving drafts of reinforcements - 'unfortunately inexperienced' – but they still weren't able to take the entire hill.

Chuikov and his own headquarters had already relocated to a temporarily safer position near the river, and now, in what became almost emblematic of the Soviet attitude to Stalingrad's defence, Chuikov ordered Alexander Rodimtsev's 13th Guards Rifle Division over the Volga and onto the hill, with orders to hold it or die. The division had already made a gruelling forced march to reach the ferry station on the Volga's eastern bank late in the afternoon, only to be told as soon as they arrived that they couldn't rest but must go straight across the river and into action. With no time to familiarise themselves with the ground – they had no maps anyway – the guardsmen climbed aboard the waiting ferries in the gathering gloom and headed over to the burning city. A thousand of them weren't even armed and had orders to take weapons off the dead. There would be plenty of those. Thirty per cent of its officers and men were killed within the first 24 hours, and within three days almost all the division's 10,000 men were dead. But the hill was not surrendered. For the young Josef Goblirsch, the experience had been horrific: 'Our entire bataillon was disbanded. My *kompanie* was totally exhausted.'[1]

Goblirsch's division wasn't the only one ground down by the fighting in the southern half of the city. A *feldwebel* in the neighbouring *71.ID* reported to his headquarters that he was now in command of his *kompanie,* and its strength stood at just nine men. One *landser* wrote home about the 'days and nights of resigned desperation ... the insurmountable fear you continue to accept even though your brain has ceased to function normally.' He described the 'slaughterhouse' he had survived and then asked the folks back home to 'read about war standing up, late at night, when you're tired, as I am writing about it now at dawn while my asthma attack wears off ... writing from a hole in the mud.' Like so many others, he was now openly comparing Stalingrad to Verdun back in the First World War, a horror that had lasted for nine months and cost over a third of a million German casualties for precisely nothing. 'Those who read about Verdun and Stalingrad and expound theories later to friends over a cup of coffee haven't understood anything.' Helmut Groscurth was another to view the Stalingrad fighting as akin to the blood-sodden fields and forts of France more than two decades earlier. 'Will Stalingrad turn into a second Verdun? That's what everyone's asking here with great concern.' The comparison was the stuff of nightmares drummed into every German child by their parents and teachers, as one German NCO understood: 'Stalingrad is hell on earth. It is Verdun, bloody Verdun with new weapons. We attack every day. If we capture 20 yards in the morning the Russians throw us back again in the evening.'

Nevertheless, *6. Armee* had battered its way forward in the south, which was now almost all in German hands. Not that the newly captured territory was much to look at, as Willi Eising remarked; 'The city centre, with the main railway station and Red Square, was a heap of rubble, the multi-storied buildings shell-damaged and gutted. Here and there half a chimney stack stood surrounded by the ashes of wooden dwellings. The population had either fled or taken shelter in ruins, cellars and caves.'

Paulus now decided to complete the city's capture by seizing its northern industrial half and specifically the four giant factory complexes of the Lazur, the Barrikady, the Red October and the Dzerzhinsky. As in the south, Paulus's plan was little more than a meat grinder reliant on massive firepower and Soviet acquiescence in doing little more than perishing where they stood. After weeks of some of the bitterest street fighting seen in the war so far, *Der Lord* had learnt nothing. Miles outside the city in his remote and peaceful headquarters out on the steppe he was entirely disconnected from his men who were fighting and dying in the choking dust of Stalingrad. He might have served with him in the *Reichswehr*, but clearly Paulus was no Rommel.

The battle to which Paulus was now committing his already weakened divisions would decimate his fragile army and leave it dangerously off balance and exhausted at exactly the time the Soviets were ready to pounce. Not that Paulus alone was to blame. Hitler piled the pressure on his narrow shoulders, repeatedly demanding he take every square metre of the city as soon as possible, while Weichs for his part stayed silent. Increasingly, the key relationship for *Heeresgruppe B* would now be between Paulus and Hitler himself, with the army group commander relegated to the position of impotent bystander.

With Hitler baying for final victory, the Germans once again went into the assault in the north. Immediately it proved itself as tough a nut to crack as the south. A *landser* described one Soviet trick:

> We would spend the whole day clearing a street, from one end to the other, establish blocks and firing points at the western end, and prepare for another slice of the salami the next day. But at dawn the Russians would start up firing from their old positions at the far end! It took us some time to discover their trick; they'd knocked holes through between the garrets and attics and during the night they would run back like rats in the rafters and set their machine-guns up behind some topmost window or broken chimney.

The enemies were almost close enough to smell each other, the Germans always saying the Soviets gave off a distinct aroma from the shag tobacco makhorka cigarettes they incessantly smoked. Willi Kreiser described how 'Our trenches were often only as far apart as you could throw a grenade. Ivan tried to push balled charges tied to long poles into our strongpoints ... if I crawled along my trench the Russians would hurl grenades at me.' This was a deliberate tactic. Under Chuikov's orders, and, knowing they couldn't match the weight of German firepower – especially from the air – they sought to nullify it by getting so close to Kreiser and his comrades that they couldn't use their heavy weapons. If the Germans withdrew in preparation for an air strike, the Soviets would infiltrate forward, mirroring their movements to deny them a safe gap – it worked.

Reinforcements. That's what the battle in Stalingrad needed and that's what the Soviets had and the Germans didn't. Between 15 September and 3 October some six fresh and fully equipped rifle divisions – two of them élite Guards units – were ferried to Chuikov over the Volga, while Paulus got nothing except a dribble of men. One of those few, precious, German reinforcements arrived at his new unit and was met by its commander, 'a *leutnant* whose name I don't remember, I think it might have been Hirsch. He was delighted to have me as a reinforcement to his *kompanie* which had shrunk to just ten men.' Going out that night to lay barbed wire obstacles Hirsch's new man was shot in the leg: 'They cut open my trouser leg to expose a large and bloody wound on my outer right thigh. There was material and metal splinters in the wound – it was a 'Blighty one' as the British would say.' He was evacuated soon afterwards and *Leutnant* Hirsch's *kompanie* was back down to ten men.

Chuikov – who seemed to possess an almost inexhaustible well of quotable *bons mots* – famously said of the fighting, 'time is blood,' and he was prepared to spend the latter liberally to buy the former. No-one was exempt from the northern battle. Staff officers were ordered away from their desks to take command of ad hoc combat groups, and the lightly wounded were patched up and kept in the line rather than being evacuated to field hospitals on the river's eastern bank. Five thousand factory workers from the Red October were told to pick up the guns they had just made and march out of the gates and into the frontline. Those who put up their hands when asked if anyone knew how to actually fire a rifle, were given white armbands to mark them out as instructors for the rest. Many of the press-ganged workers were single men whose life was regimented and semi-militaristic anyway, but even so it was a different matter to heft a rifle over your shoulder, form up in ranks and march en masse towards the sound of the guns with no training and scant chance of survival. Wilhelm Adam, a staff officer in Paulus's headquarters, saw how 'the population took up arms. Lying on the battlefield were workers in overalls still clasping a rifle or pistol in their stiff hands. The dead in workers' clothes leaned over the controls of smashed tanks. Never ever have we seen anything of this kind.' A post-war study of Soviet methods during the fighting found that:

> The inhabitants of a threatened city, or perhaps the entire male population … were gathered up quickly, regardless of age, nationality or fitness and used to fill out units. With no training at all – or at most only a few days – and often without weapons and uniforms, these 'soldiers' were thrown into battle. They were supposed to learn in combat all that was necessary and to gather the weapons from their dead comrades … this was a game played with human lives.

Soviet units committed to the battle were not rotated out of the line either, instead being kept in action until totally burnt out; the 244th Rifle Division, for instance, had been whittled away to just 1,500 men by early October, and the same went for division after division fed into the city's ruins.

While many Soviet soldiers and citizens were prepared to accept such draconian measures to help defeat the Germans, the sentiment wasn't universal, as Hans Heinz Rehfeldt saw first-hand when his mortar team captured 'a youngster from the 110th

Cavalry Division, scarcely 17 years old and just three months a soldier! He told us that boys were now being called up at age 15 and received little training. He was sick of it.' One German NCO wrote that 'Morale among the Russians is really bad. Most deserters are driven over to us through hunger.' The irony of that statement was yet to hit home.

Brutal as Chuikov's methods obviously were, it was a clear signal that the Soviets were simply not prepared to give up and abandon Stalingrad. Many Germans thought the battle was more or less over, with one *landser* remarking he was already 'dreaming of underground winter quarters, glowing Hindenburg stoves and lots of post from our beloved homes'. Franz Wertheim in his hospital, far to the rear of the army group, heard only good news. 'The big objectives of the summer campaign were either attained or within our immediate grasp. The Caucasus had been occupied and the capture of Stalingrad, where the final mopping up was in progress, would crown the offensive.'[2]

As the Germans began to believe it might all soon be over, their enemy was adapting. A force known for its centralised control and rigid adherence to orders now started to experiment with new formations and tactics. Red Army rifle sections became 'Assault Teams' of eight to ten men led by an NCO and almost all armed with fully automatic PPSh-41 submachine-guns, whose 71-round drum magazines and rapid rate of fire gave them the nickname 'burp guns'. Two such Assault Teams would form a Storm Group, with each Storm Group supported by a Reserve Detachment of two additional Assault Teams for flank protection, and a Reinforcement Group equipped with anti-tank guns and rifles, mortars, flame throwers, machine guns and defensive kit including picks, shovels and mines.

The idea was that one or more Storm Groups would be used to attack the most forward German position, and on reaching their objective and killing the Germans, the Reinforcement Group would push forward to fortify the newly won position, so the moment the inevitable German counterattack materialised the Soviets would be ready and waiting. The Soviets even practised these tactics in the city itself, in dry runs so to speak, under the watchful eye of experienced officers and NCOs, before the Assault Teams went forward and into action. This was the genesis of the Red Army's soon-to-be famous 'street fighting academy'.

The Germans were slow to understand, and then react to, the changing way the Red Army was fighting. Possessing an excellent submachine-gun themselves in the MP40, the Germans were unwilling to re-equip the mass of *landsers* with them, and so they remained a one per squad weapon. In truth, the creaking German supply system and inadequate manufacturing facilities would probably have prevented such a major change anyway, but the reality in the streets of Stalingrad was *landsers* with bolt action rifles facing squads of Red Army submachine-gunners deluging them with fire at close quarters.

For their Soviet enemies the fighting continued to inspire waves of new thinking. Having brought in the Storm Group concept, Red Army commanders began to see bigger buildings like office or apartment blocks as breakwaters which could be used to channel the attacking Germans down selected streets into prepared killing zones. Those same buildings would then be garrisoned with fifty or more heavily armed men with orders to lay low until the advancing Germans had passed them by, before opening fire at them from behind with machine guns placed on the roof and top floor, and infantrymen on all the other floors. When the exasperated Germans then brought up their supporting panzers to try and blast them out, they would be confronted with a mass of closely laid mines and anti-tank rifles hidden on the ground floor.

Even when the Germans managed to gain entry to the buildings, their usual sure touch in combat often deserted them. They would typically enter on the ground floor and then attempt to fight their way up the stairs, handing their opponents an advantage from the start, and would fail to clear the cellar or the sewer underground, allowing hidden Soviets to wait until they were embroiled above them and then attack from below. Likewise, on reaching the top floor, many German units considered the job done and would leave the roof space undisturbed. Needless to say, the Soviets would be there too, waiting for an opportunity to knock through to the adjoining loft and get behind the hapless Germans to create more havoc. Diaries, memoirs and survivor accounts are full of German frustration at being shot at from positions they believed cleared.

Karl Strecker – one of Paulus's senior commanders - realised what his men were facing and yet seemed almost powerless to try and counter it; 'The enemy is invisible. Ambushes out of basements, wall remnants, hidden bunkers and factory ruins produce heavy casualties among our troops.' For the first time in the war in the East, it was Soviet and not German commanders who were beginning to call the tune.

The *Ostheer,* and in truth the Wehrmacht in general, was now under enormous strain. Nowhere on the far-flung Russian Front was an oasis of calm; in the north the Red Army was once more attempting to break the siege of Leningrad and was fighting fiercely at Sinyavino, while in *Heeresgruppe Mitte*'s sector Moscow launched attack after attack to try and destroy the Rzhev salient and crush Model's 9. *Armee*. Already scarce supplies were having to be ferried hundreds of miles to the Caucasus, and in the deserts of North Africa Erwin Rommel was screaming for fuel, panzers and ammunition as Montgomery's British and Commonwealth forces turned the screw at El Alamein. Even the West was a drain on Nazi Germany's limited resources, with the Dieppe raid of 19 August frightening Berlin into transferring some of its best formations out of Russia and back west to France to ward off the non-existent threat of a further attack.

All Berlin could spare for Paulus were five specialist *Pioniere* (assault engineer) battalions; the 50th, 162nd, 294th, 366th and 672nd. Put under the command of the senior combat engineer in Paulus's headquarters; *Oberst* Herbert Selle, each unit was some 600 men strong, with the *pioniere* specially trained in demolition, close quarter assault and obstacle clearance. Arriving in the second week of October, they were a useful addition to 6. *Armee* but were far too few in number to make a decisive difference. Selle – an early convert to Nazism who later became disillusioned – observed:

There is bitter fighting in Stalingrad for every house, every hut, every skyscraper, every silo, every factory, with an effort of blood and material that is in no relation to the successes of either side in attack or defence ... hidden behind each projecting wall, each staircase entrance, each door recess, each lathe ... could be a machine-gun ... literally every inch of ground is being fought for here.

Over the years a myth has grown of Soviet superiority in urban fighting over a supposedly hapless German foe. The myth itself is very powerful and has been fed by the *landsers'* own memoirs, *feldpost* letters and diaries like Willi Hoffmann's. Every line and sentence cursing the ferocity of the fighting and the tenacity of Soviet resistance has helped build a narrative of Soviet skill versus German ineptitude. Urban warfare, house-to-house fighting, is a truly dreadful experience for combatants, where casualties are almost heaped on top of each other and where the nature of the battle is claustrophobic and belt buckle to belt buckle. So it is little wonder that the men enduring it speak and write about it in such lurid terms.

In truth, the soldiers of the Red Army – most of whom were born and brought up in the countryside – were far less at home in the sprawl of a city like Stalingrad compared to their German opponents, most of whom by contrast were city dwellers themselves and far more used to an urban environment. Equally, much has been made of the Soviet willingness to embrace the assault squad as the basic tactical unit, and while this was indeed an evolution for the Red Army, the argument seems dubious at best, given that German tactical doctrine was based on the squad, that huge emphasis was placed on excellence in junior leadership, and that all ranks were taught to exercise command when necessary and achieve success the best way they saw fit on the ground at the time – the very essence of what the Germans termed *auftragstaktik* (mission orientated tactics).

If it is accepted that the Red Army was no better or worse than the Germans in house-to-house fighting, why has the myth survived for so long? Firstly, the Red Army in Stalingrad had relatively few heavy weapons, their only artillery was far away on the east bank and they had very little air support as the Luftwaffe maintained aerial superiority until the latter stages of the battle. What they did have was a profusion of small arms and manpower. In those circumstances, the only viable option for the Soviets was to fight face to face and accept the appalling casualties that came with such an approach, as one German machine-gunner saw for himself: 'The sun was so bright that their helmets shone. The two of us [his loader] then swept the area with machine-gun fire. From a distance the mass of Russians looked like black clouds. If you kept pouring fire into them many would fall ... in the evening when I looked out, ach! So many Russians lay there.' The Germans in contrast had the full panoply of weaponry and tried to use it to achieve victory at an acceptable cost in lives. This precedence for firepower over blood was not a uniquely German approach and throughout the war tended to be the option adopted by the attacker in an urban battle. Perhaps the best example would be Berlin in 1945, where it was the German Army – or at least the remnants of it – that defended the capital with small teams using automatic weapons, while the Red Army opted for the application of massive weight of fire including massed tanks and heavy artillery firing point blank over open sights.

The Stalingrad urban fighting myth also suited the German Army, as it could ascribe its failure to what it saw as the uncivilised brutishness of the Soviet peoples. The argument was simple; urban fighting was vicious and degrading, therefore a foe that is vicious and degraded will have an advantage. This was pure Nazism, and this racist outlook permeated all ranks from top to bottom, with one panzer general saying that 'disregard for human life and contempt for death are characteristics of the Russian soldier.'[3] A far more junior officer wrote:

The Russian soldier was more prepared for man-to-man fighting ... our soldiers being western Europeans didn't like this type of fighting so much, they relied more on automatic weapons and using their brains [whereas] most Red Army divisions were composed of Asiatic peoples.[4]

In the end, the myth served both sides well. The Soviets could laud their success as being down to their military prowess and an indomitable will to win, while the Germans could throw up their hands and say they were beaten by the sheer brutishness of Slav racial inferiority. But a far more plausible explanation for the Red Army's success amidst the ruins of Stalingrad was that they simply had to adapt as they did due to the circumstances they were operating under, and in the end numbers told. Moscow could afford to lose the 10,000 men of Rodimtsev's 13th Guards Rifle Division and many more besides, whereas the 40,011 officers and men Paulus lost from late August to mid-October[5] were almost irreplaceable.

The fighting for Stalingrad's ruined factories would prove the point. Suffering dreadful losses, Paulus's infantry divisions were increasingly having to resort to desperate measures to maintain some sort of cohesion and fighting power, with whole *bataillonen* disbanded and the survivors used to fill the gaps in their sister units, but even that just papered over the cracks. One division reported an average strength in each of its nine *bataillonen* as being three officers, 11 NCOs and just 62 enlisted men. When Hitler reinforced his increasingly beleaguered army commander in early November with four more *pioniere bataillonen*, Chuikov was by contrast receiving divisions, ten in all. There was no comparison.

One of those four German units, the *Heeres-Pi.Btl. 336*, arrived in the city to be assigned a position across the street from the Barrikady factory, whereupon its commander – *Major* Josef Linden – reconnoitred the battlefield and found 'Loosely hanging corrugated steel sheets that creaked eerily in the wind, T-beams, huge craters ... cellars turned into strongpoints ... and over everything a never-ceasing crescendo of noise from all types of guns and bombs.' Ordered to reinforce *305. Infanterie-Division's Major* Eugen Rettenmaier, Linden found the tooth-brush moustached Rettenmaier leading just 37 men from a battalion whose nominal roll was over four hundred. Rettenmaier himself was grief-stricken, not only because of the horrendous casualties among his men, but also because his eldest son, Ottokar, had been killed at the front back in May.

Regardless, the *pioniere* reinforcements were swiftly sent into action to clear Soviet strongpoints near the Barrikady. Well-trained and experienced though the *pioniere* were, they were unprepared for what awaited them. Loaded down with satchel charges, flame-throwers, grenades and MP40s, they assembled in the eastern end of the factory waiting for the off. Tightly bunched up, one of them inadvertently tripped a booby trap. The resulting explosion killed eighteen of them and horrified the others. When finally ordered into the attack they were met by an incredible weight of fire from the tenacious Soviet defenders. In two days of fighting, from Monday 9 to Tuesday 10 November, the assaulting *pioniere* did indeed succeed in taking their assigned objectives – nicknamed the Chemist's Shop and the Commissar's House – but their losses were horrific, as one officer noted after a failed attack:

> Were these men all that was left of our units? Fresh *bataillonen* had gone into the attack, just as at home on the training ground. And what was the result? Most of them had been killed, some were wounded, and all the rest were routed, utterly routed. A cursed place!

In less than five days, over a thousand *pioniere* were lost. Herbert Selle wrote a bitter letter home; 'There will be many tears in Germany... Happy is he who is not responsible for these unwarranted sacrifices.'

As far as the German people and world opinion were concerned, completing the capture of Stalingrad was rapidly morphing into the most important goal in Nazi Germany's war. Sixth Army, originally just the lead formation of the subsidiary offensive to cover the all-important seizure of the Caucasus oil fields, was now the apex of the struggle between Stalin and Hitler, as both men increasingly put their own prestige on the line amid the burning city's ruins. As Hitler declared in a speech broadcast to the German people; 'You may be assured that nobody will ever drive us out of Stalingrad.' For Paulus, the days of directing sweeping movements by entire corps were long gone as his focus narrowed alarmingly to just four factories and their adjacent suburbs. Now, solidly chain-smoking, still troubled with recurring bouts of dysentery, and increasingly dominated by his sharp-elbowed Chief of Staff, Arthur Schmidt, the army commander was doing nothing more than feeding regiment after regiment into the fighting and responding to minor administrative routine; 'Herr General Paulus gives permission to *Oberleutnant* Georg Reymann, Regiment 549, to marry Fraulein Lina Hauswald. Neustadt ... Please forward.' Hans Doerr, chief German liaison officer with Constantin Constantinescu-Claps's Romanian 4th Army south of the city, lamented that:

> The time for conducting large-scale operations was gone forever, from the wide expanses of steppe land the war moved to the jagged gullies of the Volga hills with their copses and ravines, into the factory area of Stalingrad, spread out over uneven, pitted, rugged country covered with iron, concrete and stone buildings.

In a topsy-turvy strategy that made no sense and smacked more of desperation than military logic, he ordered one of his three precious armoured formations, *24. Panzer-Division*, to attack and seize the Barrikady and Red October workers settlements. Highly trained specialists – panzer crews, drivers, signallers and gunners – advanced into rubble-strewn streets where their expertise counted for nought. Losses were dreadful. 'We're attacking! Metre by metre we crawl forward, following the bombs that the Stukas are dropping in front of us... Unbelievable, we cannot understand anything anymore... Enemy snipers hit us in the flank and inflict bloody losses ... we cannot see them.' A senior officer described how 'the mile as a measure of distance was now replaced by the yard.'

Günter Koschorrek was with a batch of newly trained replacements heading for the division from the railhead to the rear: 'We march onwards ... hour after hour ... we sweat, we swear, many of us shout out just to lighten our spirits, but we still have to drag ourselves forward – kilometre after kilometre.' Finally nearing the city, they could 'hear the rolling thunder and the sky is glowing red – that's Stalingrad all right.' Along with about thirty others, Koschorrek was sent to a heavily depleted *Schwadron* (*squadron* – as a former cavalry division 24. *Panzer-Division* still used its old designations) where their arrival doubled its strength but still left it at less than 50 per cent of its establishment. Waiting to go forward into the frontline, Koschorrek found that 'my sleeping place has been taken by a *landser* back from Stalingrad. I can hardly make out his face – it's covered with beard stubble, his peaked cap almost covers his eyes and the earflaps are pulled down over his ears, he's in a deep sleep.'[6]

Similarly to the ex-cavalrymen of 24. *Panzer-Division*, the Saxons of 14. *Panzer-Division* found themselves fighting in the unfamiliar surroundings of the Dzerzhinsky tractor works alongside the infantrymen of Erwin Jaenecke's 389. *Infanterie-Division*. Jaenecke's Hessians had been destined for occupation duties in western Europe before *Blau* intervened and whisked them away to Russia, and now they were choking on brick dust and smoke as they inched their way forward through the twisted girders and debris of the cavernous three-kilometre-long production halls. One of them stared in alarmed fascination at the Stukas overhead: 'The whole sky was full of aircraft, every flak gun firing, bombs roaring down, aircraft crashing, an enormous piece of theatre which we followed with very mixed feelings from our trenches.' Who could blame him? He and his comrades knew that once the bombing was over they would be ordered into the attack once more.

The *Signal* magazine war correspondent Bruno Wundshammer went forward to see for himself what the situation was like at the front:

> We cross a communication trench. A glance across the parapet reveals the Volga as it flows behind fences and factories … we take cover in a cellar … a ladder leads up to the loft of the wooden house which has no back wall … the enemy is only 100 yards away. I see only wooden huts and behind them a large factory – the Barrikady.

Under increasingly heavy Soviet fire Wundshammer moved back and came across 'a soldier behind a brick wall writing a letter on a box. He takes no notice of the artillery and the shell impacts.' But then Wundshammer was brought crashing back to the brutal reality of the battle when 'shell splinters crunch into rotten wood and two infantrymen pass by carrying a third whose head is hanging down motionless. His fine fair hair moves in the wind.' The infantryman was just one casualty among many.

'It was a terrible, exhausting battle on and below ground, in ruins, in cellars and factory sewers.' The panzer crewman described how his tank 'climbed mounds of rubble and scrap, and crept screeching through chaotically destroyed workshops and fired at point-blank range in narrow yards. Many panzers shook or exploded from the force of an exploding enemy mine.' Working alongside the panzers, the German assault squads would try and root out the locations of Soviet strongpoints, machine-gun nests and gun positions, calling in the flying artillery of the Luftwaffe to smash them to pieces. The Stuka commander, Paul-Werner Hozzel, recalled that Richthofen himself stressed that

> ... our *geschwader* had to deliver precision bombing so as to avoid danger to our troops entrenched close to the target area. He wanted to watch our sorties and judge the accuracy of our pilots ... this was a very delicate order ... we couldn't risk making a dive-bombing attack from 4,000-metres altitude because of the wide area of dispersion, so we had to fly a slant range attack, releasing the bombs directly over the roofs. We had to push the bombs into the target like loaves of bread into an oven.

With the factories themselves built like fortresses – much as the grain elevator was – the Stukas carried special payloads of 'one 500-kilo bomb with a tank busting head and delayed action fuse for piercing the roofs. Each aircraft also carried two 250-kilo bombs under the wings, so each carried a load of 1,000 kilos.' Once the dive bombers had done their work, then – and only then – would the infantry and panzer-grenadiers move forward, liberally throwing grenades and spraying fire at every conceivable enemy position. However, even after being on the receiving end of such treatment the surviving Soviets would hit back, 'Fierce Soviet counterattacks as though nothing had happened, as if we'd dropped toy torpedoes instead of bombs.' On the ground Willi Hoffmann was just as amazed as his Luftwaffe comrade in the air: 'A lot of Russian tommy gunners have appeared. Where are they bringing them from?' Erhard Raus had the answer. 'A specifically Russian battle technique was infiltration … it especially suited the Russian and he was a master. Despite the closest observation of the avenues of approach, the Russian was suddenly there, no-one knew where he came from, nor for how long he'd been there.' But there they were, and determined not to give an inch:

> For every house, every workshop, water tower, railway embankment, wall, cellar and every pile of ruins a bitter battle was waged, without equal even in the First World War with its vast expenditure of munitions. The distance between the enemy and us was as small as it could possibly be. Despite the concentrated fir from aircraft and artillery it was impossible to break out.

Hoffmann's unit – the Saxons and former Czech Sudeten Germans of 94. *Infanterie-Division* – had had a brief rest after capturing the grain elevator a few miles to the south, but with unit after unit effectively burnt-out, Paulus had no choice but to order it back into the fray at the Barrikady alongside Günter Koschorrek and his fellow panzer-grenadiers. After marching through the night to reach their newly assigned sector Hoffmann was horrified to see 'so many crosses with our helmets on top. Have we really lost so many men?' He got his answer a day later when they attacked the Barrikady. 'Our *bataillon* has gone into the attack four times and been stopped each time.' He noticed that 'the Russians have stopped surrendering … if we take any prisoners it's because they're hopelessly wounded and can't move by themselves.'

Hoffmann found himself fighting near Jaenecke's Hessians, one of whom recalled how,

With dry mouths we moved forward into the factory buildings which were littered with hundreds of large objects ... the relatively large size of our force was in no way reassuring. Even if we overwhelmed them in the end each bullet they fired was bound to hit someone and if I should be the only casualty in a victorious army of a million men the victory would be without interest to me... The first two sheds were empty. Perhaps our prisoners had been telling the truth. But our orders were to check the whole place ... we surrounded the entire factory complex and then began to move towards the centre. We passed through a series of enormous barnlike buildings which seemed to be on the point of collapse. The wind was blowing hard and the buildings echoed with sinister creaking sounds. Otherwise, everything was quiet except for the occasional clatter made by one of our men deliberately shoving aside some metal object or overturning a pile of crates.

He knew this was too good to last. '[The place] was ideal for snipers and as bad as possible for us.'

'Snipers!' – a word guaranteed to spread fear among the attacking Germans, and understandably so. The sniper – a marksman (or woman) firing with a specially adapted rifle, often from great distance and always concealed – had been a feature of armies since the invention of gunpowder, but the Red Army took the concept to a whole new level. Developing a doctrine colloquially known as the 'cult of the sniper' the Soviets provided almost half a million of their soldiers and partisans with some sort of sniper training during the war, and almost 10,000 went on to achieve higher level sniper qualifications. The most famous graduate of the Soviet 'sniper cult' was the former Navy clerk, Vasily Zaitsev. Having learned to shoot by hunting wolves and deer in his native Urals, Zaitsev, whose name means 'hare' in Russian, found himself in Stalingrad where his deadly accuracy brought him to the attention of both his superiors and the Soviet propaganda machine. By early November he had notched up thirty-two kills and was also instructing other sharpshooters at an ad hoc sniper school near the Lazur chemical works, where his pupils were known as *zaichata*, leverets, as a play on his surname.[7] His fellow Stalingrad sniper, Anatoly Chekov, described his first few sorties to the Soviet war reporter Vasily Grossman.

> When I first got the rifle, I couldn't bring myself to kill another human being. A German was standing there for about four minutes talking and I let him go. When I killed my first one, he fell at once. Another one ran out and stooped over the dead one, and I knocked him down too... When I first killed, I was shaking all over; the man was only walking to get some water! I felt scared: I'd killed a person.

Chekov's scruples disappeared swiftly, as was evident in a later interview where he explained his preference for head shots: 'When I shoot, the head immediately jerks backwards, or to one side, and he drops what he was carrying and falls down.' One German officer saw for himself what this meant for his men:

> My *kompanie* has suffered heavy losses. The men mostly had shots to the head, neck and arm. The Russians have snipers and they are very watchful. They have the rifle clamped firmly in place and aim at the strip of trench past which our relief comes and goes, and because the trench isn't deep enough ... if a German helmet appears above a depression the Russian counts off the seconds until he comes into view again and then shoots... My *kompanie* has lost three more men to snipers – all shot through the head.

During the *Rattenkrieg* the Soviet sharpshooters came into their own, as Arthur Krüger acknowledged: 'They had good snipers, moving about by day was suicide.' The same *landser* remembered the neighbouring *kompanie* 'had shortages caused by men being shot in the head'. His own team received a fresh draft of men returned from leave and the military hospital. 'They came to us with the ration carriers, mentally they were probably still in Germany. They failed to hear our warning shout; "Achtung! Snipers, keep your heads down!" They didn't make it.'[8] A gunner in Wolfgang Pickert's flak division recalled a draft of six replacements arriving at his battery one night, whereupon they were duly warned about the sniper threat. Regardless, one by one the newcomers sated their curiosity about their new Soviet foe by trying to catch a look at them across the lines. By dawn only two were still alive.

Using a tactic Zaitsev came up with called the 'sixes', three teams of two – a sniper and a scout – would cover a large area from three separate firing points, ensuring that every inch of ground was under one of their guns. These killing grounds were death traps for the *landsers*, with the likes of Chekov and Zaitsev amassing tallies of 225 and 256 kills respectively, and many others reaching the one hundred mark. The Soviets perfected the come-on attack, cutting the telephone lines the Germans depended on for communications at a selected location to entice out a signaller who was forced to follow the line until he found the break to repair it – he would be shot dead as he worked. Anyone else sent out to find out what happened to the first man would follow him to the grave.

Franz Kumpf had trained as a hairdresser before the war but found himself a linesman in Stalingrad; 'Snipers made our journeys difficult.' His close friend Wilhelm Hönnige had gone out to fix a line break and had not returned, so out went Kumpf and another comrade to try and find him. 'Wilhelm lay on his stomach … the wound was the size of both my hands… I told him, "Lie still we're taking you to a doctor." The shooting kept our heads down all the time as it was daylight and the enemy could see clearly.'

Commanders were priority targets too. It was relatively easy to mark out an officer by his rank epaulettes, but soon any German sporting a pair of binoculars or a pistol holster was in the same category, something the Germans were slow to realise. The result was an ever-growing list of junior officer casualties with NCOs hurriedly promoted to try and fill the gaps. Alongside commanders and signallers, other priority targets for Zaitsev's trainees were food carriers, *Essenträgers*. The Germans stuck with their freshy prepared ration system meaning that each day units would send men back to the *gulaschkanonen* to fetch a hot meal. The *Essenträgers* would carry double-skinned aluminium containers on their backs that would be filled with the fresh food and an infusion of hot water between the two skins to keep it warm. Thus burdened, the *landsers* would head back to their comrades under the snipers' sights; the Soviets were all too keen to deprive the hungry *landsers* of their best meal of the day. Water carriers got the same treatment too, with soldiers going to and from the Volga prioritised as targets until the Germans switched tack and started to pay the city's children to fetch it for them. The half-starved youngsters were willing to make the round trip for a mess tin of food, until the snipers cottoned on and started to shoot them too – mercy was in short supply in Stalingrad.

Back in the Barrikady, the luck of the anonymous Hessian diarist ran out as hidden Soviets suddenly opened up on them and poured fire into the hapless attackers. In the end, an enterprising officer got his men to set up an MG34 machine-gun to spray the roof space with a torrent of bullets. One by one the Soviet defenders were killed and their bodies fell to the factory floor amid its smashed glass and debris.

The fighting went on. The Red October metal works was attacked no fewer than 117 times – twenty-three separate assaults were launched in just one day, only for all to end in bloody failure.[9] Willi Kreiser watched with horrified fascination as one attack was preceded by

… a hurricane of fire, we had never experienced anything like it before. After 30 minutes it all stopped and to our rear infantry jumped up, crossed the embankment and headed for the Volga. We thought that nobody on the other side could possibly have survived that barrage … now we waited to advance. Hardly any of the men who formed the advance platoons were ever seen alive again … the Russians had crept into previously prepared cellar sand bunkers, let our infantry pass overhead and then had come out of their positions to shoot them in the back.

Just to the Red October's north in the ruins of the Barrikady, Willi Hoffmann saw for himself the Soviet tactic of 'hugging the enemy'. 'The Russians are so close to us that our aircraft can't bomb them.' Ordered into the attack regardless, 'Our regiment has failed to break into the factory. We have lost so many men; every time you move you have to jump over bodies. You can scarcely breathe in the daytime, there is nowhere and no-one to remove the bodies, so they are left to rot… There are very few men left in the *kompanien*.' Barcelona-born Paul Wortmann – a former student at a technical college in Germany – wrote to his brother Eberhard about the fighting: 'Thank God you're not expecting Russia to fall by the end of the year. Nothing is worse than false hopes. You can't imagine how strong the Russian is.'[10]

Neither Hoffmann nor Wortmann felt it was worth mentioning in their letters that by order of OKW, from 15 October all Wehrmacht infantry regiments would henceforth be called grenadier regiments, and that they were correspondingly now known as *grenadiere*. What the 20-year-old Wortmann did mention though, was the tremendous fire the Russians were bringing to bear on him and his comrades; 'The Russian often attacks with tens of Stalin Organs. Imagine the barrage: 20, 30 or 40 rockets! This is the weapon of the future! Fortunately for us she needs a lot of ammunition.' Amazingly, in the middle of all the fighting some Red Army men were still deserting to the Germans. 'Yesterday a Russian tank lieutenant built us a latrine! He came over to us with a white rag on his tank gun. He said he didn't get enough to eat and has tremendous respect for the German anti-tankers. He said: "Njemetzki tank karosch"' (German tank good).[11]

The carnage at the Dzerzhinsky was just as bad as in the Barrikady and the Red October. Helmut Walz was in the Swabian *305. Infanterie-Division* as it battled to capture the massive construction sheds: 'We went into the tractor factory … the fighting there had become very bitter and ruthless … the casualties were enormous. Many of my comrades had fallen or were wounded, always in close-quarter fighting.' Moving forward with his comrade, Schappel, a shell blast forced the two of them to take cover, but Schappel was a moment too slow.

> I cleaned him up and searched for his wound. When I opened his jacket and saw the size of it I doubted he would survive. Blood and air bubbles were coming out of a gaping hole. A shell splinter had entered near the backbone, passed through his left shoulder blade and lung and exited from the right side of his upper torso. It looked as though his innards were only being held in place by his uniform.

Walz bandaged his friend as best he could and then went to find a medic, only to find a bunker full of Russians instead. After throwing in a grenade, he watched as a wounded Red Army soldier climbed out, bleeding from his mouth, nose and ears. Unbelievably, the gravely injured Soviet lifted his pistol to try and kill Walz. 'All that mattered now was who was faster... as I tried to draw my pistol, I suddenly saw stars.' The Russian had been quicker. 'The Russian's bullet had smashed my chin, and my upper and lower jaw. He'd shot me in the face. When one of my comrades saw this he went into such a rage that he threw himself at the Soviet, knocked him to the ground and trampled him until he stopped moving.' Even then Walz's ordeal didn't end. While his officer, *Leutnant* Hermann Hennes, applied a dressing to his face, '[Hennes's] helmet flew off; a sniper had shot him in the head... I watched horrified as brain matter flowed out of his shattered skull. It was a clear liquid, no blood.'[12] Little wonder that one *landser* wrote home despairingly: 'I've only got one big wish left and that is that this shit comes to an end...we're all so depressed.'

More *pioniere* were drafted in to bring their specialist close-quarter assault and demolition skills to bear, with *Pionier-Bataillon 179* commanded by *Hauptmann* Helmut Weltz among them:

> Finally you noticed some movement. A soldier jumped over the edge of a gully. A German soldier. He was running back. Of course he could be a runner carrying a message, but no,

he was followed by another soldier, yet another and others too. They were all running back... In two or three minutes we sighted the first few Russian helmets. The Russians assembled and regrouped to pursue the German *pioniere* retreating in disorder. [Weltz's men] opened a hurricane of fire on them as we had done that morning. The Russian advance halted, the line was consolidated and everything returned to its original state.

At a truly horrific blood cost the Germans inched their way towards the sluggish yellow-brown waters of the Volga. An entire German field army was now focused on a few hundred square metres of land. One of Günter Koschorrek's senior NCOs told him, 'This is the craziest place imaginable. The Russians are often only 20 or 30 metres away, sometimes at hand grenade range. No more than 200 metres in front of us there's a deep trench that leads right down to the Volga.'

Under enormous pressure from Hitler, who bombarded him from Vinnytsia with demands for the latest situation reports, Paulus demanded more from his men and called for another all-out effort from the Luftwaffe. In response, Richthofen recalled more units from the Caucasus to reinforce those already hammering Stalingrad. Operating from fields a few short miles from the city, the result was a significant uptick in attacks, building to a crescendo of 2,000 sorties and 600 tons of bombs dropped on one day alone. Paul-Werner Hozzel recalled: 'As if on a string of pearls one aircraft followed another within an interval of a few seconds, dropping their bombs on the target area divided among us. Not a single bomb missed its target. This brought high praise from the infantry.' Günter Koschorrek saw the effect: 'The sky is glowing over Stalingrad... There must be a lot of aircraft up. Bombs are ceaselessly raining down on a city that has been condemned to death ... black smoke and smouldering fires – a terrible sight, and we can feel Stalingrad's hot breath. This must be how Rome looked after Nero put it to the torch.' But this enormous effort could not be sustained. Indeed, with Hitler increasingly worried about the phantom Anglo-American threat in the West, Richthofen was forced to despatch desperately needed fighter and bomber *staffeln* back to the West. By the end of October, he'd had almost 140 bombers and 160 fighters stripped from his roster.

Now, as Hans Doerr, wrote, 'It was the last hundred yards before the Volga which held the decision for both attacker and defender.' There was no subtlety, no cunning plans, just smash, smash and smash again. Rolf Grams of *14. Panzer-Division* recorded his view of the fighting in the factories: 'It was an uncanny, enervating battle above and below ground, in the ruins, the cellars and the sewers – a battle of man against man. Tanks clambering over mountains of debris and scrap, crunching through chaotically destroyed workshops, firing at point-blank range into rubble-filled streets and narrow factory courtyards.'[13]

Then, finally, on the day of the Luftwaffe's maximum bombing effort on 14 October, the Hessians of *389. Infanterie-Division* and Grams's panzers took the last holdouts in the Dzerzhinsky tractor works and reached the Volga. The mammoth tractor-cum-tank factory was in German hands at last.

Without pause, *14. Panzer-Division* was then switched to the remains of the Barrikady, where its few remaining panzers and panzer-grenadiers went into action alongside Willi Hoffmann and his comrades of *94. Infanterie-Division*. In a mad rush, a handful of *landsers* somehow managed to reach the high bluff overlooking the Volga after seizing the factory's administration block. But there were only two dozen of them and one officer, *Leutnant* Joachim Stempel.

Stempel had been sent forward from headquarters that morning; 'Early in the morning I am ordered to brigade command; *Oberst* Freiherr von Falkenstein gives me a new mission, "Take over the remains of the panzer-grenadiers as company commander, all the best, Hals-und-Beinbruch"' [literally 'break your neck and legs', meaning best of luck]. Making his way forward he found his new command and reported for duty, to be 'greeted with joy – at the front there is no officer to lead the regiment, now reduced to *kompanie* strength.'

Leading his men from the front, Stempel's attack was a nightmare:

> Everywhere bullets and shells strike the walls... We're deafened
> by the howling of sirens and explosions. Fountains of mud
> caused by the exploding bombs erupt all around us, forcing
> us to take cover. More howls overhead – our own artillery!
> But also salvoes from the other side! The noise is like that of
> an underground train entering a station ... we continue to
> jump from shell crater to shell crater, from earth pile to the
> remains of a wall. Now quickly to the remains of a house, to
> the next cover.

Dreadful it may have been, but Stempel and his men had taken
the vital high ground. Now they had to prepare for the inevitable
Soviet counterattack.

Taking up defensive positions he and his surviving soldiers tried
to prepare for the next day's action. 'There is no rest, we are all
wide awake ... throughout the entire night the devil is loosed on
us, our food carriers have been taken out by the Russians behind
us.' The next day brought no respite.

> In a bomb crater we collect our wounded and pull the dead
> out of the hail of Russian bullets. We are lying here now, so
> close to our final objective, so close to the Volga, it's only
> 50 metres away but we simply cannot advance any further, it
> is impossible ... the Russians are lying 30 metres away from
> us, and behind them their commanders and commissars, and
> behind them the wide Volga.

He sent back a runner with a simple message, 'I cannot hold
out without reinforcements.' The division managed to scrape
some up from somewhere; 'They are 80 young soldiers from the
Feldersatzbataillon [field replacement battalion] led by a young
officer, *Oberleutnant* Ferch. All of them are just 18 or 19 years
old and haven't fired a shot in anger. Added to that are more
men from the rear area; convalescents and soldiers returned from

leave.' With the sudden influx of new blood, Stempel felt renewed optimism: 'My God, how strong we are again.' Then the Soviets attacked once more.

> They attack, they're jumping from cover to cover ... we suffer frightful losses, especially among the 'new boys'... The Russians break through, we launch an immediate counterattack. *Oberleutnant* Ferch leads it ... he jumps out of the trench next to me and immediately falls back into it. A 20mm shell has shattered his skull ... of the lads who arrived last night many have been killed in their first firefight. They were killed as soon as the first bullets flew.

Stempel's rapidly dwindling command spent the next two days fighting off attack after attack from fresh Soviet units ferried across the Volga during the hours of darkness.

> Across the river in the thick forests of the lower, eastern bank of the river, the enemy lurked invisible, his batteries and his infantry hidden from sight. But he was there, nevertheless, firing, and night after night in hundreds of boats across the river he sent reinforcements into the ruins of the city [coming up from] the deep ravines of weathered sandstone dropping sheer down to the Volga ... the Soviets would throw ever more new forces into the fighting.

Those fresh troops were under orders to attack, attack, and attack again, and under no circumstances to yield an inch of ground. As Chuikov – who else – told them; 'There's no ground left behind the Volga! Fight or die!' The often-terrified Red Army conscripts responded magnificently. 'The Russians are hanging tough and bitterly contest every hole in the earth and every pile of rubble – and snipers hit us in the flank, inflicting bloody losses. They lurk everywhere. They are hiding all around but can't be spotted at all.' Young Joachim wasn't the only Stempel in Stalingrad. 'At my father's division, *371. Infanterie-Division* [Richard Stempel was the divisional commander] the Soviets are attacking day and night ... they are trying with all their strength to penetrate into the southern part of the city, but *371. Infanterie-Division* has repulsed all these attacks. If only I could talk to father once more.'

Casualties among Stempel's ever-shrinking command were 'frightening ... we have lost 17 killed and 33 wounded in the *kompanie*.' It was all too much for the handful of *landsers* still able to fight. With the majority of his new boys dead or wounded, and precious few of his original band still alive, *Leutnant* Joachim Stempel led his tiny group of survivors back into the ruins of the Barrikady. The high bluffs that had exacted such a cruel toll from *94. Infanterie-Division* were given up, and the grateful Russians carefully moved forward to occupy the craters, holes and trenches so bravely held by Stempel's grenadiers. The ruins of the nearby factory were theirs, but the Germans had been denied complete victory. As Willi Hoffmann remarked, 'Our troops have captured the whole of the Barrikady factory, but we can't break through to the Volga... We are absolutely exhausted; our regiment barely has the strength of a *kompanie*. The Russian artillery on the other side of the Volga won't let you lift your head.' In one piece of good news for Paulus, the northern suburb of Spartakovka – so long held by the Soviets – fell at last into German hands.

The baker turned gunner Karl Nünninghoff wrote to his parents on Friday 30 October: 'Stalingrad in and of itself is in German hands, only a factory site and a village on the outskirts of the city are still tenaciously and doggedly defended. The Stalin Organs fire at us all day and also at night, but our own guns also play their songs every day. The struggle for the last corner of houses continues unabated.'[14]

For the first time in weeks, that Friday saw no significant fighting in Stalingrad. While not peaceful by any means, the city seemed to catch its breath as both sides sank back, exhausted. Ninety per cent of the city was now in German hands. Chuikov's men only held the tube mill, the steel foundry and sorting department, and the ruins of the eastern block of the Red October. They were also clinging onto most of the Lazur chemical plant and a tiny bridgehead around the ferry landing stage. As Erhard Raus wrote, 'The Russian defended every inch of his soil with incredible tenacity.'

In Vinnytsia, Hitler was preparing to fly back to Munich to appear at the Bürgerbräukeller on the anniversary of the failed Nazi Beer Hall Putsch. Having received the latest reports from Paulus he wrote in his speech:

> I wanted to reach the Volga, to a definite place, to a definite city. It accidentally bears the name of Stalin himself, but do not think that I went after it on that account. Indeed, it could have had an altogether different name. But only because it is an important point... I wanted to take it. And do you know ... we have it; there are only a couple of very small places left untaken... Now other people say: Why aren't you taking them? Because I don't want a second Verdun and would rather do it with very small shock units. Time plays no part here. No ships come up the Volga anymore – that is the decisive thing.

He went further, declaring that some people say '"It is absolutely a mistake for the Germans to have gone to ... Stalingrad... For Stalingrad is a capital mistake, a strategic mistake." We will just wait and see whether that was a strategic mistake.'

Hitler's trivialization of the situation at Stalingrad was of course ill-judged. Sixth Army had performed well at Izyum but its near 400-mile advance east to Stalingrad had taken its toll on both men and machines. It had lost 20,000 men at Izyum, and more at Kalach-na-Donu, even before it reached the city. Along the way its logistics had been stretched to the utmost, with fuel in particular in short supply. With the demands of *Heeresgruppe A* laying claim to much of what was available, the German supply system had been unable to establish and build up significant depots near Paulus's front, as was common practice. The result was that 6. *Armee* had to live something of a hand to mouth existence with any and all supplies distributed to the troops and used as soon as they arrived. This was especially true of ammunition, the house to house fighting in the city using up truly eye-watering amounts of munitions that had to be replaced by factories all the way back in the Reich and then brought hundreds of miles east on a single-track railway line.

The inadequate levels of vital supplies had been self-evident since the beginning of *Blau*. What was also now coming to fruition was the corresponding lack of major reinforcements. Sixth Army had lost 7,700 killed and over 31,000 officers and men wounded so far in the fighting for the grain elevator, Mamayev Kurgan, the main railway station, Red Square, the Barrikady, the Dzerzhinsky, the Lazur, the Red October, Spartakovka and half a dozen other suburbs and landmarks. Those losses were concentrated – as ever – in the frontline *kompanien*, resulting in a 6. *Armee* ration return in mid-October listing a strength of 334,000 men, of whom only 1 in 5 – some 66,500 – were combat troops. The inexperienced divisions in 6. *Armee*, for whom *Blau* was their first real taste of action, had fared worst in the savage fighting, and Paulus had compounded the seriousness of the army's position by his ill-judged decision to use his precious panzer troops inside the city itself.

Fresh drafts of men were forthcoming from the training depots in the Reich and were – as with Stempel's mini-command – sent to bolster the ranks, but their inexperience cost them dear and they too often disappeared in a welter of blood in a matter of days. What 6. *Armee* needed wasn't a drip-drip of recruits but a steady stream of rested, combat-experienced divisions taking their place in the line as tired and ravaged formations were rotated out to refit. But the *Ostheer* had no strategic reserve; Manstein's 11. *Armee* had been decimated in the Crimea and subsequently disbanded, leaving the barrel scraped clean. Paulus would have to make do with what he had.

The reality then, was a great deal different to Hitler's triumphalist vainglory of the Bürgerbräukeller. For the first time in the Russo-German war, a city had become the focus of a major battle (even the epic struggle of Brest-Litovsk the previous year had only involved the citadel rather than the wider city), and it was proving calamitous for the Germans. Taking Stalingrad had literally burnt out 6. *Armee*, and what had arguably been the Wehrmacht's most powerful field army four months earlier was now a brittle blade riven with cracks. One young frontline officer vividly described what it was like fighting in Stalingrad at the time

> Faces black with sweat, we bombard each other with grenades in the middle of explosions, clouds of dust and smoke, heaps of mortar, floods of blood, fragments of furniture and human beings... Imagine Stalingrad, 80 days and nights of hand-to-hand fighting. The streets are no longer measured in metres, but in corpses. Stalingrad is no longer a city. By day it is an enormous cloud of burning, blinding smoke, a vast furnace lit by the reflection of the flames, and when night falls – one of those very hot, noisy, bloody nights – the dogs plunge into the Volga and desperately try to swim to the other bank – the nights in Stalingrad are a terror for them. Animals flee from this hell, the hardest stone can't bear it for long, only men endure.[15]

Young though he was, his feelings on the nightmare struggle he was involved in were symptomatic of many of his seniors, who found themselves overwhelmed by the nature of the fighting in Stalingrad. Having been trained and brought up in classic military fashion, the German regimental, divisional and corps commanders were practised experts in the type of manoeuvre warfare at which the Wehrmacht excelled. On the open steppe they moved their regiments and *bataillonen* around with masterly control but faced with an unyielding enemy willing to spill oceans of blood to defend a cellar or pile of ruins, they found themselves at a loss. Eccard Freiherr von Gablenz, commander of the Saxons of 384. *Infanterie-Division*, sent a signal to all his officers acknowledging just how bad things were; 'I am well aware of the state of the division, I know it has no strength left ... the fighting is cruel and becomes crueller every day. It is impossible to change the situation.' Gablenz then exhorted his commanders to display more 'active leadership', by which he meant punishment:

> The lethargy of the majority of soldiers must be corrected by more active leadership. Commanders must be more severe... Those who fall asleep at their posts in the frontline must be punished by death... In the same category is disobedience ... expressed in the following ways: lack of care of weapons, body, clothing, horses and mechanised equipment.

It is hard to imagine this signal went down well with his exhausted, lice-ridden soldiers.

Contrary to Gablenz's concerns, the mass of the army's *landsers* were still fighting and fighting hard, as Arthur Krüger, a native of the city of Danzig on the Baltic coast and a member of Otto Kohlermann's *60. Infanterie-Division (mot.)* described: 'We began to go short of rations and ammunition, we were weak and exhausted.' Yet they still managed to repulse Soviet attacks, 'Generally we mowed them down.' The aftermath of such mini-slaughters was disconcerting even for the veteran *landsers*:

> We would hear weakening cries from the wounded. Three defectors came to our positions and I asked them: 'Why don't you help your wounded?' They replied, 'they only treat those who can keep fighting. Those who get back to our lines are helped, those who can't, stay where they lie.'

There was real cause for concern with a key part of the German fighting machine, the Luftwaffe. The Germans were used to having control of the air and in modern military parlance using their aircraft as 'force multipliers', making up for the lack of men and machines on the ground. While this had worked well during the first few months of the campaign in the south, *Luftflotte* 4 had now been stripped of unit after unit as precious aircraft were sent West. That left Richthofen with fewer and fewer planes having to fly more and more sorties, with resultant losses and consequent falls in serviceability meaning the balance of strength in the air was rapidly changing in the VVS's favour. As *Major* Paul-Werner Hozzel succinctly noted of his own Stuka *geschwader*; 'Four months, 120 days, 120 losses.'

The aircraft that were left were even running short of bombs, with ground crew resorting to loading scrap metal, old agricultural equipment and tractor parts into aircraft bomb bays in the hope that they might land on a Red Army soldier and kill him – it was ludicrous. Those same ground crewmen were exhausted. With the flight crew having to carry out six or seven sorties a day, sometimes even more, mechanics, bomb loaders and maintenance gangs were at full stretch, working long into the night on improvised airfields desperately trying to keep their charges air worthy. The special rations which they were meant to get – which unsurprisingly infuriated Paulus's hungry infantrymen – rarely appeared and even their uniforms were 'so worn out that they were frequently obliged to wear items of Russian uniform'.

Richthofen himself remonstrated with Zeitzler, declaring that 'Both the command and troops are so listless ... we shall get nowhere ... either we fight or abandon the attack altogether ... the days are getting shorter and the weather worse.' Privately, he held out little hope: 'The truth is that our own troops are both few in number and listless in spirit, and the high command already has its eyes turned towards Astrakhan.' (Astrakhan was a city on the Caspian Sea coast and the ultimate objective for *Heeresgruppe A*.) Zeitzler agreed with the combative Luftwaffe general but could do nothing in the face of Hitler's obsession with Stalingrad and the failure of the likes of Keitel and Jodl to stand with him.

All German eyes were now on Stalingrad; Hoth, Paulus, even Weichs, all of *Heeresgruppe B*'s senior officers were focused almost exclusively on the city itself and paying little if any heed to what was going on out in the steppes south of the city, or along its dizzyingly long flank along the River Don to the northwest. Those flanks were held by four Axis allied armies, and they were frail. With understandable reservations about their performance, Hitler had initially decreed back in early spring that his allies should be 'corset-boned', with German divisions interspersed within their formations to stiffen them up. The concept – and the lack of trust it implied – united Rome, Bucharest and Budapest in outrage, and Hitler caved. On 15 April, he abandoned his previous order and instead conceded that the Axis allied armies should fight independently under their own national commands. All Hitler now insisted on was that the Romanians and Hungarians were as far apart as possible and so unable to fight each other.

> As the Don front becomes increasingly longer in the course of this operation it will be manned primarily by formations of our allies... These are to be employed in their own sectors as far as possible, with the Hungarians being farthest north, then the Italians, and then, farthest south, the Romanians.

The Second Hungarian Army had reached its allotted segment of the river line back in August and since then had been desperately trying to destroy the dangerous Red Army bridgehead at Uryv-Pokrovka. István Balogh was in the forefront of the first failed assaults: 'Half of us have already died... My friend died in hospital. He was badly wounded, but if he had received better treatment he might have been saved... Our rations consist of looted corn and potatoes.' Three days later his unit was told to ready itself once more. '6 September. We're preparing for a new battle. All of our armoured division and a few German regiments are advancing... We were given the best meal possible – chocolate slabs, preserves, lard, sugar and goulash.'

The new offensive began with massed Hungarian and German artillery fire blanketing the Soviet defences and making Balogh quite optimistic; '9 September. At 5am the advance begins... Hungarian and German tanks are moving forwards and taking death to the Russians... Wounded are continually being carried to the rear. The Russians are holding hard.' For four days the joint Hungarian-German force fought its way towards the river, entering the village of Storozhevoy: 'Many German and Hungarian bodies. The village is smoking. The Russians are resisting strongly... The

Russians have retreated into a wood. The battle isn't over yet...
Our shells bounce off their tanks.' The attackers could go no
further. With losses of 1,200 killed and another 7,000 wounded,
the offensive was called off and much of the hard-won ground
given up. Trudging back, Balogh wrote despairingly in his diary;
'If anybody dies here nobody weeps over him.'

The Hungarian Catholic priest *Oberleutnant* Stephen Ritli was
also in the Don line: 'My regiment was the southernmost regiment
in the Hungarian army at Stalingrad.' He was shocked by the
losses the ill-equipped Magyars were taking; 'Our regiment went
to war with 3,500 men and we would return to Hungary with
only 400 left alive.' One of Ritli's duties was 'to take the ID tags –
the dog tags – from each body, which were supposed to be worn
round the neck but were most often kept in the breast pocket.'

Ritli's neighbours to the southeast were the infantry and cavalry
of the Italian Eighth Army. Their march east had been memorable
in several ways, not least for one of the last – if not *the* last –
full-blown cavalry charge of the war, by riders from the *3a Cavalry
Division Principe Amedeo Duca d'Aosta* (3rd Cavalry Division
Prince Amedeo Duke of Aosta). Much of the division's officer
corps was drawn from the Italian, notably Roman, nobility, who
longed for the thrill of the charge, as one young captain related:

> In the ranks the enthusiasm was unstoppable, especially when
> in the early stages of the gallop we were joined by Major
> Manusardi followed by his orderly... The enemy was drawn
> up in two lines: 'Sabres!... To hand... Charge!' It was the cry
> we had waited so long to hear, the cry that we had dreamed
> of since childhood. Now at last it had come amidst the roar of
> battle, the explosions, and the howling of the machine-guns.

Thrilling as it all seemed for a handful of young Italian noblemen
brought up in palazzos and au fait with thoroughbreds and sports
cars, those same feelings of elation were not echoed among the
ranks of the infantrymen who made up the bulk of the army,
a full six of the ten divisions deployed. For them the lack of

motorised transport meant a gruelling advance on foot over hundreds of miles through the baking summer heat and choking dust of southern Russia. When they finally arrived on the Don, footsore and exhausted, their army commander quickly realised he did not have enough troops to man the one hundred miles of line they had been allocated. In a vaguely understandable but still extraordinarily poor decision, Gariboldi insisted the three divisions of the much-lauded Italian *Alpini Corps*, which were en route to fight in the mountains of the Caucasus with *Heeresgruppe A*, instead be rerouted to him, hundreds of miles north. The decision was greeted with horror within the ranks of the *Alpini*, and for good reason, as Rinaldo Dall'Armi, a battalion commander in the *3a Divisione Alpina Julia* (3rd Alpine Division Julia), outlined:

> We arrived in Russia destined to go to the Caucasus, where our training, armaments, equipment and deployment would be natural, and where we could have competed sportingly with the best German and Romanian mountain troops. Suddenly we were redirected to the Don in flat territory and denied proper weapons – 1891 rifles and four laughable small cannon against 34-ton Russian tanks. There are only a few Alpini – this is not human materiel with which one can play lightly.

Unwilling to deny Gariboldi's request, the Germans acquiesced and the mountain troopers went north, filled with trepidation as to their lack of preparedness to fight a possible static defensive battle they were ill-equipped for. Their position wasn't helped by a supply line that seemed to do little more than furnish the local black market with goods, as one of their officers – *Tenente* (lieutenant) Bruno Zavagli – saw:

> The black market has achieved full legitimacy in Rikovo… behind the lines, there's everything, but everything doesn't go further; the supplies remain here for some time, passing through predatory clutches that choose and plunder, reducing the amount until only the leftovers arrive at the front.

The results were predictable, shortages in just about everything, especially food, but it was the lack of heavy weapons – particularly modern anti-tank guns – that was most concerning. 'As usual, the anti-tank weapons available to us consisted of the 1891 rifle, some hand-grenades, and the agility of our legs. After two days, I got myself a Russian PPSh-41 submachine-gun instead.'[16] Zavagli wasn't alone. As photographs of the time testify, increasing numbers of frontline troops of all nationalities began to arm themselves with proven weapons like the PPSh-41, and German quartermasters even began to issue them out to their units from captured stocks.

The Soviets played on the Italian soldiers' minds too, using the leader of their pre-war Communist Party, Palmiro Togliatti, to broadcast endless radio and loudspeaker transmissions to his fellow-countrymen:

> Every Italian soldier has the right to a pass allowing him to cross the Russian lines and turn himself in as a prisoner. Every soldier in the Red Army and every Soviet citizen is obliged to accompany him to the nearest Red Army command post. The commanders of the USSR guarantee the prisoner's life and will return him to his country at the end of the war. This is a message to all the Italians continuing to fight on the Germans' side – surrender!

The bulk of the Italian soldiery saw through this for the charade it was, but for some of the more gullible it seemed to offer a way out of their misery in the frontline.

Further south, and girdling Paulus's *6. Armee* on either side of Stalingrad itself were the biggest allied Axis contributors to *Blau; Armata a 3-a Română* and *Armata a 4-a Română* – the 3rd and 4th Romanian Armies. The capture of the Black Sea port city of Odessa the previous October had decimated Romania's two largest field armies and necessitated the call-up of waves of poorly trained reservists to try and fill the gaps in the ranks after the 90,000-plus casualties sustained in the battle. Even then, the seventeen Romanian divisions were all under-manned with the *Divizia 1 Infanterie* (1st Infantry Division) worst off at barely a quarter of its established strength. Like the Hungarians and Italians, the Romanians also lacked heavy weapons and anti-tank guns, as the panzer officer Friedrich von Mellenthin knew:

> The Romanian artillery had no modern gun to compare with the German and, unfortunately, the Russian artillery. Their signals equipment was insufficient to achieve the rapid and flexible fire concentrations indispensable in defensive warfare. Their anti-tank equipment was deplorably inadequate, and their tanks were obsolete models bought from France ... my thoughts turned back to North Africa and our Italian formations there. Poorly trained troops of that kind, with old-fashioned weapons, are bound to fail in a crisis.

It was problems with their morale that their German allies noticed even more. A *gefreiter* in the Swabian *305. Infanterie-Division* observed in disgust: 'The Romanian field kitchens always prepared three different meals; one for the officers, one for the NCOs, and one for the men, who only ever got a little to eat.' One of the NCO's young officers thought that 'The [Romanian] officers were no good ... they took no interest in their men.'

Back in Stalingrad the German rank and file had no idea of the situation out on their flanks and were only concerned with what was going on in their immediate surroundings. Rudolf Oehus wrote to his family from his gun battery's position to the west of the city.

> We are now preparing for the winter, but that does not mean we will stay here, we can still be relieved. We build stables for our horses ... they're mainly built into the ground so that the roof still peeps out... We seem to have learned a lot from last winter and are now starting to build shelters in good time so that there aren't as many cases of frostbite. Our situation hasn't changed by and large, we are still in Stalingrad, but it

has become much quieter as the Russians are being pushed more and more out of the city... You can tell that it is slowly coming to an end here.[17]

Willi Hoffmann felt little of Oehus's optimism. 'There are very few men left in the *kompanien* now... The soldiers are calling Stalingrad the mass grave of the Wehrmacht.' But he had a glimmer of hope to fasten on to: 'We have been told we are soon going to be withdrawn to be brought back up to strength.'

The two young soldiers may have believed that relief was coming, or that this winter they would be prepared and would not have to face the nightmare they endured the previous year, but one of their officers wasn't as optimistic: 'The days were shortening again, you could definitely sense it, and in the mornings the air was quite cool. Were we really going to have to fight through another of those dreadful winters?' He felt there was only one option – victory. 'It was worth anything, at any price, if we could get it over before the winter.'

Across all *6. Armee* – out on the steppe and among the ruins of the city – work gangs of *landsers* and *Hiwis* were busy building *halbgruppenunterstände* (half-section shelters) in preparation for the coming snows, and German *feldgendarmerie* (military police nicknamed *kettenhunde*, chain dogs, on account of the metal gorget they wore around their necks) rounded up surviving civilians for compulsory labour. Most were put to work within the city limits but according to Soviet sources some 60,000 of Stalingrad's depleted civilian population were transported to the Reich as forced labour during this period. This number looks conspicuously high, given the parlous state of the German transport network at the time, and as it's an official Soviet figure its veracity must be questioned, but nevertheless thousands did indeed suffer this fate. Very few returned.

The shelters all this labour was building were the last word in luxury, according to one enthusiast: 'They were really incredible given the circumstances; all the trenches connecting one to the other were deep, we had a bunker with a stove on which bread could be toasted, there were pans on the wall, everything was beautifully done.' They weren't just for the Germans either. One *landser* remembered the *Hiwis* 'chopping wood, building earth bunkers, doing laundry and working as vehicle mechanics. They lived in their own bunkers and showed no inclination to rebel.' Hardly surprising if their accommodation was anything like as sumptuous as described.

Back in Berlin, the Reich Press office circulated a briefing to all home media outlets; 'For the time being we are maintaining silence about the theme of "winter."'

In the city itself, Paulus issued a congratulatory communication to his exhausted soldiers: 'The summer and autumn offensive is successfully terminated after taking Stalingrad. The 6. *Armee* has played a significant role and held the Russians in check. The actions of the leadership and the troops during the offensive will enter into history as an especially glorious page.' He himself then mentioned the 'w' word. 'Winter is upon us. The Russians will take advantage of it.' However, he quickly glossed over whatever the Russians might do. 'It is unlikely that the Russians will fight with the same strength as last winter.'

Whether Paulus actually believed this nonsense is difficult to tell, but it seems both he and Nazi high command thought the fighting was just about over. Hitler even went as far as commissioning a special Stalingrad arm shield that would be awarded to all veterans of the battle. The war artist and soldier Ernst Eigener was given the job of designing it and chose to place a picture of the grain elevator at its centre. In the end, the shield was never made, and Eigener himself was killed in action shortly after submitting his idea for approval. His design was turned down anyway, his inclusion of a dead German soldier crowned by barbed wire clearly didn't find favour at headquarters. Written in the margin of the drawing by some unknown staff officer was the comment; 'Too demoralising'.

The belief that was infecting Paulus, Hitler and everyone else at the top, that the battle for Stalingrad was at last finally over, wasn't felt by one unknown *landser* who wrote home in misery from his trench amidst the city's rubble 'Don't worry, don't be upset, because the sooner I am under the ground the less I will suffer.' His anger was palpable.

> We often think that Russia should capitulate, but these uneducated people are too stupid to realise it.

Stalingrad wasn't finished with 6. *Armee* quite yet.

9

URANUS –
THE RED ARMY STRIKES

At a senior officers' conference on Sunday 1 November, Friedrich Paulus primly berated what he saw as a lack of effort by the Luftwaffe in supporting his troops in the city. Wolfram von Richthofen exploded. 'Our aircraft are now dropping their bombs within hand grenade range of the infantry – who are doing nothing ... following an attack by an entire *geschwader* the Army launched its attack with just 37 men, and they promptly stopped again after initial losses!' When Paulus and his chief of staff Arthur Schmidt tried to rebut Richthofen's claims, he accused them of 'trotting out all the same old stupid excuses ... numerical shortfalls, lack of training in this type of combat and shortages of ammunition.' The conference broke up with everyone in a foul mood. The Luftwaffe general returned to his headquarters and – still incensed by Paulus's accusations – contacted Zeitzler, railing to him that 'The commanders and combat troops in Stalingrad are so apathetic that only an injection of new spirit can get us anywhere.' He also said that 'those at the top lack the guts to do it.' Clearly, he had lost confidence in Paulus.

But Zeitzler wasn't listening – and neither was Hitler. Instead, both men were listening to Martin Ranft, a gunner with *220. Artillerie-Regiment* near the tiny train station of El Alamein in North Africa's western desert:

On 23 October at nine in the evening we heard terrible artillery fire from the British line. I was facing the frontline and suddenly the whole sky was red with gunfire. The shells were howling over you and exploding all around you – it was just horrible. We thought the world was coming to an end.[1]

The young aristocrat Tassilo von Bogenhardt was under the same barrage as Ranft: 'I had never experienced anything as intense as this before; until the barrage lifted we could do nothing but crouch in the dugouts and hope for the best.'[2] As Paulus and Richthofen clashed, Hitler was locked in confrontation with Erwin Rommel as his favourite general demanded he be allowed to withdraw his battered forces to escape disaster at the hands of Bernard Montgomery's British Eighth Army. Hitler's reply to the Desert Fox was uncompromising: 'It would not be the first time in history that a strong will has triumphed over the bigger battalions. As for your troops, you can show them no other road than that to victory or death.' Five days later, Anglo-American forces began to land in French North Africa far to the west. *Operation Torch*, as the landings were codenamed, signalled the beginning of the end of the Wehrmacht's presence in Africa.

The day after the first Torch landings, *Hauptmann* Hansgeorg Bätcher led a wave of Heinkel He 111 bombers in an attack on the Red Army's bridgehead on the western bank of the River Don at Serafimovich, some 160 kilometres northwest of Stalingrad. The bridgehead was in the Romanian 3rd Army's sector, but Petre Dumitrescu's men had been unable to destroy it and instead had reported a worrying build-up of fresh Soviet forces being ferried across the river. As the German bombers got near the target area, Hans Hormann, Bätcher's observer, recalled: 'We came under fierce attack from three Russian fighters and were subjected to rifle fire from the ground. We took several hits. Roos [Unteroffizier Fedor Roos] lay in the underside cabin and I went back to check if he was alright… I found him dead.' The raid wasn't a success and more Soviet infantry and tanks crossed the river. Johannes Kaufmann and his fellow pilots saw the Soviet build-up too, and knew exactly what it meant; 'It seemed clear to us that the Russians were planning to take a leaf out of our book by launching a giant pincer movement to the west of Stalingrad to isolate the city and trap 6. *Armee*, but we were ... invariably instructed to attack other targets altogether.'

Leutnant Karl Ostarhild, a young intelligence officer with Edler von Daniels Bavarian *376. Infanterie-Division*, was tasked with briefing Paulus and his chief of staff on the Soviet build-up. 'We have seen a large number of men and a lot of *matériel* concentrated in the region of Kletskaya. Our orders to conduct a reconnaissance of the concentration were fulfilled.' Ostarhild had no doubt about the reason for the Soviet build-up: 'This is an attack army, heavily armed and of considerable size. We have information about the units ... their weapons, where they've come from, up to the names of their commanders. We also know their attack plans.' Paulus thanked the young Ostarhild for his report, asked if his own intelligence staff were privy to the same information, and then dismissed him.

Why Paulus didn't react to this most crucial of briefings is a mystery. Without doubt a sense of disbelief that the Slav *untermenschen* could envisage, let alone mount, any such operation played its part, and Friedrich Paulus now added sticking his head in the proverbial sand to his list of achievements. At the same time, Chuikov was told by his superiors that the ammunition allocation to his army was to be reduced by half with immediate effect. The normally aggressive general accepted the decision without a murmur – he knew that such a move was standard Red Army practice before a counter offensive, as the attacking troops were given priority.

Henry Metelmann was a panzer crewman and anti-tank gunner and was clear on his own unit's role: 'Our division, 22. *Panzer-Division*, was attached to a Romanian army whose task was to protect General Paulus's long northern flank.' Metelmann was a former member of the *Hitler Jugend* and a committed Nazi. 'Russia was simply the enemy and its people were of a lower racial order ... we'd been told that often enough at school, in the *Hitler Jugend*, in newspapers and on the radio.' The 19-year-old had been in Russia since the start of the year, and now he and his crew were based near Millerovo, some 180 miles west of Stalingrad, 'with so little petrol ... we dug holes into the ground and drove our panzers into them and then covered them with straw to protect them from the frost, we even refrained from running the engines.'[3] Totally understandable at the time, the actions of Metelmann and his fellow panzer men would later cruelly rebound on the men of 6. *Armee*.

Hundreds of miles south of Henry Metelmann and his straw-covered panzer, Gustav Böker was writing to his family from his unit in the Caucasus: 'We've now formed a bridgehead over the Terek [river] near Mosdok. Fierce battles are taking place here, just like between the Dnieper and Desna at this time last year. Our *kompanie* alone has already shot up 11 Russian tanks with our 7.5cm guns... From here we have a wonderful view of the snow-covered heights of the Caucasus and we can see Elbrus in clear weather.'

It wasn't all going the Germans way though, as Böker admitted:

Russian bombers visit us day and night... Willi Krüger has been badly wounded by shrapnel ... another friend of mine is wounded, Martin Jaskowski from Odesse, and another comrade from the *kompanie* troop, motorcyclist Erich Schrader from Hillerse, has died. Now all of my comrades from the Peine district have been wounded or fallen. The bottom line is that things are getting worse and worse.[4]

Jagdflieger Edmund Rossmann agreed.

The battle grew harder, both in the air and on the ground. The Russians received new and better aircraft and some of their pilots were quite good. Since there were still relatively few fliers on both sides in the Caucasus by then, we met the same pilots on several occasions. We even learned to recognise some of their faces. I particularly remember the pilot of a La-5 [Lavochkin Soviet fighter]. I learned to recognise his face and we met in combat at least six times within a few weeks. He was too good to get shot down, and always countered my attacks by climbing steeply.

It was getting tougher on the ground too, as the Norwegian Waffen-SS volunteer Ornulf Bjornstadt remembered:

> We set up a bunker in an abandoned house, establishing our mortar positions with infantry support, mine was near a creek – ideal because beyond was flat land leading to the village and it was good for observation. One night there was a Russian scout patrol right in the path of my mortar position. Our men opened up. Next morning I discovered the body of a Russian officer slumped across my bunker. He had been caught in a burst of machine-gun fire. The enemy was very active, striking out from the village again and again, mostly by day. The latest mortar bombs we were issued were very effective against them. They would land on the flat ground and then bounce up into the air before exploding with a deadly cascade of shrapnel splinters.

His fellow *SS-Wiking* volunteer Ivar Corneliussen was positioned nearby.

> I remember the first time I came under artillery fire, they were Katyushas – *Stalinorgeln* we used to call them, and I was very scared. We had to run through the explosions, but I took cover and stayed on the ground, and when I looked up there was this big, black boot next to my head, it was a Dutch *Rottenführer* [corporal], and he was shouting at me; 'What are you doing? Get up and get running!' So, I got up and ran, but I was scared I can tell you. It was a terrible time. We were very far from home and our supply lines were very long, so supplies only got to us very slowly; food, ammunition, fuel and so on. We had a field kitchen that did their best to serve us one meal a day but they didn't always manage to do that, so we had to buy, trade or steal food from the local Russian civilians.

Alarmingly for the SS men and their Army comrades, the temperature in the mountains began to plummet, and Bjornstadt was one who suffered. 'When I settled down for the night in my foxhole it was raining hard. The temperature dropped and the water trapped in the foxhole iced over while I slept. When I awoke it was iron hard and I was literally frozen to one wall. I couldn't move at all and my left side was totally paralysed ... there were doctors around and one managed to get to me after he heard me yelling.' Corneliussen, a Dane from the small village of Davinde, found that:

> Going to the toilet wasn't easy either. If we could we made a trench, either by digging if possible, or if not, we used explosives to blow a hole. If we couldn't do either then we just had to go off with a shovel on our own... We hadn't been issued winter clothing or boots and this proved to be a real problem as many of us got frostbite in our feet or toes because the iron nails in our boots would attract the cold – our boots were 'drawing-in' the cold like magnets so we soon learned either to wrap cloth around our feet to keep them warm, or to find felt boots on dead Russians and take them for ourselves.

Winter had arrived in the southern Soviet Union and it was scant consolation for both men when it was announced their unit was to be upgraded to become one of the newly designated panzer-grenadier divisions.

Hundreds of miles to their north, on the night of Wednesday 18 November, fresh snow began to fall on the already freezing soldiers of the Romanian 3rd Army, and the thermometer showed a temperature of minus twenty degrees Celsius. The German liaison officer with the Romanian IV Corps at the time was *Leutnant* Gerhard Stöck. A physically imposing figure, Stöck had won gold at the 1936 Berlin Olympics in the javelin and bronze in the shot. Now he was listening to an excited Romanian intelligence officer telling him that a major attack was about to begin in the Kletskaya sector. Not given to flights of fancy, Stöck nevertheless gave enough credence to the report to call 6. *Armee* headquarters to pass on the information. The call was logged in the record: 'According to the statement of a Russian officer captured in the area of the 1st Romanian Cavalry Division, the expected attack should start today at 5 o'clock.' The ex-*Afrika Korps* duty officer who took the call, *Hauptmann* Winrich Behr, checked his watch – it was just after five on the Thursday morning, so where was the attack? He decided against waking his boss, Arthur Schmidt, especially given how many times the Romanians had already cried wolf and how prickly Schmidt was about getting his beauty sleep. Outside the headquarters, 'We had our first snowfall, and now a white blanket covers the steppe as far as the eye can see ... even the rumble of battle is barely audible.'

Back on the Don opposite Stöck, the codeword *Syrene* was passed to the 3,500 Soviet artillery pieces on the waiting gun-lines, and minutes later the battery commanders blew their issued trumpets as the signal to their gunners to let rip. Some thirty miles away Henry Metelmann and his comrades were rudely awoken; 'All hell broke loose! The whole bunker trembled, clods of earth fell on us and the noise was deafening.' Scrambling out of his bunk and into his uniform, he felt 'a draught on my backside, I'd put my trousers on the wrong way round.'

Eitel-Heinz Fenske was that rarity, a German in the Austrian 44. *Infanterie-Division*, and that morning he was the duty signaller for his *bataillon*: 'All of a sudden there was an infernal racket to the left of us among the Romanian 3rd Infantry Division. A bombardment by artillery and Stalin Organs – I had never heard the like of it! We watched the inferno from our low hill. We saw the rolls of fire slowly shift from the communications trenches to the command posts.' The bombardment lasted just under an hour, with thousands of shells, rockets and mortar bombs deluging the Romanian front every minute. Stöck called Behr once more, who this time didn't hesitate to wake up Schmidt. Over the phone the Olympian said, 'I have the impression that the Romanians will not be able to resist, but I will keep you informed.'

The moment the bombardment finally lifted, four Red Army rifle divisions leapt into the attack, to be met by determined resistance from the Romanians. Unable to accurately direct fire due to the drifting snow and freezing fog, many of those thousands of shells per minute had blown craters in the steppe but missed the Romanian positions. Now, the stunned but still living Romanian draftees were getting their revenge and pouring rifle and automatic fire into the ranks of charging Red Army soldiers. The Romanians even managed to launch a counterattack, but with just six modern 7.5cm anti-tank guns in each infantry division their lack of heavy weapons soon told when the Soviets gambled and threw in their T-34 tanks, their steel hulls driving straight over the Romanian trenches. The only real hope of stopping the Soviet offensive was air strikes and plenty of them, but as Wolfram von Richthofen bemoaned in his diary; 'Once again the Russians have made masterly use of the bad weather. Rain, snow and freezing fog are making all Luftwaffe operations on the Don impossible.'

Operation Uranus, as the Red Army's offensive was called, was a stunning success. The outnumbered and outgunned Romanians put up a much tougher fight than they are usually given credit for, but their lines were soon broken and the survivors streamed away to the southwest in panic, as Hans-Ulrich Rudel saw as one of the few Luftwaffe pilots to get into the air that day: 'The weather is bad, low lying clouds, a light fall of snow… What troops are those coming towards us – are they Russians? No. Romanians. Some are even throwing away their rifles in order to be able to run faster; a shocking sight.' Worse awaited him as he overflew the Romanian gun lines: 'The guns are abandoned, their ammunition lies beside them.' After attacking the Soviet spearheads, Rudel flew back to base to rearm and refuel. 'On the return flight we again observe the fleeing Romanians, it's a good thing for them I have run out of ammunition to stop this cowardly rout. They have abandoned everything.'[5] Horst Ramstetter also managed to battle the elements and fly over the Romanian positions.

> They were to the north of Stalingrad, two of us flew over the area to find out what was going on as the frontlines were a bit confused. I looked down and saw these greyish brown uniforms; the Romanians! I dived down but they fired at me, and I thought, 'These crazy Romanians, what

are they doing?' but it was the Russians. I flew straight back to Pitomnik [airfield east of Stalingrad] and reported. I showed them where the Russians were but they said that was impossible as that was where the Romanians were. Another flight confirmed it and we began to prepare the airfield for defence. We knew that if the Russians kept advancing like that they'd reach us within a day, we had nothing, no infantry, nothing.

Rudel and Ramstetter were lucky to return safely to base. *Major* Hans-Joachim Gabriel's He 111 medium bomber was lost as it began an attack run against an advancing Soviet column. Hit by ground fire it crashed in flames. There were no survivors.

News of the Soviet offensive spread like wildfire. 'We are now at the highest alert level, the Russians have attacked the left flank of the front with strong tank units and broken through the Romanian lines at Kletskaya, apparently the whole Romanian front has caved in.' Henry Metelmann was wrong; not all the Romanians had caved in. Subsequent to the Stalingrad disaster it suited the Germans to lay the blame for the calamity on their allies and not accept the fault as their own, when in fact a significant portion of the Romanian 3rd Army fought bravely, none more so than the 40,000 surrounded in the town of Raspopinskaya some twelve miles northwest of Kletskaya. Under the command of 52-year-old General Mihail Lascăr, the Romanians held out for four long days and nights, as Walther Wenck acknowledged on arrival in the sector:

> I reported to General Dumitrescu [commander 3rd Army], and through his interpreter, *Leutnant* Iwansen, I was acquainted with the situation. It looked pretty desperate. The following morning I took off in a Fieseler Storch to fly out to the front in the Chir River bend. Of the Romanian formations there was not much left. Somewhere west of Kletskaya, still on the Don, units of Lascăr's brave group were still holding out. The remainder of our allies were in headlong flight.

In Raspopinskaya the Soviets offered the trapped Romanians terms, only for Lascăr to reply; 'We will continue to fight without thought of surrender.' However, with no chance of relief or resupply, and with his men down to just forty rounds of ammunition each, the brave general gave the order to try and break out. One column left that night as it became dark, led by the Moldovans of the 15th Infantry Division, while the second escape column was headed by Lascăr's own 6th Infantry. In the end, only a few hundred managed to make it back to Axis lines. Lascăr himself opted to stay with the wounded and went into captivity.

Henry Shapiro, United Press's Moscow correspondent, was taken to view the aftermath of the battle by his Soviet babysitters and remembered seeing 'no end of corpses, both Germans and Romanians'. Overflying the snow-covered landscape, he saw

> ...thousands of Romanians wandering the steppes, cursing the Germans, desperately looking for Russian feeding-points and anxious to be formally taken as PoWs. Some individual stragglers would throw themselves on the mercy of local peasants, who treated them charitably, if only because they weren't Germans. The Russians thought they were just poor peasants like themselves. Except for small groups of Iron Guard [the 'Iron Guard' was Romania's home-grown fascist militia movement, much like the Italian Blackshirts) men who, here and there, put up a stiff fight, the Romanian soldiers were sick and tired of the war, and the prisoners I saw all said roughly the same thing – that this was Hitler's war and the Romanians had no business being on the Don.

He also noted that '[the steppe] was full of dead horses, while some were only half dead, standing on three legs and shaking their broken one.'

Regardless of the Romanian soldiers' feelings, many of their German comrades viewed such behaviour as straightforward desertion, and on several occasions angry *landsers* took the law into their own hands and shot fleeing Romanians. News of such incidents made it back to Bucharest, prompting an angry response from the Romanian dictator Antonescu, who fired off a letter to German high command threatening retaliation; 'I feel obliged to draw your attention to the fact that unless this attitude and these occurrences cease forthwith, I will have to reconsider the situation of our troops with regard to your Front.'

Another American, the bespectacled Brigadier-General Thomas Hurley, was a liaison officer with the Soviets and wrote a report for President Roosevelt: 'The Romanian troops, judging by the dead we saw on the field and by the appearance of the prisoners, were far below the standard of the Soviet troops. The Romanians were equipped for the most part with second-rate arms and horse-drawn artillery. Throughout the entire salient we were hardly ever out of view of dead horses and dead Romanian soldiers.'

Andreas Engel's experience of the disordered Romanians was nowhere near as bleak as Hurley's. Engel was a former typesetter from the town of Bebra in the hilly country of central Germany and was now a *feldwebel* in Hans-Georg Leyser's 29. *Infanterie-Division (mot.)*. When *Uranus* was launched, Engel's unit was behind the line: 'A surprise operational order interrupted our well-deserved rest. At once the fighting arm set off for an unknown destination, and for the time being the baggage train and services remained behind.' Tasked the following day with taking a lorryload of mortar bombs and machine-gun ammunition forward, Engel and his co-driver *Gefreiter* Michels set off and came under air attack. 'I was hit on the upper left thigh and instinctively I let myself drop free of the vehicle. Michels had also been hit in the heel.' Somehow the attack didn't set off the ammunition in the lorry and it came to a halt about 100 metres away. Lying in the road, Engel saw 'a disorderly mob of soldiers in earth-brown uniforms approaching. Our assumption that they were Russians was happily disproved – they were Romanians, deserting. They applied emergency dressings and drove our vehicle back to us ... at our request they lifted us back into the cab and we set off.'

One young officer in Carl Rodenburg's *76. Infanterie-Division* admitted that 'As the Germans like to do in the face of such setbacks, we heaped all the blame on our allies.' Another German wrote in his diary: 'The Russians broke through the 20th Romanian Division ... unfortunately there are only Romanians and Italians ... the slogan is being loudly repeated and copied from the Italians; "Avanti – retreat!".' Not all Germans thought as the diarist did, and many agreed with the former, understanding exactly what the Romanians had gone through: 'These people lost everything they owned [during *Uranus*] and had no winter clothing, hardly any good footwear, no rear services and they were very hungry. I ordered that the Romanians should receive the same rations as my German soldiers.'

With the front torn asunder, Axis hopes lay with Ferdinand Heim's *XXXXVIII. Panzerkorps*. Consisting of Romania's one and only armoured division and Henry Metelmann's *22. Panzer-Division*, *XXXXVIII. Panzerkorps* had been positioned to counter an operation like *Uranus*, but when Metelmann and his comrades ran to their vehicles, 'We finally took the straw off and catastrophe! However much the drivers pressed the starting buttons not a squeak came from the motors ... mice, ordinary field mice having nested in the straw [had] ripped the insulation off the electric cables.' Unbelievably, Metelmann spoke the truth, dozens of panzers were left immobile with their electric cabling ruined by rodents. Worse was to come when many of those still able to move crashed into ditches and *balkas* from a lack of winter track sleeves – the division's stock had been lost somewhere in transit several months earlier.

The Romanian tankers – almost all in obsolete French and Czech models – fought as hard as their infantry brethren but were overwhelmed, as were the few dozen remaining German panzers. Henry Metelmann's anti-tank gun crew were caught cold by the Soviets. 'Our PaK [anti-tank gun] was rammed into the ground as if a tank had gone right over it. Kitt and Balbo lay behind the gun shield, squashed out of recognition, and further back lay Lazar with his shoulder and half his head torn away.' His final crew mate, Fritz, lay dead some metres away. Metelmann was the only survivor.

Despite the unfolding disaster out in the steppe to the west, 6. *Armee* command was still focusing on the fighting in the city itself, believing the Soviets were only trying to cut the northern rail link to the army and that Heim's panzers would win through. The young Günter Koschorrek was on a resupply mission into the city at the time:

> There can be no talk of an HKL [Hauptkampflinie – main battle line] in Stalingrad as amid all the ruins the front shifts hour by hour ... we drive through shallow craters and over heaps of rubble ... thick acrid smoke chokes our lungs, to the left and right are burnt-out wrecks and abandoned vehicles. [Going forward on foot] a fire flares behind us – a vehicle has been hit, there's another big blaze nearby, probably a petrol dump ... we move in zig zags, clambering over stones and beams, lie flat on the ground, get up again and continue on ... some hand grenades go off, several figures run past us, bent double.

Trying to navigate through the moonscape around them, Koschorrek found an officer and asked him where his unit was. 'We've got to move further over to the right, a couple of hours ago they threw Ivan out of this area and now there's hell to pay as he wants it back.' Koschorrek tried to square the situation he was in with the propaganda churned out every week in the *Wochenshau*, the weekly news broadcast in cinemas and on the radio in the Reich: 'They are forever going on about the "proud, successful German advances" in the army news bulletins, but in Stalingrad I haven't seen anything like that ... we are holed up in ruins like cowering rats, fighting for our lives.' Finally, Koschorrek and his comrades found their own unit and could hand over the meagre supplies they had brought in. The senior NCO they reported to told them, 'The one remaining officer became a casualty this morning, so he was now in charge of the sector.' By now there were just eighteen men left alive in Koschorrek's *Schwadron*.

In an attempt to exert more direct control over the situation, Paulus ordered his headquarters moved from Golubinsky to Nizhne-Chirskaya – still well over fifty miles from Stalingrad itself. By now even Paulus and Schmidt were beginning to understand the gravity of the situation to their north and the day after the move an overwhelmed Paulus realised that Nizhne-Chirskaya was way too far from the action to be of use and ordered another move, this time close by the airfield at Gumrak a few miles east of the city. There – near the railway station – a dozen earth bunkers had been constructed for the purpose, with Paulus himself occupying a dugout some 12-feet square underneath six feet of frozen soil. Heated by a homemade clay stove, with blankets hung across the doorway to keep out the worst of the cold, the commander of 6. *Armee* made himself at home on a small cot with a rough-hewn wooden table upon which to work. The headquarters vehicles were all kept well away lest they mark the position as a target for the VVS or Soviet long-range artillery.

For the Wehrmacht's other Axis allies, the destruction of Dumitrescu's 3rd Army was a shock. The Italian liaison officer, *Capitano* (Captain) Giorgio Geddes of the Army Intelligence Service, saw the effects of the Romanian collapse in his own district behind the old frontlines:

> The roads were obstructed with all sorts of wreckage; the carcasses of dead horses, along with the metal frames of burnt-out tucks and overturned cannon. The corpses of dead soldiers lay in the bloodstained snow, thrashed by the relentless wind. [Coming across wandering bands of survivors he saw] emaciated faces, tattered uniforms, without either officers or discipline, tortured by the ice, hungry and terrified by battles of one against ten.

In one tragic incident, Geddes watched, transfixed, as a Romanian machine-gunner took offence at the attempts of two German gendarmes to order him to a troop collection point, and instead shot them both dead, only to be shot himself seconds later by one of his own comrades.

Military discipline can be a fragile thing and it wasn't just bewildered Romanians who began to take the law into their own hands. Eitel-Heinz Fenske and his unit had been ordered out of their comfortable positions outside the city and told to retreat back to its suburbs. On the way, 'We came to a giant clothing and equipment depot and almost every *landser* disappeared inside to find what he could ... sentries tried to force us back at gunpoint but they were told they would simply be gunned down if they didn't stand aside. The sentries disappeared.' Whilst many of his comrades made straight for the cartons of cigarettes stacked chest high, he did not.

> I filled the legs of my protective winter clothing with tins of Portuguese sardines with a key attached to the underside to open them... Two bottles of cognac went into my haversack, I was thinking if it stays cold a drop of cognac in melted snow might be a real life saver... A can of sardines in oil per day was a diet rich in fat, all the better to resist the cold.

Friday brought more calamity for the Germans and their allies when Andrei Yeremenko's men crashed into the badly understrength Romanian 4th Army south of Stalingrad. Günter Koschorrek and his comrades listened to the news with a growing sense of trepidation: 'Alarm! The Russians have broken through the Romanian lines in the south and are now coming at us from both sides.'

The defenders south of the city had indeed crumbled and the Soviets charged ahead, although it wasn't just the Romanians who ran as Helmut Spieth of 4. *Panzerarmee* made plain: 'The territory was full of fleeing Germans, they were jumping aboard vehicles onto the running boards and radiators – sheer chaos!' The Red Army's objective wasn't hard to fathom. The two giant pincers from north and south were aiming to link up behind the city and trap as many Axis soldiers as possible. When Winrich Behr had taken over his new post in 6. *Armee* headquarters back in October, the man he was replacing briefed him on the scenario of a possible Red Army offensive and pointed to Kalach-na-Donu on the situation map saying, 'They will meet around here.'

Three days after the launch of *Uranus*, on 23 November, the Red Army's 19th Tank Brigade approached the very town and its bridge over the River Don that Behr's predecessor had highlighted. Troops had been streaming west over the bridge for several days already, and the German garrison were used to it by now. Although the term garrison is a loose one, given there were only a handful of *pioniere* from an ad hoc engineer school, some two dozen *Organisation Todt* workers and a single 8.8cm anti-aircraft gun with eight shells to its name under the command of a *Feldwebel* Wiemann. So, when two of their own panzers appeared from the east heading to the bridge, no-one batted an eye. It was only when the panzers opened fire on the Todt workers that the Germans realised their mistake. It was a Soviet trick – the panzers were manned by Russians. 'Suddenly firing began on the Don heights and machine-gun salvoes shattered the silence.' Wiemann and his crew manfully tried to hold them off, firing off four of their rounds and hitting three Soviet tanks before being blown to pieces by T-34 shells. 'After a brief, violent struggle the bridge and bridgehead fell into Russians hands, and now everything German streamed through the town southwards.' The Soviet link-up was complete. Stalingrad was now at the eastern edge of a pocket measuring almost forty miles from west to east and twenty-five from north to south.

All around Kalach-na-Donu were a number of Wehrmacht depots, vehicle laagers, maintenance workshops and rear area service stations, all blissfully unaware of the unfolding disaster. *Feldwebel* Hans Krumfuss had delivered a number of damaged vehicle engines to a nearby railway branch line, where they would be sent west for repair. He and his co-driver were billeted for the night in a local house when they were rudely awakened by mortar and machine-gun fire. 'The Russian women in the house shrieked and cried; "The Russkis are coming!" In the streets was wild confusion.' Running to their lorry, the two men got under way: 'But in what direction? We went southwest to Chir and from there headed east once more towards Stalingrad.' Krumfuss remarked ruefully on that decision: 'Later we discovered that we had taken quite the wrong route: the other truck drivers had headed west and avoided being trapped in the Pocket.' Krumfuss would go into captivity on 31 January and be one of the very few to survive and go home.

As for the news reporter Henry Shapiro, after landing on the former Luftwaffe airfield near Kalach he went to inspect the town and found it was 'a shambles with only one house standing'. The few German prisoners who'd been taken were 'mostly young fellows and very miserable'. He noticed that whereas the Red Army men were well kitted out with winter coats, warm gloves and the ubiquitous Russian felt boots – *valenki* – the Germans by contrast only had their summer tunics and blankets wrapped around their shoulders.

News of the encirclement hit like a thunderbolt. Franz Wertheim couldn't believe his ears; 'Then came the stunning news that the entire 6. *Armee* had been surrounded...'[6] The Soviets were shaken by their own success, and unsure of what they'd actually achieved. Initial reports to the STAVKA estimated that some 90,000 Germans had been trapped, while the Romanians had taken serious losses – but the reality was far worse for the Axis. In truth, the Romanians had been shattered. Their 3rd and 4th Armies had suffered 55,000 and 35,000 casualties respectively; half their operational strengths. Some 39,000 Germans had managed to escape over the bridge at Kalach-na-Donu before it was lost, but stuck inside the Pocket were over 250,000 Germans, 15,000 Romanians, over a thousand Croats, 2,000 guns, a hundred panzers, 10,000 other motor vehicles and thousands of horses – in effect all of 6. *Armee* and a good deal of 4. *Panzerarmee*.[7]

Günter Koschorrek was one of the lucky ones, having found an available bridge, albeit one crammed with hordes of other would-be escapees. 'The vehicles converging on the bridge have built up a huge traffic jam trying to get across, everyone is pushing and we barely creep along … we stay where we are and freeze.' Somehow making it across the following morning, the tumult didn't end. 'Now only three vehicles left, with 14 of our men and three others from different units.' Hastily assembled into an alarm unit by an engineer officer, Koschorrek wasn't optimistic about their chances: 'Most of the demoralised soldiers and NCOs have no combat experience, while those from the Stalingrad area mainly served in supply, maintenance and administrative units.'

As Koschorrek and his fellow panzer-grenadiers tried to form some sort of defensive line amidst the chaos, Henry Metelmann was trying to make sense out of the disaster that had overtaken his gun team. Gathering up all the food he could find, he cooked himself 'a good rich meal of butter, meat and eggs', slept for a few hours and then collected the ID discs and paybooks of his dead comrades. Arming himself as best he could, he 'heard some wailing and following the sound – pistol in hand – came across a number of dead Romanians and Germans in a hollow.' Not all were corpses. 'I saw a Romanian officer with his arm almost torn off, looking at me with pleading eyes, and then I saw some more – including some Germans – who were still alive and all badly hurt… I'd never had any medical training and didn't have either bandages or cotton.' Without hesitating, the 19-year-old 'said nothing to any of them, gave none any comfort, not even a drink, and quickly turned and walked away.'

Metelmann would eventually make it back to his own lines having endured an epic slog across the snow-covered steppe, including a three-day stint hiding in a haystack from nearby Red Army troops.

As the desperately wounded men in the hollow shouted abuse at Metelmann's fast disappearing back, Wehrmacht high command were arguing as to what to do next. There were two choices: Paulus could gather his forces and try to break out west, or he could set up all-round defence – a hedgehog – and await relief. Neither option was particularly attractive. Having used up vast amounts of munitions to take Stalingrad, bullets and shells were now scarce, as was fuel for the panzers, prime movers and trucks. The city's field hospitals contained almost 10,000 wounded men and most would almost certainly have to be left behind during any break-out – and everyone knew what that meant. Much heavy equipment and weaponry would have to be abandoned too, perhaps as much as several thousand vehicles, a thousand or more guns and maybe as many as a hundred panzers.

The sitting tight option was also fraught with risk. The *Ostheer* was under enormous strain along much of its front and would struggle to assemble a relief force capable of reaching Stalingrad. Neither *Heeresgruppen Nord* nor *Mitte* had reserves of any size that could be sent south, Manstein's *11. Armee* had been formally deactivated on 21 November, three days after *Uranus* was launched, while the divisions of *Heeresgruppe A* were hundreds of miles away in the Caucasus.

The same day *11. Armee* was disbanded, Arthur Schmidt telephoned Martin Fiebig, the commander of *Fliegerkorps VIII*, and astonished and horrified him in equal measure by demanding he start supplying *6. Armee* by air. With Paulus listening in on his end, but leaving the talking to his pugnacious subordinate, the Luftwaffe general made his opposition to such a course very plain indeed. 'A whole Army? That's impossible! Our transport planes are heavily committed in North Africa and on other fronts. I advise you not to be so optimistic.' Breaking off the call, Fiebig immediately rang Richthofen, detailing exactly why an airlift was impossible – Richthofen completely agreed and rang Jeschonnek as the Luftwaffe's Chief of Staff. 'You've got to stop it! In the filthy weather we have here there's no hope of supplying an Army of 250,000 men from the air, its stark staring madness!'

The most enduring of all the Stalingrad myths has it that at this point Hermann Goering interceded and sealed the fate of *6. Armee* by insisting an airlift would succeed. The truth is more nuanced. During the early stages of *Uranus* Goering was actually on one of his mammoth plundering raids in Paris, pillaging art with wild abandon from the city's museums and galleries to be shipped to his multiple palatial residences in the Reich. When the scale of what was happening in the East dawned on the corpulent head of Nazi Germany's air force, he reluctantly left the City of Light and headed to Rastenburg in East Prussia where Hitler, having finally abandoned the misery of Vinnytsia for the relative comfort of the *Wolfsschanze,* was once more holding court.

In Stalingrad, meanwhile, all was chaos at army headquarters. Having finally grasped that the Soviet assault wasn't simply aimed at cutting the rail line in the north, Paulus's flaws as a commander were proving fateful. Should 6. *Armee* break out or stay put? Paulus dithered, and while he dithered some of his subordinates' made plans of their own. For several of his corps and divisional officers it was obvious they needed to escape the pocket while it was new and at its weakest. In preparation for just such an operation they ordered their men to abandon their winter bunkers and concentrate for an attack out westward. Some other commanders were not nearly as convinced and their men stayed where they were. Paulus remained silent. When he did gather all his corps commanders together to agree a plan of action, the result was inaction. In effect Paulus – as the diligent staff officer he naturally was – presented Rastenburg with options outlining the pros and cons of each and left the ultimate decision to them. Paulus was now powerless to direct the fate of his own command; it was down to Hitler.

According to Zeitzler's own account, at a meeting with the dictator to discuss what to do, the moustached Chief of the General Staff bluntly told the dictator that Paulus could not be kept supplied by air. Hitler replied: 'The *Reichsmarschall* [Goering] has assured me that it is possible.' When Zeitzler persisted, Goering was called into the conference room in person. 'Can you supply 6. *Armee* by air?' Goering flung up his flabby right arm in a Nazi salute: 'My Führer I assure you that the Luftwaffe can supply 6. *Armee.*'

His voice dripping with scorn, Zeitzler responded: 'The Luftwaffe can do no such thing... Does the *Reichsmarschall* know the tonnage that must be flown in each day?'

With evident discomfort Goering responded, 'No I do not, but the officers on my staff will.' Knowing Zeitzler's background in logistics, the dictator asked him how much the entrapped forces would require. Zeitzler said Paulus would need 300 tons per day, and Goering shot back; 'I can do that!' His face mottled purple with rage, Zeitzler exploded: 'My Führer that is a lie!' Goering gaped in shock at the retort. An embarrassed Hitler quietly told Zeitzler that as Goering was his official deputy and confirmed successor, he had no option but to take him at his word and therefore the airlift would go ahead.

Back at the front Paulus had now decided that perhaps a break-out was the best option and had enlisted Weichs's support by informing him that he only had a small amount of fuel and ammunition and food enough for just six days. Sixth Army couldn't survive on such meagre crumbs, it had to get out of the pocket. Transmitting the request to break-out to the *Wolfsschanze*, the reply came back at 0830hrs on Tuesday 24 November; *6. Armee* was to stay where it was. Paulus was also ordered to move his headquarters into the city itself.[8] Weichs, hitherto pretty much an absentee landlord in *6. Armee*'s struggle for Stalingrad, was now firmly relegated to the margins for the remainder of the struggle.

Willi Hoffmann noted in his diary:

We are encircled. It was announced this morning that the Führer has said, 'The Army can trust me to do everything necessary to ensure supplies and rapidly break the encirclement.'

10

KILL THE HORSES!

The Stalingrad airlift was one of the worst Wehrmacht disasters of the war; it is also a source of immense controversy even today. To be clear, a large-scale airlift operation was nothing new to the Luftwaffe in Russia in the winter of 1942. In January that year, 5,500 German soldiers had been surrounded in the northern Soviet city of Kholm and had to be supplied solely by air. Unable to land in the pocket due to its small size, the Luftwaffe had been forced to fly over the city and air-drop supplies, which then had to be recovered by the defenders. In an epic battle lasting 105 days, Theodor Scherer's garrison held out until relieved in early May. Even more impressive a success was the siege of Demyansk that was occurring at much the same time sixty or so miles to the northeast of Kholm. There, some 100,000 Germans were trapped under constant Soviet attack. In its largest airlift operation to date, the Luftwaffe managed to fly in 300 tons of supplies per day and take out thousands of wounded. It was a huge achievement, but altogether too beguiling, endorsing the argument that said if the Luftwaffe can sustain Demyansk and Kholm, why not Stalingrad?

The answers to that question should have been self-evident to Nazi high command. First and most important was the sheer scale. More than a quarter of a million men in Stalingrad needed infinitely greater tonnage in terms of supplies than the 100,000 at Demyansk and the relative handful at Kholm. Those airlifts also had the advantage of taking place against a backdrop of milder spring weather on the horizon, while Stalingrad's air bridge would have to function in the dead of winter. Added to that was the fact that the German front lines in the north were solid and secure, allowing the Luftwaffe to operate unhindered from bases relatively near to their landing zones – not so in the south where the entire army group was in flux and no frontline existed. With 6. *Armee* trapped, 4. *Panzerarmee* in disarray and the Romanians crushed, the Soviets were able to carry on advancing, liberating previously occupied territory and forcing the Luftwaffe's transport effort to continually move further west away from the city. The mouldy icing on the cake for the Germans was the sorry state of the Luftwaffe's transport arm itself, at exactly the moment 6. *Armee* needed it most.

Never a glory branch of the Luftwaffe, the transport fleet had been ignored and neglected since the very inception of the air force. Its workhorse was the ageing, three-engine Junkers Ju 52, first flown back in 1930 and already obsolete by the advent of war. Painfully slow – its top speed was just half that of the British Hawker Hurricane – it was poorly armed and most importantly had a limited cargo capacity of just two and a half tons and was difficult to load and unload. But needs must and with the focus on new fighters and medium bombers rather than dull transports, the Luftwaffe had begun the war with 552 *Tante Ju*s (Auntie Jus) as they were affectionately nicknamed by the *landsers*. Used in all the Luftwaffe's paratroop operations in 1940, it was the revolutionary airborne invasion of Crete the following year that decimated the fleet; 146 aircraft lost and a further 150 damaged. Demyansk was even worse with 256 aircraft destroyed and 387 experienced aircrew killed. Since German industry only manufactured a total of 2,804 Ju 52s during the war, losses on that scale were simply unsustainable.

As it was, the entire Ju 52 complement in November 1942 was 750 and a third of those were already committed in the Mediterranean to ferry troops and supplies from Sicily to Tunisia to try and combat the *Torch* landings. That left approximately

500 spread out across the Soviet Union and the rest of occupied Europe – the same number the Luftwaffe had dedicated to the Demyansk operation, in the knowledge that serviceability issues would reduce the available number of aircraft to around 150 on any given day. That was the magic number. If the Germans could keep 150 Ju 52s a day flying into Stalingrad, they could deliver the 300 tons Zeitzler had told Hitler the encircled army needed. But of the 500 not involved in the Mediterranean, Richthofen was only given control of the 295 in the Eastern theatre, with many of those grounded for a lack of spare parts and maintenance.

Given the poor logistical position in the south during the summer offensive – and the fact that the nearest major German-occupied railhead to the forward troops was 350 miles away at Stalino – Richthofen's overworked Ju 52 fleet had already flown 27,000 reinforcements forward since *Blau* began, along with thousands of tons of fuel, ammunition and other supplies. Those same aircraft had returned with 52,000 wounded, often swooping down onto the baked earth of the steppe to pick up injured men from right behind the battle line. This rolling airlift had left little time for maintenance and repair, with exhausted ground crews struggling to keep the aircraft flying. So, when Goering declared his Luftwaffe was up to the task, and Jeschonnek stood back sucking his teeth, Richthofen checked his flight rosters on the official opening day of the airlift – Wednesday 25 November 1942 – and noted with despair, 'Of all our Ju 52s, we only have 30 available for that [airlift]... Of yesterday's 47 available Ju 52s, 22 made sorties [into the pocket], of today's 30, nine made sorties. We flew in 75 tons instead of the 300 tons ordered.' The next day was the same, and when bad weather closed in on 27 November only twenty-eight tons of fuel managed to get in.[1] The following three days were better but not by much. Monday 30 November was the best day thus far, with 129 tons flown in, still 171 tons short of a number that was increasingly under scrutiny.[2]

Zeitzler's 300 tons claim to Hitler and Goering had been off the cuff, in reality. Just like the buffoon-like Luftwaffe boss, he didn't know offhand what tonnage Paulus needed. In fact, a figure was never agreed by the commanders involved at any stage of the operation. In a telex at the time, Erich von Manstein – who would play a major role in the Stalingrad battle – stated that in his opinion the minimum required per day was actually nearer 700 tons; 400 tons of fuel and ammunition and another 300 tons of food and other supplies. The noted German historian and Stalingrad expert, Joachim Wieder, pointed out that such a load meant '350 Ju 52 aircraft would have had to land in the pocket each day; one landing and one taking off every four minutes around the clock, during the short winter day and the long winter night!'

As for Paulus and Schmidt, they demanded 750 tons. Their calculation was simple maths; if the 100,000 troops at Demyansk needed 300 tons a day, then their 250,000 men would need 750 tons.[3] Like Manstein's figures, the bulk was to be ammunition and fuel, with the rest as food and the myriad other supplies a functioning army requires. Although as they still had some stores, iron rations and thousands of horses to eat, the priority for them was fuel and ammunition.

That tonnage would need an infrastructure; airfields able to operate day and night with loading/unloading facilities, navigational aids, refuelling points and the all-important fighter protection without which the lumbering transports would be easy pickings for VVS fighters. There were seven airfields within the Pocket's initial perimeter, but only two, Pitomnik and Basargino, with radio beacons to aid navigation, and only Pitomnik had proper lights and flare paths for night flights. The rest – Karpovka, Voroponovo, Bolshaia Rossoshka, Stalingradski and Gumrak – were little more than flattened grass strips on the open steppe. Martin Fiebig, hastily put in charge of the entire operation, selected Tatsinskaya as the hub for the airlift. Located some 160 miles west of Stalingrad, *Tazi* as it was universally known among Luftwaffe flight crews and ground staff, was approximately one hour fifteen minutes flying time from Pitomnik. Organised into *Kampfgruppen zu besonderen Verwendung* (KGzbV – special purpose bomber groups), the slow-flying Ju 52s would be based at Tazi as would much of the fighter cover they needed and usually had, except when flying over German-controlled airspace. That protocol – and the fact that VVS fighters very rarely went hunting behind German lines – meant that only three transports had been shot down on the whole Eastern Front in the month of June.

A number of fighters from *JG 3 Udet* were based at Pitomnik before the city was surrounded, but once encircled the decision was taken to withdraw the bulk of them and instead institute what became famous as the *Platzschutzstaffel Pitomnik* (Airfield Defence *staffel* Pitomnik) whose job was solely to protect the incoming transports. The pilots were all volunteers and were meant to be based there on a rotational basis. The facilities at Pitomnik were far from ideal, so often only two or three Bf 109s were airworthy at any one time, but fliers like Hermann Graf, Kurt Ebener and Georg Schentke toughed it out and did their best to guard the vital air bridge. Never short of opponents, the *jagdflieger* began to rack up some big scores, with Schentke claiming twenty-nine and Ebener thirty-three out of a total kill count of 130 until Pitomnik was lost. Happy hunting it might have been, but Kurt Ebener for one did not remember his time at Pitomnik with much enthusiasm.

> One day – it was the beginning of December – I led four aircraft to Pitomnik for a week's flying. What I found there was bad. My bed was a medical stretcher and we slept and ate in a smoky earth bunker. Thank God I'd taken a sleeping bag with me. I knew of course there'd be no luxuries but I'd never spent the night in such quarters. I managed to get two old blankets from my comrades to avoid freezing. The initial week was then extended until the airfield was abandoned as we were never relieved and had to stay until the bitter end in the Pocket.

Ebener described the pressure he and his fellow handful of pilots were under: 'At Pitomnik there were 12 fighter pilots from different *staffeln* of *JG 3 Udet*, our duties were to protect the ground troops and the few German aircraft from enemy air attack, and to protect the landings and take-offs of the transport aircraft. With only one or two fighters operational at any one time often it wasn't possible to both protect the airfield and the transports unloading supplies and loading wounded.'

However brave those few fighter pilots were, they were significantly outnumbered and could only fly escort to a few of the incoming flights. The majority of Ju 52s flying into and out of the Pocket had to rely on their pilots' flying skills and their solitary top-mounted machine-gun. There were gun mounts in the fuselage for an additional two machine-guns, one on each side, but they took up valuable space and weight and made loading and unloading even more difficult than it already was and so were rarely, if ever, fitted.

Under Fiebig's leadership a modus operandi was soon established at Pitomnik to try and make the airlift process as efficient as possible. Firstly, an approaching Ju 52 would be guided towards the airfield by a radio beacon, making navigation far easier and cancelling out poor weather to a certain degree. Once within visual range the red landing lights in the shape of a cross were switched on and then green Very flares were fired into the sky to bring the lumbering plane down onto the hard-packed snow runway. From then on, everything was done to complete the turnaround as quickly as possible to get the aircraft back into the sky.

Firstly, the pilot was manually directed off the main runway to an unloading area where teams of *Hiwis* and German ground crew would use the aircraft's side doors to take off the cargo; ammunition boxes and fuel drums mostly, a process which required wooden planks wedged on the ground and up to the side door to act as a ramp. At the same time other teams were siphoning off excess fuel, not needed for the return flight, from the wing tanks; from the left tank the fuel was directed to the likes of Kurt Ebener and the fighters of *Platzschutzstaffel Pitomnik*, and from the right it went to a central store for rationing. Wounded would then be brought forward from the airfield hospital and loaded on board. Stretcher cases took priority, but that meant only around a dozen men could be taken out by any one aircraft. Once that was done the aircraft was cleared for take-off, with the aim being not to be on the ground longer than around three hours.'

Pilots would look to join together for safety for the return flight without forming too large a target for the VVS – pods of three were seen as the optimal number – but when weather or time was against them the Ju 52 crews had no choice but to risk it and head off back to Tazi alone. If all went well, they would touch down no longer than six hours after first taking off, theoretically enabling them to complete two sorties per day. Kurt Ebener witnessed the grim reality of what actually happened: 'We had to watch as Ju 52s, Ju 88s and He 111s were shot down as they tried to gather together in the air for the return flights and fell burning to their deaths on the ground with the wounded on board.'

It took time to put the operation in place, even with Fiebig working round the clock, hence the load lifted in during the first week only averaged fifty tons per day, and then sixty tons the second week. By week three the daily average was 100 tons but that was still only a third of what Zeitzler thought was required, and far less than Paulus wanted.[4]

Some of the senior German officers involved began to realise the airlift was an unfolding calamity. Walther von Seydlitz-Kurzbach – the owner of one of the most famous names in Prussian military history and the much-decorated commander of *LI. Armeekorps*, the largest formation in *6. Armee* – submitted a report to Arthur Schmidt on 25 November detailing a daily supply need for his corps alone of 50-100 tons of munitions dependent on the level of fighting, 16.5 tons of food, plus nine tons of fuel as 'current stocks are as good as exhausted.' Seydlitz-Kurzbach acknowledged just how much he was asking:

Where the large numbers of Ju 52s required for the supply of the Army are to come from is a mystery. If they are available at all, the machines must first be flown in from all over Europe and North Africa. Given the vast distances that must be covered, their own fuel requirements would be so enormous that in view of past experiences with the fuel

situation, its satisfaction appears to be highly questionable...
To attach hopes to this [airlift] means grasping at straws.

The Prussian would have been even more doubtful had he heard pilot *Feldwebel* Hans Grünberg, transferred with his transport wing from up north near Lake Ilmen and arriving down south: 'Landing in deep snow [many] aircraft nosed over ... lots of forced landings.'

Unsurprisingly, as Wieder pointed out, 'During the first three weeks of the airlift the daily average flown in was 70 tons; six tons of food (20 grams per man per day) and 64 tons of ammunition and fuel ... 10 per cent of the minimum set out by Manstein.' The precariousness of the situation for Paulus and his army was a direct result of the autumn fighting that had depleted their own stocks to a shocking extent, with the whole 6. *Armee* relying almost on a day-to-day basis on what could be brought up to the city from the depots far to the west, so when the supply line was severed shortages in pretty much every category of need started to be felt within days.

Clearly, a huge increase in lift capacity was urgently required and the call went out to concentrate any and all available aircraft and crews in southern Russia. Tazi was confirmed as the main hub and the Junkers Ju 52 fleet was based there, but with the Cretan losses still not replaced and the Tunis operation ongoing, the only viable option left to Jeschonnek was to strip the flight schools of staff and any student even half-ready to fly. The loss of any of these crews would rob the Luftwaffe's transport arm of not only the next generation of pilots but also the instructors needed to train future cohorts, but this was a crisis. *Oberfeldwebel* Rudolf Hener was one such draftee:

An additional transport *geschwader* of 180 Junkers was set up in great haste to aid in supplying 6. *Armee*. The pilots were all instrument flying instructors. I was commandeered for this unit and for four months I flew at the front under the harshest conditions, laden to the gills with ammunition on the way in and wounded on the way out. When only 40 of the 180 Ju 52s and crews were left the *geschwader* was disbanded.[5]

One pilot vividly remembered the air effort: 'Transferred flight instructors, scarcely fledged trainees and pilots plucked from some operational unit or other ... a colourful mixture tossed to the front, hastily conjured up from somewhere.'

Karl Wilhelm Hoffmann was a 20-year-old part-qualified co-pilot who found himself one of 340 trainees ordered immediately east to the airlift. Originally based at the Breslau-Gandau flight school in Silesia, he was soon flying into the Pocket where he was told on landing it would take enough time to load the wounded onto his aircraft for him to grab a hurried bite to eat. 'The spoons nearly dropped from our hands ... whole parties of walking wounded hobbling to the airfield over the thin covering of snow.' Hoffmann's Ju 52 was 'loaded to the limit with 25 to 30 men because they could all sit up ... we could only take 12 stretcher cases because of the lack of space.' He found the experience heartbreaking, especially when he 'had a few short conversations' with the *landsers* who brought the wounded. 'They looked at me with their honest blue eyes and said, "The Führer will soon have us out of here!"'[6]

With Tatsinskaya already overcrowded, Morozovskaya – Moro as it was inevitably called – was chosen as home base for all the other newly designated transports, chief among which were Heinkel He 111 medium bombers. Crudely converted to carry cargo in their bomb bays, they were a valuable addition to the airlift fleet. 'The bomb bays were crammed with bread and ammunition and the wing tanks were filled with fuel for the vehicles in the Pocket.' The converted bombers were joined by Ju 86s (originally designed as a civilian airliner), Focke-Wulf Fw 200 Condors more used to anti-shipping patrols in the North Atlantic, Heinkel He 177s and even a handful of Ju 290s – Hitler's favourite personal transport plane. No type of this airborne menagerie was a heavy transport aircraft. The four-engine He 177, for one, had been developed as the Luftwaffe's answer to the British Lancaster and

American B-17 strategic bombers but had an unfortunate habit of bursting into flames in flight and incinerating its own crew. The multiple variety of models arriving at Moro inevitably complicated maintenance and repair, with even the usually dependable Heinkel 111s suffering mechanical problems and avoidable accidents, as one pilot remembered all too well. 'Because of the unevenness of the grass runway, and the gross overloading, the undercarriage collapsed shortly before take-off as we taxied along, and the aircraft slid hundreds of metres on its belly. By some miracle it didn't burst into flames.'

In a letter home, Rudolf Oehus explained to his family what life was like inside the Pocket.

> Our Army has been surrounded by the Russians for a good few weeks now, in the first few days it was very mixed up, everyone was preparing for an escape from the kessel [literally kettle], all the secret files and all superfluous stuff was burned. But luckily the Führer didn't order a breakout and instead ordered that the city and all positions had to be defended to the last, and that's worked ... the Russian has suffered terrible losses again... However, we have also suffered a lot of damage and losses as a result... The transport pilots have done great things here again, but they've mainly brought gasoline for our panzers ... not much food and post has come in, but we're quite well, as long as we can still slaughter horses.

He didn't think he and his comrades would have to carry on with their equine slaughter for long. 'In the next few days we'll probably not need to eat horse meat anymore as food and parcels will start arriving regularly.'[6]

Freshly butchered horse meat was how Oehus and his compatriots were surviving in Stalingrad. While countries such as Britain and the United States were developing the concept of easily stored and transported pre-packed rations that were designed to provide the required calories, vitamins and minerals a soldier needed, the Germans were still using a fresh food system that relied overwhelmingly on local procurement and preparation of foodstuffs. That meant supply officers ostensibly purchasing livestock, flour, fruit and vegetables from farmers and then having the men and equipment to kill, prepare and cook it all on the spot. For example, at 6. *Armee*'s main pre-*Uranus* supply base at Bolshe-Nabatov, thirty miles south of Kletskaya, some 800 head of cattle intended for the pot were lowing away as the Soviet tank spearheads roared towards them.

This was the approach that lay behind the famed *Gulaschkanone* and its horse-drawn, wood-burning stoves and massive cooking pots, as well as the bakery and butchery *kompanien* that were essential to all German divisions. The *Gulaschkanone* came in two main sizes, the larger version served anywhere between 125 and 225 men, and the smaller one half that number. Each field kitchen had a minimum of two trained cooks and a number of assistants commonly called *Küchenbullen* (kitchen bulls) by the *landsers*. Those *landsers* would typically eat three meals a day starting with a cold breakfast of bread and jam or marmalade, perhaps with some cheese and ham, all kept in the soldiers *brotbeutel* (bread bag) haversack and carried with him, washed down with a mug of coffee – by this stage of the war usually *ersatz* coffee made from acorns or chicory. Next would be the soldiers' main meal of the day, a *Gulaschkanone*-cooked hot meal comprising fully half his daily rations, with the evening meal of one-third his *Portionsatz* (daily ration), again centrally prepared, leaving the final one-sixth for the following morning's breakfast.

Food was divided into ten separate classes such as meats/soy-bean flour, cheese, fish and eggs, which were all one class, with fats – butter, lard, and so on – being another.[7] But it was bread that was the staple of every German soldier's food intake, and more specifically the standard Army *kommissbrot* loaves baked fresh by the division's own bakery *kompanie* every day and weighing 750 grams each. Every soldier in combat would expect to receive one such loaf every day as part of his allotted ration scale number I – *Verpflegungssatz*. Ration II was smaller and was for occupation and rear area troops, with ration III for garrison troops back in the Reich itself. Ration IV was the smallest and was for nurses and office-based military staff in Germany.

Three days after confirmation that Kalach-na-Donu had fallen and they were now surrounded, 6. *Armee* headquarters ordered a cut in the daily bread ration from 750 to 350 grams, less than half a loaf. With the cattle of Bolshe-Nabatov lost to the Red Army, the daily beef ration of 120 grams of fresh meat was replaced with horse, the Army's draught animals relied on to fill the *Gulaschkanone* cooking pots and the bellies of the *landsers*. The bread and meat were supplemented by thirty grams of assorted fats from the Army's integral stocks, which were designed to last ten days. Typically, three days' rations were stored in the Army dumps and baggage train, one in the divisional supply *Tross* (rearward services including baggage, catering and supply, workshops, armourer, smithy, paymaster, medical services etc) and two in the regimental train, plus one full and one iron ration (*eiserne Portionen*) with the *Gulaschkanone* itself, one iron ration in the *zug* (platoon) wagon and one iron ration on the man himself in his *brotbeutel*.

Those *eiserne Portionen* totalled some 650 grams with almost half the weight being hard biscuits, *Zwieback*, *Hartkeks* or *Knaeckebrot*, 200 grams of tinned meat (*Fleischkonserve*), 150 grams of preserved vegetables, twenty-five grams *Muckefuck* (official government designation of ersatz coffee) and twenty-five grams of salt. Half-iron rations (*halb-eiserne Portionen*) could also be supplied and were actually two-thirds the weight rather than half.[8]

As both iron and half-iron rations could only be eaten with the express permission of the unit commanding officer, the situation in the Pocket was initially one of making do with the existing stocks and butchering the horses for meat at the rate of 300 a day. Precious draught animals hitherto used to pull everything from baggage carts to artillery guns became horse stew, horse rissoles and horsemeat soup. Nothing was wasted, even the leg bones – once cleaned of meat and everything else edible they were stuck in the ground to act as markers for highways and tracks vulnerable to being covered by snow drifts.

Eating the horses enabled the airlift to focus on bringing in ammunition and fuel instead of food, but conversely reduced Paulus's mobility as his horse-drawn vehicles were increasingly left stranded. However, with winter worsening and no forage for them anyway, the horses were probably best slaughtered so that the airlift could concentrate on what the *landsers* needed to fight with; after all, a *kommissbrot* loaf may have only weighed 750 grams but a high-explosive shell for a standard *10.5 cm leichte Feldhaubitze 18* (light field howitzer 18) was 14.81 kilograms, and a single gun might fire dozens of those shells per day. This was crucial for *6. Armee*'s potential survival. Percentages vary – a motorised formation would naturally require more fuel than an infantry one – but on average over 60 per cent of the tonnage needed by a standard German division was composed of artillery shells. Whether in attack or defence, gunfire support was essential. Paulus's embattled *landsers* needed to call on their guns to blunt Red Army attacks and to support them in launching their own counterattacks, and that meant weight of fire.

With ammunition and fuel taking priority on the incoming flights there was precious little room for food. By the beginning of December, with stocks of flour in the Pocket decreasing rapidly, the decision was made by *6. Armee* to reduce the bread ration once more – this time from 350 to 200 grams; 'We are on hunger rations ... soldiers are suffering terribly from hunger, and they are only issuing one loaf of stale bread for five men.' In an attempt to try and make up for that reduction, the meat ration was actually increased from 120 grams to 200 grams, but the supply of horses was not inexhaustible and this was just a temporary solution.[9] Officially, the men were also meant to receive thirty grams of fats, thirty grams of cheese and three cigarettes per day, but these rations rarely appeared in the forward trenches and daily calorie intake fell to half that needed to keep an active male body healthy. What made the situation worse was that the food itself was often cooked a good distance behind the line and then brought forward by the *Essenträger*. If they made it past the snipers and through any shelling it was often cold or much worse: 'Even the relatively short haul from the field kitchen to the line sufficed to turn food into lumps of ice.' The *landsers* tried all they could to heat their meagre rations up; 'Some of us tied tins of food around vehicle exhausts. It was quick, but if they were left in position too long the tins would nearly explode when they were opened, pouring scalding liquid over hands that were freezing.' As vehicles ran out of fuel even this expedient disappeared.

Witnessing all this at first hand was *Major* Coelestin von Zitzewitz, a staff officer from OKH who had been flown into the Pocket on 24 November at Zeitzler's insistence, along with a communications team of one NCO and six men. Their job was simple: report regularly and directly back to Zeitzler personally on the situation in the Pocket. Zitzewitz's reports did not make for easy reading. Most importantly he detailed that despite the airlift giving priority to munitions and gasoline, expenditure was such that ammunition was fast running out, especially for the light and heavy field howitzers, and as only some 10 per cent of the required fuel was arriving 6. *Armee* was increasingly becoming immobile. He also mentioned that to demonstrate leadership to his men, the Luftwaffe's anti-aircraft commander in the Pocket – Wolfgang Pickert – was insisting on eating the same rations as his men; two slices of *kommissbrot* and some thin soup a day. When his reports were questioned for accuracy by some disbelieving readers at headquarters he recounted how one *landser* had fallen asleep and awoke to find rats had gnawed off two of his frostbitten toes without the half-starved soldier even realising.

Those like Goering who refused to hear any news that contravened their own delusional views even said that Zitzewitz's radio had clearly been captured by the Soviets who were feeding these absurd lies back to German high command. But Karl Wolf could attest to the meagre nature of the diet in those dark December days. 'Each man got a slice of bread weighing 50 grams and a quarter spoon sized piece of sausage.' Lack of food wasn't the only enemy in the

Pocket of course. 'One *kompanie* after another was wiped out by the enemy. There was no time to rest.'

One category where the Germans should have been in a good position was that of winter clothing. After the disasters of the previous winter where thousands of men had literally frozen to death in their thin summer uniforms, orders had been placed with suppliers in plenty of time and stocks built up in the logistics bases at Millerovo, Tatsinskaya, Cherkovo and elsewhere. Packed in the warehouses were some two million woollen shirts, 102,000 pairs of felt boots and well over 50,000 *umkehrbare Winteranzüge*, the excellent quilted reversible white and camouflaged or field grey suits of trousers and hooded jackets. One *landser* saw for himself the 'enormous stores of blankets, special winter clothing made of sheepskin, overshoes with thick insulating soles and uppers of matted hair, gloves, hoods of double catskin and portable heaters which operated equally well on gasoline, oil or solidified alcohol', plus 'mountains of rations in specially conditioned boxes and thousands of other necessities'. However, as one soldier bitterly exclaimed, 'We had neither winter clothing nor fur boots. It appeared that all stores of clothing were outside the Pocket.' Some did indeed make it to the front, but most of it was held back with priority given to ammunition and fuel.

The result was that once again the troops had to rely on the vagaries of the *Winterhilfswerk* (Nazi collection system encouraging civilians to donate money and clothing for the troops at the front) stores already in the city's supply dumps before *Uranus*. Hans Michel told his family, 'We're well supplied with winter things; I've got hold of a pair of socks, a fine woollen scarf, a second pullover, fur, warm underwear etc. They are all things from the *Winterhilfswerk*, but you have to laugh when you see one or other of the men wearing a ladies jumper or something similar.' The *kriegsberichter* (war reporter), Heinz Schröter, viewed it all with black humour as troops sported women's shawls, scarves and coats. 'The scenes which took place at the [clothing] depot were amongst the few events at which the Stalingrad soldiers were able to laugh.'

Wonderful though it was to be warm in Stalingrad's bitter cold, it also encouraged vermin, and every *landser* was riddled with lice, which spread diseases like typhus. 'Everyone has his own zoo ... they drive you mad ... the damned lice, they totally eat you up. The body is totally consumed.'[10] Another wrote home that 'there was no point in even thinking of washing. Today I killed my first batch of eight lice.' Veterans told the new boys to bury each item of clothing separately in the earth with just one corner left above ground. The lice – *kleine Partisanen* (little partisans) as they were nicknamed – would all congregate in that corner and could then be burned off.

Regardless of such measures, the lice seemed invincible; 'Totally lousy and filthy we lived like rats in our holes ... our main occupation was cracking open the largest lice. After crushing a hundred of these pests in a sleeve of my jacket I gave up counting.' One junior NCO said that: 'I scratched my legs so much that I couldn't bear to put my boots on ... once I tried to count the number of lice in a sock and gave up at 150. I could even hear them wriggling around I had so many.' Some Soviet behaviour grimly added to the *landsers*' misery: 'One evening when the rations were brought up a couple of Russians got into our trench, ate the contents of a cooking pot, shat in it, and then went back to their lines.' The cumulative effect on the mass of *landsers* can easily be imagined. 'We all had yellow, cheesy faces and were very tired and sluggish.'

Fiebig's strenuous efforts were having an impact though. With Tazi and Moro working flat out the three days of Thursday to Saturday 10-12 December were the best yet for the airlift, with a daily average of 180 tons flown in, up from 100 tons the preceding week. Despite the paucity of fighter cover, the increasingly bad weather and dire serviceability problems, the Luftwaffe and its transport crews were doing herculean work, but they were still 120 tons a day short of the bare minimum. As Joachim Wieder opined: '6. *Armee* was starving, running out of ammunition and becoming increasingly immobile. Its ability to break out was dramatically lessening day by day.' The signals officer Gottfried Greve concurred: 'The Luftwaffe, which we relied upon to keep us supplied, usually brought in less than a tenth of what we needed.'

Greve's *kompanie* was horse-drawn and he was forced to watch with great sadness as

> ...one horse after another found its way into the field kitchen. It was a pitiful sight, watching our loyal four-legged comrades, who had walked across France with us and brought us so many thousand kilometres to the east, grow ever weaker... I had been so proud of not losing a single horse of the 110 we had during the strenuous advance across the steppe.

In the febrile atmosphere of the Pocket, horses took on a currency of their own. 'There existed a black market in horses and kindling; a horse could be bought from mounted units for a wooden beam.' Those that traded their precious mounts for firewood, or anything else they could get, rationalised it away. 'Better to slaughter the poor animals straight away before they died of starvation because there was no food to give them.'

As ever in war, soldiers innovated to survive. Alexander von Hartmann's *71. Infanterie-Division* was holding a sector of the line in the southern half of the city and his Saxons soon realised that behind them was the colossal grain elevator and its still existent bounty. Some enterprising *landsers* headed off and found the silos still had some grain sitting in them. They loaded up and headed back where 'Russian families offered at once to grind it. They had a large but primitive hand mill which needed several men to turn it, which was very strenuous.' Realising their luck, they 'ground day and night. In the evening we infantry relieved the Russian civilians ... the best of it was that we had a master baker in our *kompanie*; we ate the first oven-fresh loaves with pious respect.' The bread tasted somewhat sour due to contamination of the grain 'but better bitter bread than none! We also supplied the local civilians with it.'

Amid the Stalingrad rubble, Eccard Freiherr von Gablenz was no longer exhorting his commanders to impose fresh punishments to combat their men's lethargy, instead he was writing despairingly to his wife back in the Reich: 'I don't know how it is all going to end, and this is very difficult for me because I should be trying to inspire my subordinates with an unshakeable belief in victory.'

It was now abundantly clear to even the greatest optimist in Nazi high command that Paulus and his men weren't going to be able to sit out the winter on the Volga. Their only chance was a relief attempt. All eyes turned to the remainder of *Heeresgruppe Süd* and Erich von Manstein.

11

WINTERGEWITTER – WINTER STORM

'When will Hitler take any decisive steps to free us from encirclement?' Willi Hoffmann's plea was a powerful one. At Demyansk the plan had been simple. Supply the pocket by air until the weather was good enough for a relief attempt to be successfully made. The plan had worked. The major difference at Stalingrad was the timing. Demyansk only became a pocket in February with spring just round the corner, whereas 6. *Armee* had been cut off in mid-November. Walter von Brockdorff-Ahlefeldt's men had had to face six to eight weeks of snow, ice and cold before the thermometer started to rise, but Paulus's troops would have more than twice that time in winter's steely grip – and Stalingrad is cold, even by Russian standards. Despite being hundreds of miles further south, its mean winter temperature is almost two degrees lower than Leningrad's and it stays below freezing during the daytime from mid-November until late March.

Johannes Kaufmann noticed it on his return from supporting the drive into the Caucasus: 'It had suddenly turned very cold and wintry ... the thermometer had plummeted to minus 38 centigrade.' The panzer commander Erhard Raus was clear what this meant for the *Ostheer*: 'Unless forced by circumstances to do so, the Germans did not launch offensives in midwinter.' The Germans were now being forced by circumstances, and so the Wehrmacht was going to try something it had never attempted before – it was going to launch an offensive in winter.

As early as 28 November Paulus received a telegram telling him to 'Hold on – I'm going to hack you out of there – Manstein.' So jubilant was Paulus that he shared it – with Manstein's permission – with his men. One *leutnant* inside the Pocket said, 'That made an impression on us! That's worth more than a trainload of ammunition and a Ju full of food!' This was no empty promise. Manstein was already a legend in the Wehrmacht, famed as the mastermind behind France's defeat, the *Barbarossa* charger, the conqueror of the Crimea and Sevastopol, if he said he was coming then he was coming! He was also Paulus's superior as of the week before the telegram was sent, when Hitler brushed the ineffectual Weichs to one side and created *Heeresgruppe Don* (Army Group Don), based on Manstein's old *11. Armee* headquarters and composed of *6. Armee*, *4. Panzerarmee* and the remnants of Dumitrescu's 3rd Romanian Army. This sounds like an impressive outfit, but the problem was that much of the new army group's strength was inside the Pocket, and precious little outside. In fact, Manstein only really had three formations with any punching power; *17* and *23. Panzer-Divisionen*, and Erhard Raus's *6. Panzer*, rushed back to the front from France where it had been refitting.

Nevertheless, before dawn on Saturday 12 December Manstein launched *Unternehmen Wintergewitter* (Operation Winter Storm). The attack surprised the Soviets, and at first, Hermann Hoth's 230 panzers charged forward, Luftwaffe fighters overhead shooting down some fifty-four VVS aircraft for the loss of just six of their own on the first day. At Tazi, Martin Fiebig excitedly wrote in his dairy: 'The Russians are on the run, just like old times.' Manstein, too, was pleased and instructed Paulus to prepare his troops for a break-out. Knowing *6. Armee*'s best chance was for the encircling Soviets to be hit from both sides simultaneously, Manstein's plan was to get as close as possible to the city and then order Paulus to punch out to meet him – the break-out signal was *Thunderclap*.

Willi Hoffmann was ready: 'Today the officers told us to be prepared for action. General Manstein is approaching Stalingrad from the south with strong forces. This news brought hope to the soldiers' hearts – God, let it be!' Relief couldn't come quickly enough for Franz Kumpf, a signaller in Alexander von Hartmann's *71. Infanterie-Division*. A barber in civilian life, he was called to his regimental headquarters one morning to cut his commander's hair, only to find said officer's batman hoarding a number of delicious looking fruit tarts.

'Where did all these come from? We don't have anything to eat in the line?'

'I brought them from France!'

'Don't lie to me, give me one of those tarts or I'll inform on you.'

To his delight the guilty orderly handed over a single tart. 'I ate a quarter of it in great haste with the aid of my bayonet, the rest I stuffed into my mess-tin for later.'[1] Kumpf cut the officer's hair and took the booty back to his bunker, sharing it with his four closest comrades, and for the first time in weeks the five of them felt almost full.

Back in that same regimental headquarters, the Prussian landowner and devoted husband Manfred Freiherr von Plotho, was writing to his wife: 'We are still locked in, but the situation has completely stabilized, so we can confidently await further developments … it's still difficult to get the mail because it only goes by air.' Keen to reassure her, he tried to paint an optimistic picture: 'Our soldiers have done heroic things again … and leadership and men have passed the test in full - and now we are about to turn the tables on the exhausted and widely bogged-down Russian and tackle him so that we can get some rest for the winter.' He even held out hope to see her sooner rather than later. '*Hauptmann* Mutius is supposed to come, and then my chances of going on leave increase considerably because after some training he can replace me. But first the military situation must be restored.'[2]

Out on the steppe, Hoth and Manstein pushed on. Günter Koschorrek and his comrades prayed for a miracle: 'The rumour is circulating that *Generaloberst* Hoth and his panzers are on the way to break open the pocket round Stalingrad. Is it true or is it, as usual, just gossip? Perhaps it really is the great salvation that all those surrounded are so fervently hoping for.'[3]

For the first time since the Pocket was formed, a cautious sense of optimism started to creep through the cold and hungry *landsers* trapped in the 6. *Armee* perimeter; Manstein was now less than forty miles away and a rumour was doing the rounds saying he had a huge fleet of trucks carrying every manner of food and luxury just waiting to reach the city's defenders. The rumour was partly correct. There was indeed a convoy of 800 cargo-laden trucks at the heart of Manstein's advance, but rather than bread and fripperies they carried 3,000 tons of fuel and ammunition to get Paulus moving and fighting. They would be the ace up the Germans' sleeve. On receiving *Thunderclap*, Paulus would concentrate his remaining panzers and heavy weapons and break out onto the steppe and reach the trucks and their precious supplies. Sixth Army would then be saved, and the Germans could focus on building a solid defensive line having staved off disaster.

On Wednesday 16 December, the *landsers* in Stalingrad woke stiff and cold to find themselves being given their allocated rations as the divisions distributed the 145 tons of supplies that had been flown in the previous day. Another 145 tons would arrive that same day as proof of the Luftwaffe's continuing efforts. Much of the food being handed out was pretty much the last of 6. *Armee*'s own depleted stocks. Individual divisions and regiments still held some reserves centrally, and several thousand horses hadn't been butchered quite yet, but the break-out could not be delayed much longer.

Hans Krumfuss was ordered to report for a briefing from his commander, Alexander von Hartmann, together with all the other drivers in his division. Hartmann was a Prussian from a family with a long tradition of service, his grandfather being *General* Eberhard von Hartmann who served with distinction in the Franco-Prussian War and latterly became the Governor of Ulm. Not a man given to idle chit-chat with his soldiers, he made an impression on Krumfuss by his direct questioning: '[He] walked along our lines asking here and there for the senior man, looking at our decorations, he was very friendly to us.' He then asked what the situation with the vehicles was, and how much fuel was available, as they would be needed shortly for the breakout. 'We were impressed by the urgency of his words. I'd never heard [him] speak like that before ... upon parting he offered each man his hand and looked him in the eyes.'

Far off to the northwest, that Wednesday morning dawned cold with a thick blanket of freezing fog shrouding the land. Snow was falling in gusts and visibility was 100 yards at most. Then 'the sky became red, on fire; following four bursts of Katyusha fire our village was in flames.' In an awesome display of firepower, 20,000 shells a minute began to plaster the frontage of the Italian Eighth Army. Two Soviet armies went into the assault – soon joined by a third – and hit the 3rd *Ravenna* and 5th *Cosseria* Infantry Divisions. The Genovese, Ligurians and Emilio-Romanese didn't run but fought back, pouring a withering fire into the attacking Soviet infantry. What the Italians needed was artillery support but back on the gun lines there were so few shells that permission to fire even a single round was reserved to regimental commander level. Worse still, the Italians were just as poorly furnished with anti-tank guns as their erstwhile Romanian neighbours had been, and with starkly similar outcomes.

A young Italian officer, Egisto Corradi, witnessed a Red Army tank literally run over one of the few anti-tank cannons in the line before heading in his direction. Flinging himself into a ditch he looked up at the underside of the tank as it drove over him. '"This vehicle must be filled..." That's all I read! It was an American Sherman tank, maybe it was out of order, or hit. It stopped about 30 paces beyond. We were on top of it immediately and we beat savagely on the metal with our guns. We yelled – "Come out!" They responded Niet! We were like drunks, full of pride and rage.'

The Germans were also having to fight with one arm tied behind their backs. A German *kampfgruppe* (battle group) commander was determined to destroy a house at the centre of a Soviet troop concentration.

By begging I got approval from regiment to fire six rounds and directed the fire with the infantry cannon commander. The first shot was far too short because the barrel was still cold. The next few landed around the target … unfortunately we are so short of ammunition that you have to ask permission first and only ever fire at a rewarding target … so we had to break off without having hit the house, but we enjoyed it!

Italo Gariboldi, Eighth Army's ageing and ineffectual commander, having blustered angrily at earlier attempts to 'corset bone' his divisions with German units, now desperately called for German reinforcements to come to his aid, but they had none to give as every man, panzer and gun was far to the south with Manstein. The only troops available were his own reserve, the 156th *Vicenza* Infantry Division, so Gariboldi radioed their commander Etelvoldo Pascolini and ordered him forward. It was hopeless. The *Vicenza* only had two under-strength regiments, rather than the usual three and both were filled with middle-aged reservists trained and equipped for rear-area security duties and not frontline combat. Without a single truck to their name, Pascolini's men trudged forward across the snowy steppe with no real prospect of arriving at the front in time to help their battling comrades.

Just as with the Romanians during *Operation Uranus*, the standard story trotted out by the Germans ever since is that the Italians ran away from the very first moment they were attacked, an accusation not borne out by the facts. Even as the conscripts of the *Ravenna* and *Cosseria* were fighting for their lives on 18 December, a German staff officer at OKW dismissed the Italian Foreign Minister Count Galeazzo Ciano's question on Italian losses with the words, 'None at all. They never stopped running.'

In truth, it wasn't until the morning of 19 December – the third day since *Operation Little Saturn*, as the offensive was called, had begun – that the Soviets broke through, as huge losses among the *Ravenna* and *Cosseria* took their inevitable toll. With the front comprehensively breached and nothing to plug the gap, the Soviets ran riot and tore Eighth Army to shreds. Exhausted Italians were soon shuffling westwards through the snow, hungry and desperate to reach safety. Second-Lieutenant Veniero Marsan of the *Cuneense Alpin*, the 4th Alpine Division, described the toll it took on his orderly, Ottavio:

> At a certain point Ottavio simply stopped walking; he sat down in the snow and wouldn't move. I told him to get up, and I told him that if he stayed where he was he would die. There was no response. I slapped his face, I yelled at him, I told him to get up, to get moving, to save himself. There was no response, he was immobile, like a statue … we took him to an *isba* [Russian peasant hut] where there were at least 20 other soldiers lying on the floor, also suffering from various degrees of exposure. We knew the men were beyond suffering and would die very quickly in that state.

When Berlin finally woke up to the unfolding disaster, it despatched the few troops it could spare from *Heeresgruppe Mitte* to try and stem the rout. Hans Roth of 299. *ID* had fought throughout the entire Russian campaign, taking part in Kiev's capture the previous autumn as part of 6. *Armee* before his division was reassigned to *Mitte*. Now it was sent south once more. Arriving at the front he was in no mood to judge his allies favourably: 'It becomes clear to me, these guys are taking off, they're running away … their faces are yellow and it probably doesn't look much better in their pants.' But even Roth could see that this behaviour wasn't universal among the Italians, with some 'feverishly trying to establish positions where they can regroup those who are fleeing'.

Italian losses were catastrophic. Ugo Reitani, an artillery captain, had started *Blau* with 230 men, 160 mules, and enough guns and equipment to fill an entire train on the way to Russia, and now he found himself in charge of 'fourteen men, 13 mules, a few empty rifles, a few handguns and the rage we have…' It was the same story across the entire Eighth Army. The *Tridentina* division for example – previously almost 17,000-strong – was reduced to less than four and a half thousand freezing and half-starved souls. Its commanding officer, Luigi Reverberi, recorded: 'My officers and Alpini have been heroic, but so many are missing. Mine, in comparison to those of the other divisions who are prisoners for the most part, are dead or wounded. In just one day at Nikolayevka I lost 40 officers.' Some Italians would continue retreating well into February, with one of their number; Nuto Revelli, describing how they were 'falling apart, sick, more or less frostbitten, with non-stop diarrhoea ... now we are just a mass of disarmed men ... we aren't good for anything.'

With a huge hole torn in the Axis front to the north, Manstein knew the window to reach 6. *Armee* and save it was closing rapidly. Only some thirty-five miles from the Pocket on 18 December, Manstein asked Hitler to order Paulus to launch the break-out attempt. No response was forthcoming from Rastenburg. For the next three days, as *Heeresgruppe Don* stubbornly fought to maintain its position, Manstein repeated his request, and Paulus waited for *Thunderclap*. What was going on?

The answer was in the stenographer's notes of Hitler's daily military conference held back on 12 December as *Wintergewitter* got underway. Responding to a question from Zeitzler confirming Manstein's aim of breaking Paulus's army out of their position on the Volga, the dictator replied that 'Under no circumstances can we give up [Stalingrad]. We would never win it back again ... if we abandon it, we would sacrifice the entire meaning of this campaign.'

Hitler would not countenance a withdrawal. As far as he was concerned Manstein was to reach Paulus and support him in holding the city until a renewed offensive in the spring could restore the entire southern front. Needless to say, this would have been news to Paulus, let alone Manstein. Not that Paulus felt any great urgency to act decisively. By now he was a busted flush. Never a general who felt at home visiting his men or showing his face to inspire confidence or raise morale, he was increasingly passive, allowing Schmidt to take on more and more day-to-day command responsibility and focusing instead on minutiae and irrelevant courtesies. 'My dear *Generalfeldmarschall*, may I first of all apologise for the quality of this paper and the fact that this letter is handwritten...' This is from a missive he sent Manstein at the height of the crisis.

What then of oil? What then of *Blau*'s stated aim of seizing the oilfields of the Caucasus without which the German war machine would grind to an ignominious halt? As late as 28 November, just a fortnight before his astonishing *volte face* to Zeitzler, Hitler had spoken by telephone to Manstein as the general prepared his plan for *Wintergewitter*. When Hitler refused Manstein's request to place *Heeresgruppe A* under his command, the exasperated general had demanded, 'Mein Führer, please tell me what *Heeresgruppe A* is supposed to be doing in the Caucasus.' Hitler testily replied: 'It's a question of the possession of Baku, *Feldmarschall*. Unless we get the Baku oil, the war is lost... If I can no longer get you the oil for your operations, *Feldmarschall*, you will be unable to do anything!' Now that all-pervading rationale was put aside. The original goal of the entire offensive was simply discarded, whatever was happening in the Caucasus was of secondary importance. Stalingrad – and only Stalingrad – now mattered.

Willi Hoffmann asked a question in his diary; 'We are waiting for the order, but for some reason or other it has been a long time coming. Can it be that it isn't true about Manstein? This is worse than any torture.' Unbeknown to the frustrated *landser*, the hopes of every man in 6. *Armee* were about to be dashed by the character of their commanding general.

The Luftwaffe had continued to strain every sinew and in the four-day period up to 23 December, and with Manstein repeatedly requesting *Thunderclap*, Fiebig's airlift carried in 1,077 tons of supplies at an average of almost 270 tons a day – the best performance yet, especially considering fog on the last two days had reduced flights. However, it was still less than the magic number of 300 tons minimum and it wasn't enough for Paulus. Informing Hitler and Zeitzler that he only had enough fuel for a break-out of fifteen to twenty miles maximum, he laid the blame squarely at the feet of the Luftwaffe, saying that without an additional 1,000 tons of fuel he had no option but to stay where he was. He even complained to a Luftwaffe pilot that his men hadn't eaten for four days and that they had been seen 'falling upon the carcass of a horse, smashing its head open and eating its brains raw'.[4] It was unlikely, however, that Paulus had seen this personally, as he increasingly confined himself to his headquarters. Indeed, he and the over-bearing Arthur Schmidt saw no issue in loudly decrying the state of the airlift while not once venturing to see the reality at Pitomnik for themselves; that was the Luftwaffe's responsibility and not theirs as far as they were concerned.

Wolfram von Richthofen was crystal clear in his diary what his view on the situation was: 'I no longer telephone Jeschonnek since all my recommendations are rejected... I now send only teletype messages... I ask for orders because recently I have received only criticism rather than directives. Probably they just don't know what to do.'

In this toxic atmosphere Manstein made one last plea to Hitler on Wednesday 23 December to order *Thunderclap*. His response was emphatic. 'I fail to see what you're driving at! Paulus has only enough gasoline for 15 to 20 miles at most. He says himself that he can't break out at present.' Manstein had to concede that his forces were still thirty-five miles from the Pocket and unable to advance any further. Without Hitler's consent, Manstein was unwilling to sanction *Thunderclap* himself. Amidst the loftiest echelons of Nazi Germany's high command everybody was looking to avoid taking the tough decision and instead point the finger at someone else. As for Hitler, he didn't want to relinquish Stalingrad and be forced to admit his entire strategy was a failure, and as long as his senior generals refused to join together and present a united front, he continued to play the political game he had perfected over the last twenty years and divide and rule. Manstein – so often lauded since the war as the Wehrmacht's greatest strategist and a vocal critic of Hitler – meekly accepted Hitler's objection without ever really testing it and allowed Paulus's unfounded assertions to define the argument.

One officer who did at least try to change Hitler's mind was the one-armed panzer general Hans-Valentin Hube. Ostensibly flown out of the Pocket to receive the Swords to his Knight's Cross with Oak Leaves from Hitler in person, he was determined to press Hitler to allow 6. *Armee* to try and break out. One *landser* who saw him leave was furious. 'A high-ranking officer got into a Ju 52 with two trunks, and the aircraft then took off with him alone!' Now Hube was in front of his Führer and making his case. 'The daily bread ration is 200 grams for combat troops and 100 grams for rear area personnel. The ammunition situation is catastrophic. Our artillery no longer fires on enemy positions, but fires only to stave off enemy attacks.' Hitler listened impassively and then refused, promising instead to launch another relief attempt if necessary. According to Adolf Voss – a friend of Hube's – *Reichsminister* Martin Bormann then 'came up behind him [Hube] and said he should visit again. Hube replied that he had said everything there was to say.'

That left Paulus himself. Sixth Army was his command after all, and he could have given the order to break out and accepted the consequences afterwards. Back on 27 November at the senior command conference Paulus had convened to agree on what to do about the encirclement, Seydlitz-Kurzbach, himself a veteran of Demyansk earlier in the year, urged him to 'take the case of the Lion', a reference to *General* Karl von Litzmann's famous break-out at Brzeziny in 1914. Hans-Valentin Hube firmly declared that 'A breakout is our only chance!' The pugnacious Karl Strecker was just as clear. 'We can't just remain here and die!' Erwin Jaenecke and Walter Heitz heartily concurred, and Jaenecke went so far as to claim that 'We shall go through the Russians like a hot knife through butter.' He also invoked the memory of Paulus's mentor; 'Reichenau would have brushed aside all doubts.' Paulus quietly replied; 'I am no Reichenau.'

Indeed, he wasn't. His monocled predecessor had already proven at Rostov his willingness to disregard Hitler's no withdrawal orders if he considered them ill-judged, but Paulus was not made of the same stuff. Now, almost exactly one month later, Paulus had still not found his steel. Instead of making the toughest of decisions he listened to the doubters, some of whom were in the Pocket, men like Gert Pfeiffer:

I knew that all the wounded could no longer be flown out. Break out and leave the remainder of the wounded where they lay? German officers and doctors would never have been trusted again! The majority of our soldiers would never have been able to cross the Pocket on foot carrying arms and ammunition, fight through the encircling troops and then win territory ... the greater part of the men were already too weak and wheeled vehicles weren't available.

Citing lack of fuel and an unwillingness to abandon the wounded to the tender mercies of the Soviets, Paulus primly sat on his hands and metaphorically signed the death warrant for his entire army – without having the nerve to pick up the pen himself.

The next day – with Soviet pressure proving relentless – Manstein had no option but to withdraw. *Wintergewitter* had failed. A *landser* in *71. Infanterie-Division* wrote: 'The Army bulletin reported that Manstein's army had itself been surrounded and had had to fight its way out to the south with heavy losses ... that was the end for us, *6. Armee* was being sacrificed!' Willi Hoffmann was in despair. 'The Russian radio has announced the defeat of Manstein. Ahead of us is death or captivity.' Another *landser* wrote that; '*Wintergewitter*, the break-out from the Pocket, had been abandoned... For the first time in the war I broke down and cried.'

The young Saxon spoke truer than he knew.

Proving the saying that when troubles come, they come not single spies but in battalions, the day before Manstein called off *Wintergewitter* the Red Army's still-advancing spearhead was but a few miles from Fiebig's main airlift hub at Tatsinskaya. Despite their being precious little in the way of troops to defend it, Goering stubbornly refused to let it be evacuated in good time. The inevitable result was the sound and fury of Soviet tank shells exploding on the airfield's northern perimeter at 0520hrs on Christmas Eve morning. In scenes of near total panic, aircrews scrambled to take off as shell and shot whistled around them. In the chaos two Junkers collided in mid-air as they desperately tried to gain height, others crashed into each other before getting airborne and still more were hit and set on fire as they taxied to the runway. Incredibly, some 108 Ju 52s and sixteen Ju 86s managed to escape. One Ju 52 landed at Novocherkassk, almost eighty miles away, piloted by an Army signals officer, *Hauptmann* Lorenz, who had neither a pilot's licence nor any flight training. He would receive an honorary pilots badge that very night from Wolfram von Richthofen himself.

Lorenz's amazing feat couldn't mask the scale of the disaster. Twenty-four Ju 86's and twenty-two Ju 52s were destroyed, along with another twenty awaiting repairs that had to be abandoned.[5] A full quarter of Fiebig's primary transport fleet were gone, along with masses of spare parts, repair workshops and maintenance facilities. Hundreds of tons of stockpiled ammunition, fuel and food destined for 6. *Armee* fell into Soviet hands, and perhaps most important of all, Fiebig was forced to set up his operation once more from scratch, this time another hundred miles further west, increasing flying time and using more fuel. No wonder that night he wrote, 'I was at the end of my strength, so I went to bed early, even missing the Christmas visit of the *Generaloberst* [Richthofen].'

Tazi was gone. It would be briefly recaptured on 28 December, and then finally abandoned for good three days later. Moro was in trouble too, with Soviet tanks threatening to overrun it, and the main Italian Eighth Army supply base at Millerovo was overrun as well. Johannes Kaufmann was flying from a nearby airfield; 'Quite suddenly, a whole mass of armoured vehicles appeared out of the gloom below us and we immediately came under heavy fire ... the nearby township of Millerovo was ablaze, we were surrounded by the enemy ... and in a token display of military preparedness we were ordered to occupy the slit trenches dug along the eastern edge of the airfield.'

Christmas Eve – traditionally the most joyous festival of the year in Germany. Paul Wortmann and his comrades were determined to make it so in Stalingrad, as he told his family: 'The three of us celebrated, even if we didn't have a fir tree, but celebrated a nice, contemplative and yet merry Christmas. Our plates were full, fuller than our stomach now, which is overflowing with sweets, biscuits, crispbread, mixed with a stiff grog and coffee beans.'[6] Wortmann's Christmas feast sounds more like a wish list than a reality. Hans Krumfuss's bore more relation to the norm in the Pocket: 'Soldiers from a horse-drawn unit came to ask if they could slaughter two small horses in our kitchen. They'd become separated from their unit and had no kitchen facilities of their own. Our Spiess [senior company NCO] allowed it and we were rewarded with a tongue and a liver. It wasn't much but we enjoyed it nevertheless.' Karl Wagner was a former salesman and wrote to his wife back in Berlin with a description of that Christmas Eve:

Christmas Eve is here and my thoughts linger even more than usual on my loved ones. I see your lovely tree in front of me, our little one looking at the strange lights with big, amazed eyes, Karlheinz probably has a really nice load of presents and is probably very happy, even if his dad couldn't do anything this time... My wish tonight is that you spend the holidays healthy and undisturbed and that I may be able to celebrate this festival again with my loved ones. I know that your thoughts will stay with me, especially this evening, and so we are at least a little together in spirit... We are still in a somewhat difficult situation ... still in the endless barren Russian steppe, which is now covered by a blanket of snow and an icy wind is blowing. There are 14 of us in a hole in the ground ... somewhat protected from the cold and wind. The sky is overcast today, there will be more snow, not even the stars show us the direction home ... we haven't received any gifts, not even a tree... The supply problems are huge for us with ammunition, and most importantly food, being in desperately short supply.[7]

Otto Gemünden was that rare creature in the Wehrmacht, a humble NCO with the Knight's Cross of the Iron Cross dangling around his neck. Awarded the coveted medal in October for single-handedly smashing a Soviet tank attack on the northern boundary of the Pocket, he had been flown out for treatment to the wounds he'd received and then returned to duty and flown back into the Pocket on 6 December. A *Wachtmeister* in Wolfgang Pickert's 9th Flak Division, Gemünden saw for himself the conditions in the line. 'The provisions were getting ever less and everybody had lice.' Christmas Eve brought little comfort: 'The usual sparse rations had a few sweets and six to eight small Christmas trees, made of green paper and expertly folded.' At least the night itself was undisturbed by Red Army fire and the men 'sang *Silent Night, Holy Night* with much fervour.'[8]

Incredibly, some *landsers* still believed the diet of propaganda they were being fed. One, a *Feldwebel* Kotenbar, was confident: 'The Führer said, "We shall take Stalingrad" and you can depend on it, we shall take Stalingrad.'[9] Dietrich Goldbeck, a qualified engineer in *60. Infanterie-Division (mot.)*, recalled his commanding officer – *Major* Reimann – touring the positions on Christmas Eve 'to distribute cigarettes, chocolate and some brandy. [The mood was] 'carefree, merry and full of hope ... nobody conceived of an unhappy end to the encirclement.' The Austrian *landser*, Karl Wolf, wasn't so upbeat: 'They [the Soviets] played us *Stille Nacht* [Silent Night] and *O Tannenbaum* [O Christmas Tree] and other carols and hymns from the Heimat [homeland] over the loudspeakers. There couldn't have been a single soldier who didn't dearly wish he was back home with his loved ones.' There was some good fortune though. 'That night there was no fighting.' A supply officer, having attended a makeshift church service, was walking back to his bunker past mounds of unburied corpses: 'During the past weeks all of us have begun to think about the end of everything...'

With Tazi lost, not a single aircraft landed at Pitomnik on Christmas Eve, and not a single shell, bullet, barrel of fuel or morsel of food was unloaded. Since the encirclement had become a reality on 23 November, 6. *Armee* had suffered 28,000 casualties in a single month – it was being ground into dust. Arthur Schmidt, still resolutely clinging to the illusion of some sort of miracle appearing from the steppe, wrote in the Army's war diary; 'Food and fuel are nearing their end ... the strength of the men is rapidly decreasing.' Ration rolls now indicated there were only 40,000 frontline combat infantrymen in the Pocket, along with 13,000 beleaguered Romanians and 19,000 *Hiwis*.[10] Helmuth Groscurth, a staff officer in 6. *Armee* and early member of the anti-Nazi resistance, wrote of the latter that 'It's an odd state of affairs that the "beasts" we've been fighting against are now living with us in the closest harmony.' Hans Krumfuss noted how after a Red Army advance 'his' *Hiwis* could have returned to their former comrades but showed exactly the opposite inclination: 'I tried to make [them] understand that they were free now [their] own people had arrived. To my surprise this did not go down at all well and they pressed me to take them with me. When I assented and they got into the lorry, at a stroke another ten were suddenly there.' One officer on the Pocket's northern perimeter noted that 'the estimated fighting strength of my division was only some 5,000 men, of whom a thousand were *Hiwis*.'

The relationship between the *Hiwis* and the Germans was complicated. On a personal level, many *landsers* viewed the former Red Army men as brothers-in-arms and true comrades and would happily share what little they had with them, while at the same time considering them as eminently expendable. In this the defenders of Stalingrad were no different from their erstwhile brethren throughout the *Ostheer*. Erich von Lossow – a signals officer in Richard Stempel's 371. *Infanterie-Division* – typified this moral ambivalence when he wrote in his diary about the decision to withdraw back into the Pocket after *Uranus* closed the trap around 6. *Armee*:

> Distribute stores of oats, slaughter all horses not capable of single horse harnessing and give them to the Hiwis to eat ... if any of them takes advantage of the situation or mutinies then shoot them dead. [And a day later] The Hiwis are now only given a quarter of the midday ration, no bread, coffee only once – since then most of them are only working at half speed.

In many ways, perhaps the best way to describe the German view of the *Hiwis* was as a relationship between a master and a favoured pet. What cannot be denied is that the Pocket – and indeed the Eastern Front as a whole – could never have held for so long without them.

Now, with Christmas upon them, Manfred von Plotho's thoughts were with his wife:

Christmas Eve, of course my thoughts are often turned to you... I couldn't make up my mind to write one of those deliberate farewell letters ... you have so many long letters from me and you know me so well I don't have to write a 'tragic' farewell letter... I know you'll bring up the boys sensibly for me, I don't have to worry about that... Perhaps I'll write you a few more thoughts on bringing up the boys after all... Tutzi, there will be a lot to talk about next time we see each other.[11]

For Karl Nünninghof, Christmas Eve brought a glimmer of joy as the former baker and his comrades received a welcome surprise: 'All sutler stocks that were still available were given out, we got 40 cigarettes, three bars of chocolate and some schnapps.' The respite didn't last long though, as he told his parents; 'The front was relatively calm, but that was the calm before the storm. On the morning of the 25th the Russians attacked and broke through in company strength, then we were immediately alerted, so you can imagine that one loses all Christmas thoughts. By noon the front was pretty much settled again. Well now you know what kind of Christmas we are having out here.'[12]

The Saxon gunner, Rudolf Oehus, was in much the same mood as Nünninghof, but he struggled to maintain it:

Everyone got half a bottle of sparkling wine, 350 grams of chocolate, a sausage and something to smoke... I sit here with five other comrades in our quarters and look into the desolate winter landscape of Russia ... this is now the second Christmas that we've spent apart from each other, who would've thought that two years ago? But what is there to do ... it is really time that we were relieved, but when?

Siegfried Knappe might well have been just as melancholic as his fellow gunner, but luck intervened on his behalf that fateful Christmas. Wounded for the third time in October, the young artilleryman had been evacuated back to the Reich for treatment only to find 'shortages of everything at home, especially ... meat, coffee, tea, chocolate and so on and things were starting to get worse ... now that the war wasn't going well people resented the shortages more. The population seemed a little more cowed and dispirited.' He had recovered enough by December to be sent back to the front. 'Stalingrad was in desperate need of reinforcements. My new orders were to report to 6. *Armee*.' Arriving in Rostov on Christmas Day he went to the local movement office only to be told, 'You'll have to stay here for a while, the Russians have surrounded 6. *Armee* ... the only way in now is by air and the weather has grounded all flights except those taking ammunition in and bringing wounded out.'[13] Only seven tons of ammunition reached Stalingrad that Christmas Day, and precious few wounded got out.

Knappe would stay in Rostov counting his lucky stars. Hans Staudinger, a 22-year-old Austrian from the pretty little town of Bad Wimsbach, was not so fortunate. A butcher in the Luftwaffe's famous *Immelmann* Stuka *Geschwader* based near Stalingrad when the Pocket had been formed, he was forced to watch as the flying and technical personnel had been flown out to Tazi, while he, along with several hundred other ground staff considered non-essential, was pressed into service in the ad hoc *Bataillon Immelmann* and shunted into the frontline, 'where we lay in the open with MG42s [machine-guns nicknamed Spandaus by the Allies] in foxholes.' Having had very little to eat for several days, 'just some horsemeat and soup with bread', he was overjoyed that Christmas to receive from his sister 'a kilo-packet with frozen apples which we ate immediately', even as they listened to the Red Army loudspeakers inviting them all to 'Come on over, you will get a loaf of bread every day, and don't forget your mess tins!'[14]

The bemused Germans even adopted the same tactics themselves, using their *Hiwis* to urge their former comrades to come over to them; 'You should all desert, they'll feed you well and treat you well. On the Russian side you'll die whatever happens.'

Paul Pieper was doubly unlucky, having only joined his unit fresh from training the day before the Pocket was formed. As a new boy, he experienced weeks of heavy fighting 'at the western end of the Pocket facing towards the steppe in an open field'. Then 'during a heavy attack almost my whole unit was wiped out.' Pieper was almost the only survivor; 'I lay with a comrade in a bomb crater about 50 centimetres deep. I had been wounded in the arm – it was stiff and swollen and I could no longer move it. My comrade had been killed instantly.'

In Berlin, the Propaganda Ministry had been busy and had prepared a Christmas broadcast for the nation to help lift morale. The 'Ring Broadcast' went out loud and clear, with greetings to the people from a U-boat crew out in the cold waters of the Atlantic, from a unit of the *Afrika Korps* in Tunisia, some garrison troops on the *Atlantik Wall*, and then via a crackling radio link the announcer proudly declared, 'And now here is Stalingrad.' A joyous chorus of soldiers' voices sounded across the airwaves from the 'front on the Volga'. The troops all then burst into a rendition of the classic Christmas Carol *Silent Night*. It was a masterly piece of theatre and a total con. The Ministry had faked it all.

A young officer in the real Stalingrad wrote to his mother:

Despite everything the little tree had so much Christmas magic and homely atmosphere about it that at first I couldn't bear the sight of the lighted candles... I cracked up and had to turn my back for a minute before I could sit down with the others and sing carols...

12

HUNGER AND THE RED ARMY

On Monday 21 December, *6. Armee* reported its first case of death by starvation. An officer from Bernhard Steinmetz's *305. Infanterie-Division* had been reassigned to another unit to the west and set off down the road away from the Barrikady with his orderly in tow. As usual it was freezing, and when the officer saw a soldier from his own regiment sitting huddled against the remains of a wall he instinctively stopped and asked him if he was alright. The soldier slurred a response saying he was fine but tired. The officer and his orderly helped him up and half-carried him to a nearby aid station, fearing he was wounded but didn't know it. A doctor gave him the once-over and found no visible injuries, but the man was clearly in a very bad way. An hour later he quietly died. The confused physician carried out a further examination of the body and determined the cause of death – starvation.

Unwilling to believe such a report, OKH sent a senior pathologist from Berlin into the Pocket to ascertain the truth. Selecting several corpses from a makeshift mortuary in the city, the eminent doctor had the bodies thawed out so he could perform autopsies on them. He was appalled by what he found.

Under the skin and surrounding the inner organs hardly a trace of fat; in the mesentery a watery-gelatinous mass; the organs very pale; instead of red and yellow bone marrow, a glassy, wobbly jelly; the liver congested; the heart small and brown; the right ventricle and atrium greatly enlarged.

These are all classic signs of starvation. At the same time, back in Rastenburg, a visibly agitated Adolf Hitler confronted Kurt Zeitzler about his eating habits. Ever since Jodl had sided with List in his argument about delays in the Caucasus, the Führer had stopped eating with his senior staff, preferring to dine alone, but even so he could see that Zeitzler's middle-aged frame was fast receding. With his uniform increasingly hanging off him, Zeitzler informed Hitler that the reason for his transformation was that he was eating the same rations as the men trapped in Stalingrad to show empathy with their plight. The effect had been startling: he had lost 26lbs in just a few weeks. Richthofen – aware of Zeitzler's solidarity with the soldiers of 6. *Armee* – wrote caustically in his diary about his own boss: 'It would do his [Goering's] figure a power of good to spend a little time in the Pocket.' Hitler, never a man prepared to stare an inconvenient truth in the face, conceded the fig leaf of banning the consumption of cognac and champagne in his headquarters as a gesture of support for his entrapped troops and then ordered Zeitzler to cease his diet immediately.

In the Pocket, Hans Krumfuss saw that 'Most men had frostbite to the feet and many had no footwear. Their feet were bound with rags and strips of tent canvas to protect against the cold... [We] had been without rations for days.' When rations finally did turn up 'it was yesterday's soup, frozen solid, so we needed to thaw it out.' The cold was unbearable and 'The only protection we had for our heads was a thin cap comforter under our steel helmets. The men made themselves gloves of stitched rags.' In a masterly understatement he then noted, 'All in all it was a grim day.'

Back in Rostov, Siegfried Knappe checked with the air base every day to see if he could get a flight to Stalingrad, 'but the weather remained bad'.[1] Joachim Heil, an officer in Alexander von Hartmann's 71. *Infanterie-Division*, was determined to find a way into the Pocket after returning to Russia from home leave. Told in no uncertain terms by the responsible movement officers that he would be liable to a court martial and possible execution if he flew in without orders, he – along with two of his brother officers – took the risk and somehow got themselves aboard a flight of Heinkel 111s. 'I found a crew with a wounded gunner who were prepared to take me in his place. Unfortunately he had taken his parachute with him so I would have to fly without one.' Heil would come to regret his decision as he endured the nightmare of the Pocket and subsequent imprisonment, although his two companions fared even worse; 'Dr Arno Scharf died later in captivity, I still don't know the fate of *Leutnant* Jensen. I was only released in 1949.'

The bad weather was hitting the airlift hard. With Tatsinskaya lost, Martin Fiebig had moved his main Ju 52 hub to Salsk, while the He 111s, Condors and other assorted bombers and transports flew out of Novocherkassk. Both were much further west, increasing flying time, absorbing more fuel and reducing payload. Michael Deiml was flying out of Novocherkassk:

> We now flew only supply operations. We dropped containers of provisions and sacks of bread, landing to pick up wounded men, occasionally a war reporter or a shot-down aircrew. [On one mission] we took off from Novocherkassk at 0745hrs and landed at 0955hrs at Pitomnik airfield. Here there were masses of wounded German soldiers ... we began unloading the food containers, 20 sacks of large loaves and distributed them with the help of some Organization Todt men. After that eight wounded and a war reporter got on board.

The smooth loading of the wounded onto Deiml's flight was increasingly becoming the exception rather than the norm as desperation took hold among the freezing men on the ground, who realised that their only chance of survival was to make it aboard an aircraft. Andreas Engel had been wounded back in November during *Uranus* and since then had been 'lying in a primitive, cold shack ... the wound hadn't been treated properly and a phlegmone [suppurating infection of the soft tissue] had set in... Every day the rations were reduced; a slice of bread and now and again some horsemeat broth. Morale was at rock bottom.' In despair he crawled out of the makeshift shelter and somehow flagged down a passing truck, which took him to Pitomnik. 'The crowd here was unimaginable, my hopes sank to zero.' But lady luck smiled on *Feldwebel* Engel: 'Next morning an aircraft came, and at gunpoint the crew had to stop the machine from being stormed. As a wounded man unable to walk I had the great fortune to secure a place and be flown out.' He would survive to be wounded again fighting in northern Italy in December 1944.

To reduce the strain on Salsk's overburdened facilities, some Ju 52s were quartered at Zverevo, which the air transport expert *Oberst* Fritz Morzik contemptuously described as 'a smooth field with no hangars and no billeting facilities ... the airfield is completely covered in snow ... the construction of bunkers is very difficult because the earth is frozen solid to a depth of a metre.' He didn't add that the few buildings within the airfield's perimeter had had all their windows blown out by VVS air attack, leaving them open to the elements and consequently more akin to freezers than shelters.

Two sorties per day for the aircrews was now a pipe dream and the amount of supplies flown in became erratic. On Boxing Day some seventy-eight tons got in, and this increased the following day to 127 tons, only to fall back down to a risible thirty-five tons the day after when bad weather set in. The 300 tons per day target was a distant memory and would only be achieved once more before the end.

On the same day a meagre 127 tons of supplies were flown into the Pocket, an increasingly desperate Zeitzler confronted Hitler with a plea; 'Unless you order a withdrawal from the Caucasus now, we shall soon have a second Stalingrad on our hands.' The dictator blustered as usual, but in an astonishing *volte face* the following day, he grudgingly relented. 'Very well, go ahead and issue the orders.'

This was it. *Blau* had failed. The Nazis' drive to secure the Caucasus and its oil wealth was abandoned. The gasoline, without which Hitler declared he must end the war, was conveniently forgotten. Now the race was on to withdraw *Heeresgruppe A* back through the bottleneck at Rostov before it was cut off in the Caucasus and a 'super-Stalingrad' was created. The Danish Waffen-SS volunteer Ivar Corneliussen remembered receiving the order to leave the Caucasus:

> We were ordered north... We went over the Kalmyk steppes. It was a cold journey, there was lots of snow and there were no roads, so our vehicles only made slow progress. The thing I most remember about that journey though wasn't the cold, but that we had a pig – a dead one of course – hanging off the side of the vehicle, and to cut any meat off it, so we could cook it and eat it, we had to use an axe – it was frozen solid you see.[2]

Another member of *SS-Wiking*; an *SS-Hauptsturmführer* Schneider, also remembered the retreat and the total confusion it engendered: '47,000 new sets of winter uniforms, brand-new panzers and vehicles from a depot in the homeland were simply set alight.'[3] At another town, 'Engineers blew up the railway bridge and soon the last grenadiers had gone by ... we turned around for a final look at the town, which was burning, we took our leave and followed our grenadiers west.'

Corneliussen and his comrades got within spitting distance of Rostov, and then:

> There was a problem, the route over land was cut off, so instead we had to walk over the ice of the Azov Sea to the south of the city. We were all worried about the ice breaking, and we were bombarded by Russian artillery and attacked by Russian aircraft a couple of times, so we went over that ice as fast as we possibly could. Once we got to the city the thing I most remember about the place was just how icy the streets were – we had to crawl along on all fours on the streets sometimes just to get around. The food wasn't good either; we kept on being fed the same diet of meat and bread with no

vegetables, so a lot of us got jaundice as a result and looked like Asians with yellow skin. It was always some kind of stew they fed us, and it was poured into our mess tin, and then we had relish or whatever put in the lid, and a couple of slices of bread of course, and on the odd times we got potatoes we put them in our side-caps.

Unappetizing it might have been, but at least the Dane was getting fed. In the Pocket *Oberst* Hans-Jürgen Dingler from Helmuth Schlömer's *3. Infanterie-Division (mot.)* noted that 'As a Christmas treat the Army allowed the slaughter of 4,000 of the available horses.' With little if any fodder available, those horses were mostly skin and bone, but the meat gleaned from their wretched carcasses was distributed as best as could be and each man was allocated two horsemeat rissoles to accompany their now further reduced ration of soup with no fats for lunch and dinner and just fifty grams of bread per day. Some men, however, preferred not to wait for their duly allocated horsemeat ration and instead took matters into their own hands, as one appalled *landser* saw for himself: 'At the entrance was a dead steppe pony ... a number of men were at work cutting out the soft flesh. One of them had succeeded and was holding a lump of flesh in both hands, trying to bite into it. It couldn't be eaten though, because the blood froze on his hands and face. This awful scene remained in my memory for ages.'As mentioned, certain specialists, such as panzer crew and pilots, were meant to receive better rations and this caused a deal of resentment in the Pocket, although as one Luftwaffe pilot based at Pitomnik revealed, this supposed preferential treatment was honoured more in the breach than in the observance:

There hadn't been much to eat for a long time, we pilots got a daily ration of a loaf of bread between seven and a tin of sardines between three to four men. We could take off and land on this but we couldn't turn tightly or become involved in dog fights as we would become dizzy and then couldn't see properly.

In Rostov, Corneliussen and his comrades were well looked after. 'With so many of us being ill we were all sent to the lazarett [military field hospital] to get de-loused and washed as we were filthy after our journey from the Caucasus. We were issued new uniforms and given vitamin tablets and grape sugar to help get rid of the jaundice, and after a couple of days of this treatment we were all declared fit and sent back to the regiment.' In Stalingrad meanwhile, 'We're squatting here with 15 men in a bunker ... terrible overcrowding ... one man is washing himself, a second is de-lousing himself, another is asleep.' Eberhard Pohl, whose battalion had fought so hard to keep the Soviets from reaching Pitomnik during the fighting back in late November, was pleased to receive confirmation of the award of the Knight's Cross for his men's achievement, but even more pleased to receive 'a small packet wrapped in dirty brown paper. On the paper General Paulus had written in pencil a few words of recognition. The packet contained some Army *kommissbrot* and a tin of herrings in tomato sauce.' Being the good officer he was, Pohl shared the bounty with his men.

The language Hitler now publicly began to use towards 6. *Armee* suddenly changed. Gone were constant rejoinders to hold out for a relief effort, to be replaced by stern exhortations to hold out 'to the last man and the last bullet'. The shift in tone didn't go unnoticed in Paulus's headquarters. Wilhelm Adam confronted his boss about it, only for the visibly deteriorating Paulus to declare to his subordinate:

What would become of the war if our army in the Caucasus were also surrounded? That danger is real. But as long as we keep on fighting, the Red Army has to remain here. They need these forces for a big offensive against *Heeresgruppe A* in the Caucasus and along the still-unstable front from Voronezh to the Black Sea. We must hold them here to the last so that the eastern front can be stabilized. Only if that happens is there a chance of the war going well for Germany.

Adam's fellow headquarters staffer, Herbert Selle, found himself instructed by OKH – as 6. *Armee*'s senior engineering officer – to build concrete fortifications for the troops as soon as possible to allow the Army to hold out until the following spring. Knowing the state of the airlift and that the nearest viable gravel deposit for such an endeavour was on the shores of the Sea of Azov, Selle raged at the idiocy of high command, declaring it guilty of 'a downright criminal ignorance of the local situation'.

Back in the real world – away from OKH's delusions – the Red Army was continuing its advance west and now overran a series of *Ostheer* communications relay stations. In Paulus's headquarters the teleprinter went silent. From now on, the only communication 6. *Armee* had with the outside world was via radio or written message by courier.

With a break in the weather, the airlift picked up again; 124 tons went in on 29 December, followed by 240 tons the next and 310 tons the day after that. It was a remarkable achievement given the situation. It couldn't be sustained. This was the high point of the Luftwaffe effort and the last time the 300-ton daily minimum would be achieved. The returning aircraft also managed to evacuate several hundred wounded men as well as carry out fifteen tons of mail for family and friends back home. Meanwhile, an order was sent to all artillery and gun commanders that no more than five shells were to be fired per gun per day unless expressly sanctioned by regimental command or above. A young officer in 76. *Infanterie-Division* raged at the situation: 'No possibility of getting a bit of warmth, no chance of survival for the wounded, no ammunition, no weapons to fight off Russian tanks, no prospect of relief from outside the Pocket.' He marvelled that 'the men are still willing to fight on under these circumstances!'

Lethargy started to become a severe problem, with men struggling to sleep at night as the Soviets stepped up night harassment raids on their positions with the despised *Nähmaschinen* (sewing machine) U-2VS biplanes. Powered by a tiny 100hp engine, the obsolete aircraft couldn't even reach a speed of 100mph, but at night they had the skies to themselves and flew endlessly over the

German frontline, the pilots cutting the engine to soundlessly glide into the attack and then dropping their small bombs, sometimes by hand. Joachim Feurich found himself enduring just such an attack whilst on an ammunition train on the single-track line to Gumrak. 'The attacker was following the railway line heading directly for our train. The aircraft ... would cut its motor suddenly and come at its target rather like a glider. It had no bomb racks, so the bombs were tossed out from the cabin by hand.' For some reason Feurich decided to stay on the train even after his comrades all jumped off to avoid being caught in any blast: 'There was no time for reflection, the aircraft flew over us and away without dropping anything, probably he had no more bombs left.'

Casualties from the raids were few and damage minimal, but it was the effect on morale that was the real prize for the VVS. As one *landser* described, 'I am exhausted but I cannot sleep at night, but instead dream with open eyes again and again of cakes, cakes, cakes.' To rub salt into the wound, the Soviets broadcast that many of the *Nähmaschinen* pilots were women, earning them the nickname 'the Night Witches' from the frustrated Germans. Wilhelm Eising remembered 'the "Owls of the Rollbahn" or "sewing machines", as they were known, would come screaming over in rolling attacks – not a minute passed without the roar of their motors, without the whistle and crash of their bombs. We often marvelled that the casualties weren't greater.'

Conditions continued to get worse. There weren't nearly enough *halbgruppenunterstände* built back in October and November to accommodate everyone, and many men were having to make do in improvised shelters in cellars and burnt-out buildings. The supply system was just about functioning, although with fuel desperately short, outlying units often missed out on whatever rations or ammunition were available. Even for men closer to the almost empty depots there was more luck than judgement in obtaining any food. Willi Hoffmann found himself on the wrong end of it all: 'The horses have already been eaten. I would eat a cat; they say its meat is tasty. The soldiers look like corpses or lunatics, looking for something to put in their mouths. They no longer take cover from

Russian shells and haven't the strength to walk, run away or hide. A curse on this war!'

Fritz Pabst, the 36-year-old former carpenter, was with his construction unit inside the Pocket. With no bridges or roads to build, he and his fellow workmen in uniform now found themselves virtual bystanders to a battle they could do little to influence. With nothing to do but shelter in their bunker, Pabst diligently wrote home to his wife and three children:

> We still haven't got any mail, but we reckon every day that the good old Junkers, which brings everything, won't forget us either. It's been over five weeks now since I've been able to wash any clothes, we've all got lice, I only found 15 on me today, so over time they seem to be getting less, they are like us... I haven't washed or shaved myself in the last four weeks either, no opportunity to do so, we all have centimetre-long beards, but nobody loses hope and courage, we all know that victory is ours. I now have a small bunker and even a stove, so we can at least warm ourselves up a bit.

Like any good husband and father, Pabst asked how they all were and told his family to keep warm and healthy, but even he couldn't whitewash the reality completely and told his wife of the fate of a friend and neighbour from back home.

> I have to tell you something sad... Paul Werner was fatally injured by fragments of a bomb. A splinter went through his neck and one through his chest, I was right there with him, but he was dead instantly. What a shame for him, he was a good comrade. If it is not yet known there, please keep it to yourself... Don't worry about me. I'll definitely get out of here, I'm almost convinced of that, and then everything will be fine.[4]

Not far from Pabst's bunker another *landser* wrote, 'We're mainly feeding ourselves with horsemeat, and I myself have even eaten raw horsemeat because I was so hungry.'

The new year brought no solace to the men of 6. *Armee*. Siegfried Knappe was still in Rostov on New Year's Day and thought 'the sky was bright and clear – perfect flying weather. I went to the airfield only to be told that a *Führerbefehl* [Führer Order – to be obeyed by all] had just arrived that no more troops were to be sent to Stalingrad.' The young gunnery officer realised it was an order that saved his life: 'Once again I had received a new lease on life.'

Felix Schneider wasn't as lucky as Knappe. Trapped in the Pocket, the anti-tank gunner reflected on a miserable Noel: 'The only joy we had was that we had potatoes at noon at Christmas.' A native of the town of Büchel in the Rhineland-Palatinate on Germany's western border, he was more used to rain than snow, but nevertheless found the white stuff useful; 'The ground is well covered with snow, and it's a very valuable material for us. First of all, it replaces water for us because there is none here. With snow we make soup and coffee. Then we build the most beautiful walls with it, camouflage walls so that the enemy does not see us during the day. We live here like hermits in a ravine in an open field, we have built bunkers and this is our accommodation.'⁵

Schneider, and everyone else in 6. *Armee*, was still receiving a trickle of supplies from the airlift. With the skies clear, the Ju 52s and other assorted flights continued to take off and land, still flying in mainly ammunition and fuel but having now to devote more space and weight to food as stocks in the Pocket disappeared into starving mouths. Worse still for Paulus was the news from his logistics staff that the huge herds of horses the Army possessed when the encirclement began were almost entirely gone and that all food supplies would be eaten by Monday 18 January at the latest. Fiebig and his exhausted aircrews were performing miracles given the circumstances, but even so, during the first two weeks of the new year the average daily total flown in was just 145 tons, less than half the stated bare minimum.

Pitomnik was now a scene of carnage. Wrecks littered the airfield alongside abandoned equipment and piles of assorted detritus. It was pitted with shell and bomb craters, and so many aircraft had crashed into them or been hit by predatory VVS fighters as they tried to take off or land that the frozen ground crew could no longer keep the airstrip clear. Inbound pilots found themselves swerving around obstacles on landing to avoid disaster, and as the machinery needed to clear the worst of the snow broke down or ran out of fuel the situation just got worse. Unforgivably, both Paulus and Schmidt still refused to understand the importance of Pitomnik and the other airfields to the survival of their command and left it to the overstretched Luftwaffe and a relative handful of Army staff to try and keep the lifeline functioning. In the driving snow and freezing temperatures, dozens of *Hiwis* were press-ganged into service, loading and unloading and trying desperately to keep the airfield operational.

Sitting freezing in his dug-out, Rudolf Oehus wrote to his parents on New Year's Day. 'Everything is still the same here, the Pocket is still not open, and when it will really open cannot be foreseen yet, hopefully soon ... there is about 20cm of snow. We now only have ten horses left, the others have all been slaughtered, the supply lasts for a couple of weeks, and it is good that we slaughtered some, otherwise they would all have starved to death.'

For Karl Nünninghof, the cold was the worst thing, as he told his brother Willi:

I have just come back from the station, it's so cold that my eyelashes froze together. This winter is sure to be just as cold as the last. When the sentry woke me up this morning at 0330hrs for my turn on guard I put on everything I had at my disposal, I thought to myself, I don't want to freeze to death. In addition to felt boots, a coat and an overcoat, I put on my thick winter trousers, headgear, fur hat and a woollen footcloth over my nose and under my eyes, and yet I was happy when my two hours on guard were up. If you had seen me huddled up, you would not have recognized me. As soon as I got into my bunker, my gun turned as white as lime and my fingers almost stuck to it. Dear Willi, I hope you don't need to go through such a winter in Russia. I never wish you that. After the watch I quickly fetched coffee from the kitchen because I was dressed. I tell you, I thought my fingers had fallen off. Then I came back to the bunker, undressed and warmed up at the bunker stove that my comrades had lit. After that I sat in the corner and ate my slice of bread in comfort, with a mug of coffee that I had saved from yesterday, I haven't eaten as much for some time. Now, on an empty stomach, I have to fetch a cannister of food three to four kilometres back from our fire position at noon today.

Like pretty much every member of *6. Armee* the former baker was now eating anything he could get hold of; 'Yesterday I was so hungry that I didn't know what to do. Fortunately, I'd scrounged a bit of powdered cardboard from the cook the day before so I mixed that with some milk to eat.'[6]

The Germans weren't uniquely susceptible to the cold. A Soviet war correspondent told how 'If you breathe on your glove a thin film of ice forms immediately. Even wearing *valenki* and two pairs of woollen socks you had to move your toes all the time to keep the circulation going ... and the Germans had no *valenki*.' On trying to write a report he found 'the first word was alright, the second was written by a drunk, the last two were the scrawl of a paralytic, quickly I blew on my purple fingers and put them back in my fur-lined glove.' Many Germans didn't have gloves – fur-lined or not.

Everyone was suffering in the cold, German, Russian – and Hungarian. The only surviving allied Axis army in the south still more or less functioning – Gusztáv Jány's Second Hungarian – was wretchedly sitting in its trenches, fearful for its future as it stared across the snow-covered steppe toward the Soviet lines. The ethnic German padre *Oberleutnant* Stephen Ritli saw how a dead Magyar soldier 'was brought back after lying for some time in the snow and was frozen with one arm extended over his head. Of course, this meant the body wouldn't fit in a coffin so I asked if anyone would volunteer to saw the arm off.' Unsurprisingly no-one came forward, 'so we had to cut a hole in the top end of the coffin for the arm to stick through and bury him like that.'[7]

Then Moro fell. Moscow's Third Guards Army had continued to push forward and finally reached the bustling airfield. Once again, the airlift was knocked sideways, just as it had been when Tazi fell.

With *Heeresgruppe A* still streaming back from the Caucasus through the Rostov gap, all there was available to try and block the Red Army's advance were the remnants of *Heeresgruppe B* and *Heeresgruppe Don*, both formations far more impressive on paper than in reality. No help would be forthcoming from elsewhere along the absurdly long Eastern Front either. *Heeresgruppe Mitte* had just about held on in a life-or-death struggle in the Rzhev salient – the Rzhev meat-grinder as it became known – while *Heeresgruppe Nord* was about to face another furious Soviet attempt to relieve the siege of Leningrad. Soviet superiority in men and *materiél* – and their predilection for winter fighting – was transforming the face of the war. The factories relocated east the previous summer and autumn were now churning out tanks, guns and all manner of military equipment in huge quantities, and Anglo-American aid was pouring in through Soviet ports. The figures were stark. The Soviets would manufacture 24,446 tanks and 25,436 aircraft in 1942, the Germans just 6,180 and 15,556 respectively, while the contrast in artillery production was even more striking with the Germans 23,200 guns dwarfed by Moscow's extraordinary 127,000.[8] The result was a Red Army able to mount simultaneous major offensives against all three *Ostheer* army groups, take enormous losses and still rejuvenate shattered formations and create new ones.

The day after the seizure of Moro, the STAVKA confirmed that the offensive to crush the Pocket – *Operation Koltso* (Operation Ring) – would begin one week later, on Sunday 10 January.

13

THE STRUGGLE'S END

There was good news for the airlift, the weather at Pitomnik was clear. But those same clear skies sent the temperature plummeting further, as Kurt Ebener recalled: 'The cold was almost unbearable, there were days at 25 to 30 degrees Celsius below freezing when our ground crew weren't able to start the available Bf 109s, as the heating devices were almost all defective and ripe for the scrapheap.' Supplies still flew in, but with Moro now lost the airlift hubs were even further west. The Luftwaffe continued to battle the odds but was lucky most days to deliver 100 tons of supplies.

The flights were still taking men out, and those on them considered it nothing short of a miracle. *Gefreiter* Eitel-Heinz Fenske had long ago eaten the tins of Portuguese sardines he'd pilfered from the soon-to-be-abandoned supply depot as his unit fell back into the Pocket perimeter, and now he was in the frontline fending off Soviet attacks.

I was hit by a shell splinter in the left wrist and suddenly had a swelling the size of an egg with blood beneath it. As a trained medic I treated it correctly and made a small cut with my jack-knife so that the blood could drain out. I then held the wound against the ice-cold armour plates [of a German self-propelled gun] to cool it. Fortunately, the splinter was a ricochet otherwise I might have lost my hand.

Scant days later he was not so fortunate when taking part in a counterattack. 'A shell fell 100 metres left of us, another 50 metres right of us and the third exploded right in the middle of our seven-man squad ... all I had seen was a bright, lilac-coloured light and heard a loud retort... I couldn't move my right side.' Found alive by a passing cart driver he was taken to a field hospital for treatment, where a young doctor; Hubert Haudinger, proceeded to take forty-eight shell splinters out of Fenske's right side. Scheduled for evacuation, he spent several excruciating days awaiting his flight. Eventually 'it was the day of my transfer out. We were wrapped in so-called air transport sacks, three-layered paper sacks about two metres long designed so we didn't freeze to death whilst in the aircraft.' He lay waiting, yearning for it to be his turn, but first went 'the married men with children, then those without, and if there was any room left in the aircraft after that then we others took our chance.' The minutes ticked by and the 18-year-old Fenske thought 'they'd forgotten us' when 'suddenly the sound of engines – was it the Russians or the long-awaited medic? It was the latter!' Loaded aboard, 'It was already dark when our three-engine Ju 52 landed at Salsk.' Treated in a military hospital, Fenske was deemed unfit for further service and never returned to frontline duty – but he was alive.

Realising how bad the situation was in the Pocket, and perhaps hoping to forestall the need for *Koltso*, the Soviets called a unilateral ceasefire on 7 January and offered Paulus terms if he was to surrender. The Germans and their Romanian allies were offered food, medical treatment for their wounded, permission to retain decorations and personal effects, and high-ranking officers could even keep their swords. It is extremely doubtful that the Soviets would have kept their promises, partly because their own medical and supply services were pretty rudimentary to say the least, but it didn't matter. Paulus asked Hitler for permission to agree to the capitulation, whereupon the dictator exploded; 'Capitulation out of the question. Every day longer that the Army holds out helps the whole front and draws away the Russian divisions from it.' There was no longer any need to read between the lines of Hitler's communications; in his mind 6. *Armee* was dead already and their only job now was to sell their lives as dearly as possible.

To fulfil its now designated role of tying down the Red Army in the south, the entrapped Germans needed two things above all: ammunition and fuel. Paulus still had some sixty panzers and hundreds of guns and mortars, but if the panzers and prime movers couldn't move for lack of fuel then they were easily bypassed or destroyed by the Soviets; and men without bullets to fire were even more helpless. Reports were now coming into Paulus's headquarters that Soviet soldiers were walking casually between positions in their lines, safe in the knowledge that the Germans had orders not to fire unless directly threatened; there simply wasn't enough ammunition. It was obvious that the Soviets were massing to attack the Pocket, but the Germans could do nothing about it.

In the end the Soviets concentrated nearly 10,000 guns, some 257 tanks and 281,000 men ready for the offensive. To be honest, this was a surprisingly small force given that Paulus could still muster 191,000 men.[1] The usual ratio of attackers to defenders used in service manuals to ensure victory is 3:1 and the Red Army was well short of that, although the Soviets knew that the majority of the men they were facing were service and support personnel, and though willing, they lacked training, weapons and combat experience. The Soviets also knew just how wretched the surviving Germans were, with one *landser* writing despairingly to his mother: 'I can't move my legs anymore because of hunger, and it's the same with the others. One of our comrades died, he had nothing left on his body and went on a march and collapsed from hunger on the way and died of cold.' The unnamed *landser* said his unit had received a single 750-gram loaf of stale *kommissbrot* for six men and were told it had to last three days.

In a desperate attempt to husband the tiny amount of food remaining, Paulus ordered that all Soviet PoWs were to be released and handed back to the Red Army, thus relieving the Germans of the task of feeding them. In justifiable terror of retribution, large numbers of would-be returnees – many of whom had been working as *Hiwis* anyway – refused to be repatriated and hid wherever they could in the rubble instead. Desperation was now endemic, as one man recalled in his diary: 'To my horror I saw German soldiers scraping off skin or rind from an old rotten cow carcass. It stank to high heaven and was going to be worked into leather in the summer. When I pointed out to them that it would make them ill they looked at me without understanding as if to say "then give us something else!"' That was impossible as he acknowledged. 'From now on, only 50 grams of bread – one slice – per day!'

The same morning the PoWs were due to be handed over – Sunday 10 January 1943 – at 0650hrs, with the temperature gauge reading 35 degrees Celsius below freezing, *Operation Koltso* began. A few hours later, panicked signals started to arrive at Army headquarters from the perimeter; '0940. Enemy broke through on a wide portion of the front line... Isolated strongpoints are still intact. We are trying to rally and train last available parts of supply and construction units ... to set up a blocking line.' With shells pounding every identified position within the perimeter, Paulus noticed Herbert Selle watching him intently from the doorway to his quarters.

'What do you say to all this Selle?'

'I agree with what all the other older staff officers say sir.'

'And what is that?'

'That the Herr General should have disobeyed orders, but the opportunity was allowed to slip. As early as November the Herr General should have wirelessed; "I fight this battle with and for 6. *Armee*. Until it is over my head belongs to them. After the battle my Führer, it belongs to you."'

After a pause, Paulus replied, 'I am aware that military history has already passed judgement on me.'[2]

That evening, another signal arrived at Paulus's headquarters. 'Our own losses considerable. Resistance of the troops diminishing quickly because of insufficient ammunition, extreme frost and lack of cover from heaviest enemy fire.' The Pocket – by now a sort of lozenge-shape – had a nose as it were, extending west around the town of Marinovka, which was held by Helmuth Schlömer's superb 3. *Infanterie-Division (mot.)* and elements of Martin

Lattman's *14. Panzer-Division.* The fighting there was brutal: 'Massed tanks rolled across our lines, especially the trenches, to crush the men in them, and then, finally, hordes of Russian infantry attacked.' Somehow the front held. 'From one hour to the next our ranks dwindled. Anybody who could still walk or crawl was in the forward trenches, from a general to the most junior soldier...wherever you looked there were abandoned and wrecked bunkers and vehicles in flames.'

With no reinforcements, precious few heavy weapons and little ammunition, the defenders couldn't long hold out as the Soviet main effort aimed to pinch off the Marinovka 'nose'. In less than twenty-four hours the Red Army succeeded. *3. Infanterie-Division (mot.)* was almost annihilated. To the north of Marinovka, Edler von Daniels's Bavarians were also crushed in bitter fighting. A signal to *Heeresgruppe Don* read, 'Ammunition so low that combating enemy masses in front of perimeter no longer possible... Parts of division fighting with bare steel because ammunition exhausted.'

The attack ground on. In two days, the Soviets lost 26,000 men and more than 135 tanks – more than half their total armour – but Paulus lost 60,000 men and huge amounts of heavy weapons as they were abandoned in the snow owing to lack of fuel. As for the survivors, they stumbled eastwards through the blizzards to try and reach an illusory safety in the city itself. Helmuth Schlömer witnessed it: 'The retreat ... has been a road of horror and suffering for the troops. Close to physical exhaustion the soldiers stamped through the endless snowy waste in which formless mounds lay here and there; fallen or frozen comrades, destroyed and abandoned vehicles.' The 49-year-old Westphalian general was heartbroken at seeing 'wounded, mutilated and half-frozen human beings, crying for help and asking to be taken along'. The marching men were too weak to help their fellow *landsers* and had no option but to leave them to freeze to death.

As for Paulus, he radioed Erich von Manstein as his immediate superior and told him, 'No reserves left. Enough ammunition for three days. Heavy weapons immobilised by lack of fuel.' By this time Manstein was of the same opinion as Hitler, that *6. Armee*'s function was to tie down as many Red Army troops as possible to allow the rest of the southern front to be stabilised. Just like his Führer, Manstein had written off the men of 6. *Armee*.

Having been refused permission to surrender on the eve of *Koltso*, Paulus ordered Wolfgang Pickert to fly out and explain to high command exactly what the situation inside the Pocket was in the hope of overturning the decision. On landing at Salsk the flak general was greeted by Martin Fiebig, who asked him what was going on, to which Pickert replied, '6. *Armee* is fighting its last battle ... ammunition and fuel reserves no longer exist.' The bespectacled Pickert wasn't the only messenger Paulus sent to plead his case. The final plaintiff would be Coelestin von Zitzewitz, the aristocratic OKH staff officer Zeitzler had despatched in late November to send him regular updates as to the situation on the ground in Stalingrad. Several days before the tall, young officer boarded his flight out of the Pocket, the Luftwaffe made one last attempt to transform the airlift and turn the situation round for 6. *Armee*.

Erhard Milch was a former airline executive and inveterate schemer with an easy smile and a taste for intrigue. Promoted to the rank of *generalfeldmarschall* of the Luftwaffe in the famous 1940 Kroll mass promotion ceremony, Milch had ambitions of toppling Goering and assuming the leadership of the air force. In the winter of 1942-43 he was the coming man in the Nazi hierarchy and had formed a mutually beneficial partnership with Albert Speer, as the Reich's Armaments Minister, to transform the German war economy. Now he was presented with the ultimate poisoned chalice and ordered to take over command of the airlift. The timing couldn't have been worse. Even as he was preparing for his new role, Soviet shells were landing on Pitomnik. Kurt Ebener recalled: 'On 17 January we could quite clearly hear the impacts of enemy artillery shells on the airfield and in our bunker. We knew then that the Russians had broken through the western side of the Pocket and were advancing on Pitomnik.' Only thirteen tons of supplies were flown in that day, and a lucky sixty-two wounded flown out. Another signal was sent: 'Supply situation catastrophic... If increase in supply promised again not immediately forthcoming, any further holding on hopeless.'

By now Arthur Schmidt had more or less relegated Paulus to the role of observer as he tried to shore up resistance in the Pocket's western half outside the city, but there was little he could do to save Pitomnik, as Kurt Ebener saw for himself.

I was supposed to fly airfield protection the next morning. On the previous evening *Oberleutnant* Lukas landed at Pitomnik after flying escort for supply aircraft and having got into aerial combat on the way. His Bf 109 was no longer serviceable and so there was no question of him taking off again straightaway and he had to spend the night with us. His aircraft was supposed to be the first one to be warmed up the next morning and you needed a lot of time for that, given the cold. Finally, his aircraft was started and he took off. He then flew airfield protection until my Bf 109 was ready to lift off, after a while he flew off to the west. At almost the same time the last Ju 87s took off, climbed to 300m and dived on the southern boundary of the field, dropping their bombs.

The sudden realisation of what those dive-bombing attacks meant dawned on the young *jagdflieger*:

We pilots and ground crew looked at each other and suddenly one of the mechanics said the Russians were coming. I saw only soldiers in white camouflage suits – Russian infantrymen. My Bf 109 wouldn't start and in attempting to get the engine to fire one of the mechanics got shot in the hand then shouted at me 'Quick, out of the aircraft, the Russians are here.' The airfield had been overrun and all was chaos... German vehicles and panzers drove over wounded German soldiers, in their hundreds our emaciated *landsers* threw away their rifles, fell exhausted into the snow, and died.

Pitomnik fell. However, in the ensuing chaos the news failed to get through to a number of pilots. 'That night some supply aircraft managed to land at Pitomnik as it still wasn't known outside of Stalingrad that the Russians had taken the airfield. The Russians didn't shoot at them but instead captured them.' Kurt Ebener and the rest of the Luftwaffe flight and ground crews that managed to escape Pitomnik now headed east. 'The panic was now complete, all those who could still walk left for the field at Gumrak about 25 kilometres away. We marched in the freezing cold through deep snow with nothing to eat, and constantly under attack by enemy aircraft. A forced march like this was a real challenge for us Luftwaffe men, but the will to survive made us strong and able to carry on. On 18 January, shortly before dark, we reached Gumrak.'

Back in German-held territory, Milch had arrived to be briefed by a tired and dispirited Martin Fiebig. The news was bad. None of the Fw 200 Condors were still airworthy, while only a third of the He 177s and He 111s were operational. Worse still, fewer than one in ten of the Ju 52 workhorses could fly. Milch's air armada was a chimera. Fiebig then told him that the best airfield left in the Pocket was Gumrak, some four miles east of Stalingrad city centre. Thinking ahead as best he could, Fiebig had already ordered sixteen Heinkel 111s to fly to Gumrak, land, unload and report back on the airfield's readiness to act as a lifeline for 6. *Armee*. Those reports were sombre. Predictably, neither Paulus nor Schmidt had visited Gumrak or made any preparations for it to become operational. There were no ground or reception crews, just hordes of wounded and desperate men gathered at the edge of the landing strip hoping to get aboard any aircraft that flew in. The Heinkel crews had had no option but to unload the precious supplies themselves while trying to keep the sullen masses at bay. Earlier flights had landed at Gumrak, and several aircraft had been forced to make emergency landings there or been shot up by roving VVS fighters, and now those same aircraft littered the runway – it was total chaos.[3]

As one Heinkel pilot said, 'There were wrecks of Ju 52s and He 111s bordering the narrow runway laboriously dragged to one side ... the runway was about 50 metres broad and the wingspan of an He 111 was 24 metres, meaning those steel wrecks were damned nearly at the edge of the runway.' The pilot remembered his briefing: 'Every pilot is free to act according to his own judgement.' One crewman remembered Gumrak being 'in a very dangerous condition with shell craters, machine wreckage and equipment strewn everywhere'.

After meeting Fiebig, lost in thought in his staff car on the way to Taganrog airfield, Milch didn't notice the blanket of damp fog stretching across the road and out onto the steppe. His driver was doing his best to navigate but didn't see the upcoming railway line or the train that appeared out of nowhere and sideswiped Milch's car on the unseen crossing. The Luftwaffe *feldmarschall* survived but was badly injured.

The following morning Milch, bandaged but alive, sent a Heinkel 111 to Gumrak with a bomb bay full of supplies and a passenger – Luftwaffe *Major* Erich Thiel. Thiel's job was to liaise directly with a *Major* Freudenfeld – senior Luftwaffe signals officer in the Pocket – and Paulus himself, and dramatically improve conditions at Gumrak. More Heinkels and Ju 52s followed Thiel in and some thirty-two tons of cargo landed at Gumrak that day. Another thirty tons was dropped by container in the hope troops on the ground would retrieve them. 'The aircraft were re-routed to Gumrak but instructed not to land but instead to throw the supplies out over the airfield.' The tactic was only partly successful as a report said at the time: 'Supply canisters only partially found due to snow drifts. Collection of same very difficult due to lack of fuel.' For the first time in the airlift almost all the delivery was food – hardly a bullet or drop of fuel was sent in.

On presenting himself to Paulus, Thiel detailed what he had seen at Gumrak; namely inadequate ground preparations and an airfield pitted with shell holes and in a woeful state. The result was a terrifyingly difficult landing and take-off for the transport aircraft – if they could land at all – and a turnaround time on the field of more than five hours per aircraft. Michael Deiml and his crew tried to land there but couldn't, and 'had to go round again because of obstacles on the landing strip ... so we dropped our provisions containers, opened the entry flap in the lower fuselage and, standing over it in an icy draught, tossed out the 20 bags of bread we had brought with us.' Paulus irritably waved away Thiel's report. 'You are talking to dead men here ... the Luftwaffe has left us in the lurch.' He then rounded on the handsome young flier: 'Today is the fourth day that my troops have had nothing to eat... The last horses have been eaten. Can you imagine it; soldiers diving on an old horse cadaver, breaking open its skull and devouring its brain raw? What should I say ... when a man comes to me begging "Herr *Generaloberst*, a crust of bread?"' Arthur Schmidt joined in, telling Thiel that 'the Luftwaffe has betrayed us, and this crime against *6. Armee* cannot be atoned for.' Flabbergasted, Thiel realised that Paulus and Schmidt had already given up on Gumrak and the airlift, and now only sought to lay blame for *6. Armee*'s impending demise on the Luftwaffe. To reinforce the point, a signal from *6. Armee* headquarters was sent to *Heeresgruppe Don* stating that 'Fuel situation caused by failure of Luftwaffe paralyses all movement, even for supply of men with food.' Astonishingly, the same signal also baldly stated, 'Gumrak air base fully serviceable'.[4]

One man who did find salvation at Gumrak, was the fighter pilot Kurt Ebener.

On 19 January, in the early morning, a Ju 52 landed at Gumrak between the bomb craters. The crew was made up of four *unteroffiziere* and their orders were to take off immediately. I joined them and now had a small chance to escape the hell of Stalingrad. I was able to help my Ju 52 comrades as I told them the only way to survive was to fly south and fly at low level across the steppes. Several times we shivered in fright as we saw Russian aircraft higher up until we landed to refuel at Krasnodar.

Unable to believe he had survived, Ebener carried on his journey from Krasnodar on foot and by truck until he reached his unit in the Donets area five days later. They had posted him as Missing In Action and believed him dead.

Ebener was joined in escaping via Gumrak by the young Josef Goblirsch. Wounded by shell splinters, he was transported to the airfield where he found 'a picture of horror; mountains of amputated limbs, all covered with a layer of calcium chloride – by day air attacks by *jabos* [*jagdbombers* – fighter bombers], by night the 'duty NCO' [sewing machines] came with bombs, rats attacking the wounded ... men wounded in the stomach laid out on the floor and kept quiet with morphine.' Eventually flown out, Goblirsch's Ju 52 came under attack from three VVS fighters, forcing him to take up post as the sole machine-gunner and ward them off with belts of tracer.

Remarkably, Goblirsch's stroke of luck wasn't unique. Arthur Krüger, the Danziger who had seen Soviet snipers make short work of his reinforcements a couple of months before, had been wounded in the head and left shoulder, but not badly enough to be allocated a precious place on an evacuation aircraft. However, on talking to a Ju 52 pilot awaiting help to drag one of its wheels out of a shell crater on the airfield,

> He asked if I could fire an MG because he didn't have an air gunner. I replied, 'Of course, I'm from an MG *kompanie* where I was an instructor and section leader.' He replied, 'Then I will take you as an air gunner when I'm cleared for take-off.' That was my salvation... Once the aircraft was full and more with wounded, we took off without a problem and got clear of the encirclement... I was the last of my *kompanie* to leave Stalingrad alive. Of my comrades with whom I had been in action, none survived Stalingrad.

The same day Ebener flew out of the Pocket, Paulus, a practising Roman Catholic, circulated an order to all units within 6. *Armee* forbidding suicide. In particular, the order said it was unacceptable for troops to stand on top of their trenches and entice the Soviets to shoot them. Paulus could circulate as many orders as he wanted, in reality his ability to influence the course of the battle had long ago disappeared, and now his personal authority among the men was fast slipping away. One young signals officer recounted how he was undergoing a few days very hasty re-training as an infantryman when he was suddenly despatched as a signaller to the remnants of a panzer regiment because 'my predecessor had not been able to put up with the pressure any longer and had turned his pistol on himself ... the closer the end came the more frequent were similar cases. Who would dare to set himself up as judge of those who did it?'

Regardless of Paulus and Schmidt's criticisms, Thiel and Freudenfeld threw themselves into transforming Gumrak into a useable air base. It was an impossible task and Thiel knew it. In his report back to Milch at his base at Stalino on Wednesday 21 January, the young officer admitted to his boss that 'It is already too late.' Unwilling to admit defeat quite yet, Milch ordered Thiel to continue his efforts, and even looked at options such as the use of gliders packed with food that would be towed within range of Gumrak and then released to land near the *landser*'s positions. Thankfully for the men who would have had to pilot the flimsy wooden gliders, the idea was soon dropped. As for the positions they might have landed near, there were precious few of the bunkers built back in October and November. With the crushing of the western half of the Pocket around two-thirds of those relative safe havens had been abandoned and thousands of Paulus's men now found themselves sheltering in craters or shell holes, at the mercy of the elements and with barely a blanket for warmth.

The day before Thiel sent his doom-laden report to Milch, Coelestin von Zitzewitz, now noticeably thinner than he had been back in November, finally flew out of Gumrak and was taken by his old boss to see Hitler. 'When we arrived ... General Zeitzler was admitted at once, while I was made to wait in the anteroom.' On being summoned into the dictator's presence, Hitler began by saying, 'You come from a tragic and terrible place,' before launching into a diatribe on how the Pocket was to be saved, including the possibility of sending a battalion of the new Tiger tanks across the frozen steppe to punch a hole through to Stalingrad and thus restore the front. Zitzewitz listened in disbelief, noting how 'the spacious room was only dimly lit, in front of the fireplace was a large circular table with club chairs round it, and on the right stood a long table, lit from above, with a huge situation map of the entire Eastern Front on it. In the background sat two stenographers taking down every word.' Eventually, Zitzewitz could sit in silence no longer;

> I used the first pause ... to describe the hardships of 6. *Armee*; I spoke about the hunger, the frostbite, the inadequate supplies and the sense of having been written off; I spoke of wounded men and the lack of medical supplies. I concluded with the words, 'My Führer ... the troops can no longer fight to their last round because they are no longer physically capable of fighting and because they no longer have a last round'... Hitler looked at me in surprise ... then he said, 'Human beings have great powers of recuperation,' and with those words I was dismissed.

With Zitzewitz out of the way, Hitler sent Paulus a message: 'Surrender out of the question. Resist to the end.' When Paulus responded that Leo Raubal Jr – a *leutnant* in the Luftwaffe's engineering branch and Hitler's favourite nephew – had been wounded and requested that the dictator send in a light aircraft to fly him out to safety, Hitler sent back a blunt refusal. 'Leo is a soldier.' For the first time whole German units in the Pocket began to raise the white flag and surrender.

Truth be told, the fate of 6. *Armee* was now taking up less and less time at both OKW and Hitler's headquarters at Rastenburg. In North Africa, Montgomery's Eighth Army was on the verge of capturing Tripoli, Rommel's main supply base, while the Red Army's offensive against *Heeresgruppe Nord* to break the siege of Leningrad was in full swing. Even more compelling was the launch of *Operation Little Saturn II* on 12 January. Having more or less destroyed the Romanian 3rd and 4th Armies and the Italian Eighth

Army, the Soviets now cast their eyes upon the sole remaining allied Axis army – the Hungarian Second.

Relatively intact after the tumultuous fighting in November and December, the Second was in much the same state as its fellow Axis brethren had been before their catastrophic demise. Inadequately trained for the most part, the Hungarians lacked heavy weapons – especially modern anti-tank guns – with little in the way of reserves. Nominally a force with a strength of around 200,000 men, losses and a bloated supply chain half full of men desperate to secure a safe sinecure, meant the frontline was manned by only around half that number. The Magyars did have a small armoured force, but as with Radu Gherghe's 1st Romanian Panzer Division, it was underpowered and mainly equipped with obsolete tanks and armoured cars.

The STAVKA had set *Little Saturn II*'s objective as nothing less than the crushing of the Hungarians and then the annihilation of Hans Salmuth's German 2. *Armee* to the north as well.

Filipp Golikov launched the offensive on the morning of 12 January with probing attacks from the 347,000 men of his Voronezh Front. Deszo Laszlo's 7. *Könnyü Hadosztály* (7th Light Field Division) took the brunt of the first attacks, and while his 35th Regiment held the line, the neighbouring 4th Regiment fell back in confusion. Golikov didn't hesitate and ordered a general attack the next morning into the gap where the panicked Hungarian 4th Regiment was meant to be. The Soviet attack set off a chain reaction in the Hungarian ranks and just four days later, on 16 January, it was clear the Hungarians had suffered a calamitous defeat. Stephen Ritli was caught up in the middle of it all and remembered it as 'The big run ... it was absolute chaos. I witnessed a senior officer do one of the most stupid things I saw during the whole war. He came out of his bunker and yelled "Run that way! [pointing to the west], every man for himself!"' The chaplain soon found himself 'running like everybody else through very deep snow in freezing weather. We ran for weeks...'

In scenes reminiscent of the fate of the Italians and Romanians, the petrified survivors trudged west, stealing anything they could find to keep going. 'Starving men must eat and there were many times when we took food from the locals who were very poor and hungry themselves.' After finding a calf unsuccessfully hidden by the locals, Ritli and his men cut its throat and butchered it in the snow but couldn't cook the meat, 'so we ate it raw with blood running down our faces.'[5]

Just as with the Italians and Romanians, the tale of the Hungarians was not one of an army simply running away, as a German regimental commander made clear in his report on them after an unsuccessful counterattack: 'The Hungarian troops fought very well, and the reason for the failure of their counterattack attempt lay with the helplessness of their units against enemy armour and the freezing weather.'[6] Nonetheless, the Second Army more or less vanished. In the end Ritli was one of only around 40,000 men who escaped the disaster.

This fresh calamity heaped yet more anguish on German high command, who were now far more focused on the fate of the 125,000 men of the relatively intact 2. *Armee* rather than the ragged scarecrows of 6. *Armee* – at least Salmuth's men had a chance of survival, so the gentlemen of the general staff reasoned.

Back in the Pocket, Thiel and Freudenfeld had worked a mini-miracle and somehow got Gumrak up and running – at least to some extent. Milch, too, was having an impact. An extremely capable organiser he was still managing to fly in over sixty tons of supplies a day, despite the myriad problems that bedevilled the continuing airlift. It was less than half the daily average that went in during the fortnight before his arrival as airlift supremo, but it was still an achievement given what was happening on the ground. Thiel and Freudenfeld even found time to start work on preparing the Stalingradsky airfield right next to the city to act as a base for the air bridge if anything happened to Gumrak, which was a sound idea given Soviet shells were already hitting the airfield from Red Army artillery batteries.

One man who benefited hugely from Thiel and Freudenfeld's labours was Paul Pieper, the apprentice shoemaker from the depths of Germany's famed Teutoburg Forest who had only joined his unit the day Stalingrad was cut off. Badly wounded in the arm – a bullet had fractured his left elbow joint – he had been given a precious authorisation slip entitling him to be flown out but had decided that the casualty system had broken down and so had made his own way to Gumrak. Once there, he scavenged for food and took what shelter he could find as he waited for a chance to get on board one of the dwindling number of aircraft arriving. Eventually, he was woken from a deep sleep by two comrades from a flak unit who told him that two aircraft had landed, 'and as I had the authorisation to be flown out, I should definitely go.' However, in his own mind he had 'already given up, and didn't want to make the effort anymore, and so thought to myself "it won't do any good, there will be a huge crush again."' Cajoled and encouraged by the anti-aircraft gunners, he relented and set off and 'when I got to the aircraft ... I noticed that there were hardly any wounded there. Perhaps they hadn't got their passes to fly! Two bombers had landed, He 111s ... there was no sign of the usual great throng always present on the airfield.' Not believing his luck, he scrambled aboard, 'in at the flap through where the bombs used to be dropped. Once we'd all climbed in the flap was secured from the inside. We sat pressed very close together.' Horribly overloaded, the pilot somehow coaxed the aircraft into the freezing night sky, and then it dawned on Pieper and his fellow passengers: 'We could scarcely believe we had come out of it alive, some were crying, others wanted to thank the three airmen.' Within two days Pieper was in a clean hospital bed in Stalino with freshly laundered white sheets and some of the best medical care in the Wehrmacht.

As for Freudenfeld, he met his old friend Eberhard Pohl – *bataillon* commander in the Austrian 44. *Infanterie-Division* – and had to give him some bad news: 'There was to be no relief for the soldiers at Stalingrad, the fortunes of war had changed. The loss of Gumrak airfield was only a matter of time, it was already under observed artillery fire from both north and west.' Pohl was dumbstruck by the news.

That evening, Friday 22 January 1943, Paulus sent a message to high command:

Rations exhausted. Over 20,000 unattended wounded in the Pocket. What orders should I give to troops who have no more ammunition and are subjected to mass attacks supported by heavy artillery fire? … Since 16 January only received 36 rounds for light howitzers, used up several thousand, only 30 rounds per barrel left … ammunition mostly used up, partial signs of dissolution… Ability of fortress to resist coming to an end.

The following afternoon Stalingradsky was declared operational and capable of receiving limited flights. At the same time, Soviet tanks rolled across Gumrak's snow-covered landing strip – the airfield was now in the hands of the Red Army. Josef Rosner, one of Eberhard Pohl's Austrian grenadiers, had been fighting near the village of Gontshara when 'A Mongolian came through the trench and threw a hand grenade at my machine-gun. I was hit by splinters in both hands and the right eye. He aimed his machine-pistol at me and shouted "Stoi!" [Stop!] Had his gun jammed or was the drum magazine empty? I still had two rounds in my pistol, so I shot him dead and hid myself amongst all the bodies lying around, feigning death.' Waiting until the tide of battle swept past him, Rosner somehow made his way to Stalingradsky where he was astonished to see several Heinkel's land: 'From three bunkers pitiable figures staggered towards the aircraft. When we got to the He 111s the Russians began firing at them with 10.5cm guns. One He 111 burst into flames as the aircraft gunners hauled Storva [a comrade of Rosner's] and me into the machine as the thirteenth and fourteenth to be rescued.' Rosner would lose all of his toes in hospital – amputated due to severe frostbite – but would survive to thank the likes of Thiel and Freudenfeld for his deliverance at Stalingradsky.

Michael Deiml and his crew flew into the emergency airfield 'which we called Stalingradskaya. There, a very sad sight met our eyes. In the icy temperatures – minus 30 degrees Celsius and lower – we met our soldiers, lightly clad in uniforms of thin material, starving, frozen together and almost motionless.' Deiml and his crewmates were unloading the provisions containers and bread sacks when an 'anti-aircraft *hauptmann* said he wanted to give us his will.' Deiml's Heinkel made two more flights to Stalingradsky, taking out as many wounded as they could carry, but were forced to leave so many more behind. On their final flight they unloaded the bread sacks and took on as many wounded as possible. Sent aft to carry out a minor repair prior to take-off, he noticed that a wounded man had crept into the aircraft through the open flap.

When I followed him inside he looked at me in agitation, as if fighting for his life, his eyes begging me to let him leave with us. I can never forget that look. Although we were already loaded to the limit I let him into the interior and said nothing to *Gefreiter* Adrian [the pilot] Stalingradsky fell to the Russians the same day ... the last German aircraft had left Stalingrad.

As the first Soviet riflemen reached the airfield perimeter, the men of the Twenty-First Army and Chuikov's Sixty-Second linked up and the Pocket was split in two, with no airfield now in German hands. A staff officer shivering away in the new northern mini-pocket understood the situation: 'Involuntarily the image of a dead chicken came to my mind; it had lost its head but its wings were still flapping and its legs twitched as if it could, and would still, escape its fate. Thus it was with us. Reflex movements announced the onset of our deaths.'

Leutnant Gottfried Greve reported seeing 'numerous stragglers wandering around, grey faced, their frozen limbs wrapped in bits of blanket, begging for bread'. They had no chance. By now the ration system had more or less broken down. Greve himself said 'the daily ration on those last days was 35 grams of bread, 50 grams of tinned meat and 15 grams of wheat grain for soup.

We melted snow for water, first picking out specks of rubble and splinters.' He also said they barely ever received the set rations, more often than not they were lucky to receive a single slice of bread and nothing else – the horses had all long since disappeared into the pot. One staff officer remembered, 'There hadn't been much bread for a long time. In the final days we were only issued 38 grams per head, and the iron rations had long ago been eaten.'

The northern pocket comprised the Dzerzhinsky tractor works and most of the other industrial sites upon which 6. *Armee* had bled itself white the previous year, while the southern pocket was the rubble-strewn suburbs south of the Mamayev Kurgan. At 1645hrs on the afternoon of 24 January Arthur Schmidt sent Manstein an update.

> Attacks of undiminished violence against the entire western front which has been fighting its way back eastward in the Gorodische area ... to form a hedgehog in the tractor works... Horrifying conditions within city proper. Approximately 20,000 wounded uncared for seeking shelter in ruins, intermingled with about same number of starving, frost-bitten men and stragglers, mostly without weapons, which they lost in the fighting... Heavy artillery pounding the whole city area. Last resistance along the city outskirts in the southern part of Stalingrad ... under the leadership of energetic generals fighting in the line and of gallant officers around whom a few men still capable of fighting have rallied.

He held out little hope. 'Tractor works may possibly hold out a little longer.'

As the morning turned to late afternoon he sent another message. 'Troops without ammunition and food... Collapse inevitable.' He asked Hitler for permission to surrender. Once again it was refused.

That same day, Manfred von Plotho's wife wrote to him: 'The situation is still not seen as desperate and counter-actions are in progress. And as long as there is still a spark of hope, my whole being flows to you ... we believe in you and send you all our strength that you can hold out for another day until maybe the rescue will come. And if it is our fate to part forever now, I can never lose you completely.'⁷

Karl Nünninghof's parents were far bleaker. 'The news from Stalingrad is heartbreaking and terrible for us back home. We are very worried about you... I have written so much and also sent parcels to which we still have no answer, where is the post if it is not delivered to you? But we do not give up hope... One hopes from one day to the next that the war will end, but instead it goes on.'⁸

On Tuesday 26 January Paulus formally requested that any further flights to the Pocket bring in nothing but food and drop it as near to his men as they could. He said there was no need for any more ammunition as the *landsers* had too few weapons to use it anyway. Holed up in bunkers and makeshift positions, those *landsers* who still had guns commented bitterly: 'They're attacking without a break ... and we've got to save every shot because we have hardly any ammunition. How much we wish we could really shoot properly once more.' Others, half frozen and weak from hunger, could do nothing but stare as Red Army soldiers began to walk nonchalantly through the rubble without bothering to take cover from an enemy they knew could no longer defend himself.

Amazingly, some of those same defenders hadn't given up all hope quite yet as one officer – Karl Schwarz – remarked: 'All and sundry discussed breaking out. Most were convinced it was impossible in the prevailing cold without food and ammunition, yet some thought it worth a try.' A reconnaissance of possible routes out of the city found 'every bunker and hole in the ground bristling with Russians' at which 'hope perished even amongst our optimists.' A few hardy souls weren't put off and concocted a plan to 'try and lie concealed beneath tarpaulins [in the back of a truck] while a *Hiwi* and assistant up front drove.' However, fate intervened; 'A lorry was made ready with great enthusiasm, loaded up and tarpaulins provided, but before the limited number of escapees had been drawn up a chance mortar round put paid to this last dream [by destroying the truck] with a massive explosion.'

An NCO wrote a last letter to his wife back in the Reich: 'You should not mourn my death... I am sure that everything will continue. You will have to take a job and take care of the little ones. I shall carry you in my heart until the last moment. You will be with me until I take my last breath.'

Alexander von Hartmann – still wearing the Knight's Cross personally awarded him by Paulus the previous October – had seen his beloved *71. Infanterie-Division* shrink before his eyes to fewer than two hundred combatants. Now, trapped against the railway embankment in the southern half of the Pocket, he took leave of the survivors; 'Captivity for a general is dishonourable. It is a great honour when an officer dies in battle. I will not kill myself, but I will sell my life dearly.' Armed with a carbine he then climbed the embankment and began firing at the Soviets. He was joined by his last two surviving regimental commanders, *Oberstleutnant* Kurt Corduan and *Major* Bayerlein. Their last stand was depicted in a typically heroic illustration by the war reporter Hans Liska and published in *Signal* magazine, (see page 1). In Liska's drawing however, Hartmann is pictured alongside his fellow generals Max Pfeffer and Richard Stempel deluging shadowy Soviets with submachine-gun fire and hand grenades. Liska also recounts that 'Three cooks were busy ... in their field kitchen when surprised by Soviet tanks. To defend themselves they snatched a few grenades lying nearby and leapt at the tanks, demolishing a couple of the giants. They then went on with their cooking.'[9] Having anything to cook by that stage in the Pocket would be a surprise to the remaining *landsers* of 6. *Armee,* to say nothing of grenades 'lying nearby'. As for Hartmann's last stand, he, Corduan and Bayerlein were all killed. Pfeffer would survive the Pocket but die in Soviet captivity in Voikovo Prison Camp in December 1955. Fritz Roske would lead the last few men of *71. Infanterie-Division* into captivity a few days later.

The next day *Oberst* Arthur Boje, commanding officer of *Infanterie-Regiment 134* of the renowned 44. *Infanterie-Division,* stood up in the cellar of the former NKVD headquarters in the city and faced the last of his men. 'We've no bread left and no weapons. I propose we surrender.' No-one raised an objection. Boje – wounded in the foot and with a high fever due to lack of medical care – turned and painfully started up the stairs out of the basement. His fellow Austrians stood and followed him with their hands in the air. As one of his last remaining officers pointed out, 'There was no more ammunition to be had. What else could you do in such a situation? We had practically fought to the last shell, the battle for Stalingrad had been decided.' The day after Arthur Boje and his men trudged into captivity, Arthur Schmidt sent a missive to *Heeresgruppe Don*. 'Food situation compels suspension of the issuing of rations to wounded and sick in order to keep alive fighting personnel.' It was a desperate ploy but of little if any practical use – there simply wasn't any food left anyway. One *landser* wrote, 'I only weigh 92lbs, nothing more than skin and bones, the living dead.'

With no airfield to land on, the Luftwaffe attempted one last time to help their beleaguered comrades and on the night of Friday 29 January an astonishing 124 assorted bombers and transports appeared over the two mini-pockets and threw their loads out in the hope that the *landsers* below would be able to retrieve at least some of them. Franz Rechberger was one of the lucky ones who did indeed manage to salvage something from the air drop: 'We opened our last cans of preserves which we'd gathered up after an aircraft dropped them in the snow, and we accompanied them with a "special coffee" made from the last beans in the haversack, pulverized with an axe and boiled in melted snow. Then we lay down to sleep to gather our strength for what lay ahead.' Notwithstanding Rechberger's good fortune, the vast majority of containers and food sacks were either captured by the Soviets or lost all together in the chaos and confusion, as Karl Wolf bitterly testified. 'Most [of the aircraft] dropped their provision bombs over the advancing Russians. Now and again some of them fell into our hands but we no longer had the strength to open them and had to leave them where they lay.'

Thirteen hundred miles away, on Saturday 30 January Adolf Hitler took to the podium in the Berlin Sportpalast once again to speak to the nation. Among the handpicked audience was the panzer crewman Richard von Rosen. Having been injured during *Barbarossa* he had recovered and just completed a potential officer course. Now a *Fahnenjunkerfeldwebel* (officer cadet sergeant), Rosen and his comrades had been picked up at 0700hrs by buses 'which arrived to take us to the Sportpalast to hear an address by Hitler. The place was packed with men from the Army, Luftwaffe and Kriegsmarine newly promoted to the equivalent rank of junior *leutnant*... We had to wait four long hours until the event began at midday.' It was the first time Rosen had seen the dictator in the flesh; 'I was not impressed either by the "entry" of the Führer, the introduction by Goering, nor Hitler's speech itself. The jubilation ordered was more mechanical than emotional... I wasn't stirred.'[10]

In Stalingrad the southern mini pocket had shrunk to a few streets around Paulus's headquarters in the cavernous basement of the *Univermag* department store bordering Red Square. Günther Ludwig recalled the situation: 'The defence in the Tsaritsa sector had broken down and the Russians were approaching Red Square from the south. By the afternoon only the width of a single street still separated them from the Square.' In charge of a handful of men, Ludwig knew that Paulus's command post was about 100 metres to the rear 'in the so-called "department store."' To his dismay he received an order from Chief of Staff 6. *Armee*, General Schmidt:

'No matter what, prevent the Russians from entering Red Square and taking out the Army commander in his command post.' [I] had about 50 men available who were still just about able to lift a rifle. The assignment was impossible ... the only weapons we had were rifles and pistols.

The appearance of Soviet tanks proved Ludwig's point. The panzer officer was shocked to then be hailed by name by the Soviets, who told him in no uncertain times to evacuate the ruined building he was in or their tanks would blast it to pieces. In a desperate attempt to try and save the lives of the many wounded who were lying untended in the building, Ludwig went out under a flag of truce and negotiated with the Soviets to avoid any more killing.

Now, for the first time, men who had earlier deserted suddenly turned up among their former comrades looking fed and looked after. Throughout the battle – and indeed throughout the Russo-German war – Soviet propaganda used psyops (psychological operations) to help try and break Axis resistance. This usually consisted of fairly crude measures such as loudspeakers alternately blaring martial music and German language announcements promising all sorts of inducements for any soldier prepared to cross the lines. As the war progressed the tactics became more sophisticated, and the Soviets began to use native Germans – either pre-war exiles, many of them communists themselves, or deserters and even prisoners – to broadcast to their erstwhile comrades telling them how well they would be treated, that it wasn't their war, and that all the Soviets wanted to do was to live in fraternal brotherhood with their fellow working-class German comrades. Unsurprisingly, few fell for it, many had seen at first-hand how the Soviets dealt with prisoners or had at least heard from others tales of barbarism. 'The Russians were quite near us and kept calling out for us to go over to them, there would be food and so on… nobody was prepared to go into captivity … we knew how bestially they treated people, so a lot of comrades preferred to shoot themselves.'

One *landser* remembered how a sentry from his unit had been taken alive by the Soviets one night, 'The drag marks can clearly be seen in the snow. A scouting party was sent out but received only lively fire and returned having achieved nothing.' Two days later the missing man returned; 'a German voice spoke through a loudspeaker from the Russian trenches: "Here is soldier Pollack. I am OK, the rations here are better than you have. Come on over!"' Now, amidst the rubble the Soviets tried a new approach. 'That evening two comrades came to us who had fallen into Russian hands. They reported good treatment and plenty to eat. They had been sent back to us. We stared at them as though they were some kind of strange animal … was it just a trick to obtain our trust?' The bemused *landser* and his comrades didn't take up the offer.

In Paulus's headquarters all was surreal. At noon the previous day, even as the Soviets rampaged through his shredding defences, the visibly deteriorating general had sent a grovelling signal to Berlin: '6. *Armee* greets its Führer. The swastika flag still flies over Stalingrad.' Hitler replied in a similarly ludicrous tone, ending his message with 'My thoughts are ever with you and your soldiers.' To honey his words, Hitler granted a raft of promotions in 6. *Armee*, including making Paulus a *generalfeldmarschall*. Designed to spur the recipients on to a final act of resistance to the encroaching Red Army, the elevations were of no practical use. Paulus's in particular had a sting in the tail, as he himself realised: 'One can't help feeling it's an invitation to suicide. However, I'm not going to do them such a favour.' Paulus knew only too well that no German *generalfeldmarschall* had ever been taken alive so understood fully that Hitler's expectation was that he shoot himself rather than accept capture. Indeed, Hitler would later rage that 'In peacetime Germany, about 18,000 or 20,000 people a year chose to commit suicide, even without being in such a position. Here is a man who sees 50,000 or 60,000 of his soldiers die defending themselves bravely to the end. How can he surrender himself to the Bolshevists?'

Friedrich Paulus had decided at the very last gasp to disobey his Führer. In so doing he not only believed he was following his conscience but was also following Wehrmacht regulations, specifically regulation Number 2: 'It is expected of every German soldier that he prefers to die with a weapon in his hand to being captured. But in the vagaries of battle even the bravest man may have the misfortune to be taken captive by the enemy.'[11] The debate about what might have happened to 6. *Armee* had he discovered his moral compass earlier in the battle has raged ever since.

As it happened, one of the last reports he authorised to be sent out claimed that the northern mini pocket could hold out a short while longer as Soviet strength was weaker there, while confirming that the starving, frozen, emaciated *landsers* grouped around his own headquarters would 'hold out to the last according to orders'.

The end, when it came, was more farce than high drama. Günther Ludwig's scratch defence force was spent. 'I walked around my position on the southern edge of the square. A few of our sentries lurked in the shadows of the ruins. They had been without a warming fire, without food and without heavy weapons for days. They weren't capable of withstanding a further attack.' Having spoken to Red Army representatives about surrender, Ludwig was sent for by 6. *Armee* headquarters and reported to Arthur Schmidt, fearing the worst: 'You have been in contact with the Russians. Are you aware that this is strictly forbidden?' Ludwig confirmed he had and explained his reasoning to both Schmidt and Fritz Roske, who was standing at Schmidt's shoulder having taken command of 71. *Infanterie-Division* on Alexander von Hartmann's death. Ludwig needn't have worried. Expecting Schmidt to call for his head he found instead that he seemed relieved to have had the decision to surrender taken out of his hands. 'I was speechless, completely stunned...so that was the end of the "fight to the last man and bullet" that Herr Schmidt had constantly been on about! Deeply depressed I slowly walked across Red Square to re-join my comrades.'[12]

At 0615hrs on the morning of Sunday 31 January 1943 a signaller in Paulus's headquarters radioed *Heeresgruppe Don*, 'Russians at the door. We are preparing to destroy [the radio].' Wilhelm Adam recalled: 'It was still dark, but day was dawning almost imperceptibly. Paulus was asleep.' Schmidt woke his boss with a gruff 'I have to inform you that the Russians are at the door.' At 0715hrs 6. *Armee* sent its final signal; 'We are destroying [the equipment].'

The first Soviet to enter Paulus's headquarters was a tank commander, Lieutenant Fyodor Elchenko. He was shocked by what he saw. 'It was packed with soldiers – hundreds of them ... they were dirty and hungry, and did they look scared!' Elchenko saw Paulus 'lying on his bed ... wearing his uniform ... he looked unshaven and miserable.' Adam wrote in his diary that Paulus was told by the Soviets: 'Prepare yourself for departure. We shall be back for you at 0900hrs. You will go in your personal car.' Adam was allowed out with a driver to prepare the car:

> Climbing out of the cellar, I stood dumbfounded. Soviet and German soldiers, who just a few hours earlier had been shooting at one another, now stood quietly together in the yard. They were all armed, some with weapons in their hands, some with them over their shoulders… My God, what a contrast between the two sides! The German soldiers, ragged and in light coats, looked like ghosts with hollow, unshaven cheeks. The Red Army soldiers looked fresh and wore warm winter uniforms… At 0900hrs sharp the Soviets arrived to take the commander of the vanquished German 6. *Armee* and his staff towards the rear. The march towards the Volga had ended.

Major Freudenfeld – the Luftwaffe officer who had done such sterling work with Eric Thiel to improve coordination at Gumrak and speed up the supply flights – reported to Luftwaffe headquarters, 'Soldiers run around aimlessly. Very few combatants are left. The staffs have lost their grip as leaders. Russian tanks are breaking through. This is the end.' Then, at dawn on the morning of 31 January he sent his final message, the Soviets were 'at the door'.

After Paulus refused to take responsibility for the northern mini pocket, it was left to the triumphant Soviets to batter it into submission. Karl Strecker was in command in the depths of the tractor factory, and the pugnacious Prussian fought on for another day even as the Soviets lined up artillery guns a scant three metres apart to engulf his men in high explosive and shrapnel. Dietrich Goldbeck was witness to the last act:

> The Russian encirclement was now so tight they could fire at every individual who showed themselves … there was a terrible bombardment and shelling of our trenches. We heard through the loudspeaker of our Wehrmacht receiver that the southern pocket had surrendered. Then they played us the Song of the Nibelungs [Nibelungenlied – from Wagner's

operatic Ring Cycle] to mark our final battle... We could no longer help our wounded. We began to destroy our papers... the last field kitchen was shot to hell... I was still unable to take it in.[13]

At daybreak the next morning, 1 February, realising that further resistance only meant more bloodshed, Strecker sitting in *Oberstleutnant* Julius Müller's command post deep amidst the rubble turned to his subordinate and said, 'I must go now.' Müller replied, 'I shall do my duty.' The decision made, Strecker then gathered together the remaining staff officers of the five divisions huddled around his headquarters and announced to them that 'General Paulus and everybody still alive in the southern Pocket has surrendered to the Russians. Our situation is hopeless. Therefore, as senior commander in the Pocket I give you the freedom to act from now on as your conscience dictates. Any further defence is pointless.' Strecker then sent his final signal. 'XI Korps and its divisions have fought to the last man against vastly superior forces. Long live Germany!' One of Strecker's men remembered that 'The shooting stopped. Prisoners were taken quietly without any excesses by the conquering troops... Both sides were sick to death of it all and happy that it was finally, finally, over.'[14]

Hans Krumfuss, the grizzled old *feldwebel* who had made the wrong call in November and driven back into the Pocket instead of west to safety, had earlier been offered the option of taking part in a mass suicide by an old comrade, but had refused. 'I would not die by my own hand.' Leaving the would-be suicides, he was in another bunker when 'A Russian shouted in... "Kamerad, ruki verch!" [Kamerad, hands up!], we laid down our weapons and walked into the open with our hands raised. The Russians were very joyful and friendly, for them it was a great victory!' Gert Pfeiffer remembered much the same.

Oberst Finck and I plus one messenger and one radio operator with an intact radio set capitulated with the very last remnants of *6. Armee* ... we were totally exhausted, filthy and lice-ridden, lying in a hole in the ground somewhere in the western end of the Barrikady... I fired two shots into the radio and then a Russian major armed with a pistol jumped into our makeshift bunker after I told the runner to fix a strip of white cloth to his rifle and hold it up to be seen.

Wilhelm Gereke, a young gunner in the same division as Krumfuss, had seen his regiment more or less annihilated during the preceding two months and was numb: 'We fired off all our ammunition and made our small arms unserviceable because there was no point in fighting any longer. We surrendered ... on reaching the enemy positions the fighting troops offered us cigarettes and cigars from the provisions warehouse they'd captured. These men didn't steal from us ... about 250 of us were arranged into a column and with one sentry we started off south.'[15]

Gereke's experience of decent treatment from men who only the previous day had been trying to kill him is a common one among veterans of a multitude of conflicts. Once the hot blood of mortal combat has had time to cool a soldier often only sees his own image in the face of an enemy and acts accordingly, perhaps subconsciously in the hope that were the tables turned he would receive humane consideration himself. Unfortunately, Gereke then experienced the other side of the coin from rear area troops who were only too happy to profit from the prisoners' misery: 'When the sentry was relieved after a kilometre and a half the great shake down began, in which even civilians joined in. We were relieved of everything visible ... some men even had their boots taken so they had to stand barefoot in the snow in temperatures of minus 30 degrees Celsius.' Franz Rechberger had much the same experience. Having had the cheek to drive into captivity in a still functioning car, he and his friends were ordered out by a Red Army officer they came across, whereupon 'We were surrounded by Russians who robbed us of watches and lighters with loud "Urr jest!" and "Maschinka jest!"'[16]

That same day Hitler ordered the following communiqué to be broadcast:

The Battle for Stalingrad has ended. True to its oath, to
its last breath, *6. Armee*, under the exemplary leadership
of *Generalfeldmarschall* Paulus, has succumbed to the
overwhelming strength of the enemy and to unfavourable
circumstances. The enemy's two demands for capitulation
were proudly rejected. The last battle was fought under a
swastika flag flying from the highest ruin in Stalingrad.

Regular programming on the radio was replaced by the doom-laden
tones of the Adagio movement from Anton Bruckner's Seventh
Symphony, and several days of national mourning were declared.

On Wednesday 3 February *Leutnant* Herbert Kuntz was briefed
by his boss, Hans-Georg Bätcher; 'Have a look see whether fighting
still continues anywhere or whether escaping parties can be seen,
then drop your load.' Piloting his Heinkel bomber over the city,
Kuntz noted that not a single anti-aircraft gun fired at him, nor
could any signs of fighting be seen. Dropping ever lower to try
and identify German forces, Kuntz asked himself, 'Where should
we drop our load? The altimeter read 100 metres, 80 metres, the
lowest I dare go because it might not be accurate ... we were so
close to the ground. I jerked the machine back into the fog, into
the safety of height ... we had to drop our cargo of bread blind.'
Kuntz prayed that it would 'strengthen a brave *landser* for the long
march'[17] and then ordered it dropped earthwards. As soon as it
was gone Kuntz turned his aircraft round and flew west.

The young artilleryman Rudolf Oehus disappeared in the
maelstrom of those last few chaotic days in Stalingrad. His parents
frantically tried to garner any news of him from survivors who
might have known his fate, one of whom wrote to them after his
own lucky escape from the city:

Dear Herr Oehus, now that I have seen pictures of your
son, I remember him very well; I couldn't do anything with
the name alone. I can only say of your son that he was still
alive on 22 January – the day of my wounding and my
evacuation. Unfortunately, I don't know what later became

of him and all his comrades. I assume, however, that he will be in Russian captivity... So there is hope that your son is still alive. Even if he won't have an easy time in captivity the prospect that he is still alive and may still be able to return at the end of the war is a consolation for you and your dear family.[18]

Rudolf Oehus, the 22-year-old farmer's boy from Bergen in Lower Saxony drafted into the Wehrmacht in 1940, and who fought across Ukraine and southern Russia with his battery, was gone. Officially declared Missing In Action, he wasn't identified among the thousands of men who trudged despairingly into captivity at the end of the battle, and neither was his body ever found among the ruins. Like so many others, Stalingrad became his grave.

Karl Schwarz, the 28-year-old staff officer whose comrades had thought of trying to escape the doomed city hidden under tarpaulins in the back of a truck, now shuffled pathetically into captivity along with several hundred other survivors from his unit. 'The Sixth Army ... was dead.'[19]

14

COUNTING THE COST

As the world looked on, the new year of 1943 began with the Soviet Union and the Red Army appearing ever mightier. In Britain no less a figure than Alan Brooke – Chief of the Imperial General Staff, scion of Protestant Irish aristocracy and no friend to communism – declared with joy, 'We start 1943 under conditions I would never have dared to hope. Russia has held.' The *Daily Telegraph* newspaper trumpeted that the Soviet Union had saved European civilisation, and the British government announced that 23 February was to be celebrated nationally as 'Red Army Day'. Stalin basked in the praise while renewing his calls for the Anglo-Americans to open a second front in western Europe by landing in France. Amidst the hyperbole, the Soviet dictator quietly hushed up the failure of *Operation Mars*. This offensive – far larger than its little brother *Uranus* in the south – was designed to encircle and destroy Walter Model's 9. *Armee* in the Rzhev salient opposite Moscow. Once that had been achieved the Soviet forces would go on to exploit their victory and comprehensively defeat *Heeresgruppe Mitte* – always seen by the Soviets as the heart and soul of the *Ostheer*. As it turned out, the 1,900,000 men, 3,300 tanks, 1,100 aircraft and 24,000 guns and mortars concentrated for the attack were thrown like water on rocks. The Rzhev meat-grinder cost the Red Army 1,600 tanks, 100,000 Soviet soldiers killed and 235,000 wounded. It was an epic failure, but immediately passed into the shadows, blotted out by the success at Stalingrad.

That success was truly staggering. The debate about just how extraordinary has run ever since. A global conflict like the Second World War where entire nations and empires fought each other across much of the planet could never really be won or lost in a single battle – no matter how large – but Stalingrad more than most has a claim to that title. The all-conquering Wehrmacht died in the snows of the Russian winter of 1941, but it showed remarkable powers of regeneration in early 1942 to amass the forces for *Fall Blau*. However, those forces suffered from the same flaws as their predecessors in *Barbarossa*, and after initial victories and advances, by the end of September the entire operation had run out of steam – exactly as had happened the previous year. The Germans simply did not possess the men and *matériel* to sustain an operation that would militarily defeat the Soviet Union without the communist system collapsing in on itself.

In another mirroring of *Barbarossa*'s failure, *Blau*'s lack of concentration on its objectives was calamitous. Hitler was correct in identifying Nazi Germany's lack of oil as the single biggest weakness in his bid for global power, and the seizure of the Caucasus oil fields would not only have solved the problem but would have deprived the Red Army of their bounty. But even as the strike south petered out, the fixation with capturing every last building in Stalingrad became *Blau*'s raison d'etre. As it turned out, the Wehrmacht still managed to struggle on for another two and half years without Soviet oil, despite Hitler's gloomy prophecy to Paulus back in June that 'If I don't get the oil of Maykop and Grozny then I must end this war.' Mind you, the Nazi dictator was very fond of making overblown statements, as his subordinates should have known. Just two months after declaring the critical nature of the Caucasus oil, he also announced to his own high command that 'If, due to the shortage of coking coal, the output of the steel industry cannot be raised as planned, then the war is lost.'[1] Following that up with a confession to Heinz Guderian that 'If I had known that the Russians had so many tanks I would not have started this war.'

In truth, 1942 was once again a year of strategic diarrhoea for the Third Reich. *Blau* was never the sole objective for the year, added to it were the capture of Leningrad, the defeat of the British in North Africa's desert, the ongoing U-boat war in the Atlantic and the destruction of Europe's entire Jewish population in the gas chambers agreed upon at the Wannsee Conference. Hitler and his generals prided themselves on their knowledge of the military theories of Clausewitz but seemed not to have understood what the Prussian cavalryman had actually written.

Regardless of the Nazi penchant for acting like a child in a strategic sweetshop and grabbing at everything, it is difficult not to gasp in horror at the performance of Friedrich Paulus. Given command of an army that he was told 'could storm the heavens' he increasingly ceded responsibility for decision-making to determined subordinates like Schmidt and von Seydlitz-Kurzbach, while supinely acquiescing to every communiqué from Vinnytsia and then Rastenburg. Blessed with an incredibly powerful field army possessing integral armour, masses of heavy weaponry and a cadre of veteran formations, he proceeded to show little in the way of tactical or operational flair, allowing himself to be drawn into a battle of attrition in Stalingrad that handed over significant advantages to his enemy. Was he, in effect, exactly as the eminent historian Walter Goerlitz described him, '…just a staff man … who failed in practice'? Was he alone responsible for the tragedy on the Volga? Was he a ditherer, who didn't dare venture the brave decision and the risk? And specifically, could he not rebel against Hitler's orders and save his men by an unauthorised break-out? The fallacy of the unchallengeable nature of Hitler's orders had already been demonstrated in the East by Paulus's mentor von Reichenau when he had ignored the command to hold Rostov the previous year, and it had done the monocled general's career no harm at all. True, when Hans Graf von Sponeck had done the same to save his division from almost certain destruction in the Crimea, he had been arrested, tried and sentenced to death – subsequently commuted to seven years imprisonment – but as an army commander Reichenau and his actions were the better comparison to Paulus's own. Paulus would also have agreed no doubt with Rudolf von Ribbentrop, son of the Nazi Foreign Minister Joachim and serving Waffen-SS officer, that

...the German Army disposed of the oldest and most efficient management system ... based on the fundamental knowledge that the highest effectiveness of all troops could only be attained if each soldier was capable of acting independently in the 'emptiness of the battlefield'... The basic precepts of the German military code were that German troops of all ranks must be able to act on their own initiative and independently.[2]

Der Lord failed miserably to apply this precept to his own behaviour.

The result for the soldiers of Nazi Germany and her allies was nothing short of biblical. During the vital Second battle of El Alamein in late October and early November, around nine thousand German and Italian soldiers were killed and as many as another 15,000 were wounded, and the Axis also lost some 500 tanks and 254 guns. In terms of lives lost, this was roughly equivalent to four day's fighting in Stalingrad.[3] As ever with the battles on the Eastern Front the numbers are disputed, but the one figure that isn't is that some 91,000 survivors went into captivity on surrender of the Pocket. The vast majority were Germans, but there were also some 3,000 Romanians and a handful of Croats. Of the estimated 19,000 *Hiwis* in 6. *Armee* at the time, nothing is recorded. Those who were not killed in the final days probably tried to pass themselves off as refugees with varying degrees of success. Most would have received a bullet in the back of the head from their former comrades and been dumped in a mass grave.

For the 91,000 captives, regardless of what the Soviets had promised, their ordeal was far from over. An anti-tank gunner sombrely recalled

Towards six in the morning the Russians came cautiously in files of infantry towards us, there was no shooting ... a white cloth fluttered. After a short while infantry carrying machine-pistols and wearing bright white snow smocks appeared at our bunker. Listening to their jarring demands that we should all come out and line up outside I wrecked the radio receiver with a hatchet and was then one of the last to leave the bunker. Outside we were all lined up – about 70 men, many with serious wounds and frostbite, waiting in silence for the order to march off.[4]

The British war correspondent and celebrated future historian Alexander Werth arrived in Stalingrad on 3 February to see the devastation for himself. Taken to a large burnt-out building, he saw 'in the porch the skeleton of a horse, with only a few scraps of meat still clinging to its ribs. Then we came into the yard ... more horses' skeletons.' Seeing a hunched figure scuttle down some stairs to a basement Werth followed and found

...around two hundred Germans dying of hunger and frostbite. 'We haven't had time to deal with them yet,' one of the Russians said. 'They'll be taken away tomorrow, I suppose.' And, at the far end of the yard, besides the other cesspool, behind a low stone wall, the yellow corpses of skinny Germans were piled up – men who had died in that basement – about a dozen wax-like dummies... There was nothing we could do for them.

Little if any food or medical treatment came the prisoners' way and they were marched in pathetic columns to various prison and labour camps across the Soviet Union. As one remembered, 'Now there began for us a six-day death march...' Already severely weakened by malnutrition and wracked with disease, the survivors dropped like flies. 'Countless of our comrades didn't survive ... dying of all kinds of frostbite and maladies ... and whoever couldn't keep up was shot by the ruthless guards.' The majority of *6. Armee* survivors were dead within three months, typhus killing thousands.

One prisoner remembered being given 'a loaf of bread to be shared amongst eight, and each man got a salted herring – that was our rations for the next eight days.' He was marched to a hell hole called Beketovka Camp where 50,000 prisoners were held; 'Terrible things went on in that camp because the men were starving ... you got something to eat once a week if you were lucky.' Finally shipped out to a new camp in the former Volga-German Republic of southern Russia, the prisoners began to die quickly. 'Often up to 30 per day would die, mostly of typhus, dystrophy or dysentery. [By] 'September 1943, 70 of us still able to work, and another 150 sick, were transferred to Volsk Camp – the only survivors from the original 2,000 men.' Those dead prisoners would join the 160,000 men of *6. Armee* killed from 19 November to the very last day in February. Sixth Army was wiped out, and much of *4. Panzerarmee* went with it. Hans Salmuth's *2. Armee* was lucky to survive but lost almost 80,000 men. The Wehrmacht had never experienced anything like it.

Horrific as German losses were, they didn't compare in percentage terms with those of their ill-fated European allies. Romania had suffered dreadful casualties capturing Odessa the previous year but that was as nothing compared to what it suffered now. Its 3rd and 4th Armies were more or less destroyed after losing 150,000 men between them and had to be withdrawn from the front. The Hungarians lost 100,000 men as their Second Army was annihilated, and the Italian Eighth Army lost much the same. The reinforced regiment Zagreb had sent was immolated too. The fascist Croatian regime had sent some of its best men east and now had to ponder on a growing civil war with Tito's communist Partisans with its armed forces shorn of several thousand of their very finest. Four entire armies, the core of the Axis ally's contribution to the war in the East were gone. They would never recover.

The young Italian *Alpini* officer, Nuto Revelli, had been wounded in the fighting and evacuated back to Italy. On his train journey home down through the recruiting areas for his beloved *Julia* Division he saw 'In every station there's a small crowd of women dressed in black, already marked by mourning, imploring us for news. They show us photographs of their relative; they want to know the fate of the *Julia* Division. We only know the *Julia* almost vanished completely on the Russian Front. We don't know what to say.'

Equipment losses were high, too. German industry – never as efficient in reality as in the popular imagination – was undergoing something of a revolution in 1942 due to Albert Speer's dominant position as armaments supremo and his successful collaborations with the likes of Erhard Milch, but that was almost from a standing start and it was unable to fulfil the needs of a Wehrmacht that was becoming more and more reliant on the horse to function. Some 1,600 panzers and over 9,000 guns and mortars were lost, along with as many as 60,000 precious motor vehicles.[5] As Paulus tramped into captivity the *Ostheer* couldn't muster 500 operational panzers across its entire front, with *Heeresgruppe Nord* having just three.

It was, however, the situation in the air that was most dangerous for the Third Reich. German military success in the West and East was based on the twin pillars of manoeuvre and air power, and the latter was gutted after Stalingrad. The losses suffered during the Battle of Britain had been particularly high among bomber and ground attack crews and had never truly been made good. The fighter arm – the *jagdwaffe* – had also bled heavily but its core of *Experten* were able to paper over the cracks by becoming virtual scoring machines, achieving ever higher kill numbers that Joseph Goebbels and his propaganda machine could laud to the heavens. But *Blau* stripped away the Luftwaffe's veneer of supremacy. Yes, the Luftwaffe reduced Stalingrad and its suburbs to rubble, and yes it held its own against the VVS fighter arm, but it couldn't decisively affect the outcome of the battle and it singularly failed to successfully intervene on behalf of the allied Axis armies during the *Uranus* and *Little Saturn* offensives. To cap it all, the airlift was a catastrophe.

That airlift effectively destroyed the Luftwaffe's transport arm – already debilitated by the losses incurred during the invasion of Crete – with some 266 Ju 52s lost. That amounted to more than a third of the entire fleet and added to them were the wreckage of 165 Heinkel 111s, forty-two Ju 86s, nine Fw 200 Condors, five Heinkel 177 bombers and a single Ju 290 transport liner. In total, some 488 aircraft were lost, in effect an entire *fliegerkorps*. For context, the Luftwaffe lost just eighty-four aircraft during the Second battle of El Alamein.[6]

A thousand highly trained and experienced multi-engine pilots and aircrew were killed during the airlift, including dozens of irreplaceable flight instructors, leaving the air academies and training schools back in the Reich desperately short of qualified staff and further reducing the flow of new pilots to the frontline *staffeln*. Those losses had enabled the Luftwaffe to fly in some 8,350 tons of ammunition, fuel and food in the seventy-one days from the airlift's launch on 24 November 1942 to its closure on 2 February 1943. That was just over one-third of the basic requirement of 300 tons a day and not nearly enough to keep 6. *Armee* fit, healthy and fighting. The returning aircraft did, however, manage to bring out over 30,000 wounded men and specialists deemed important enough by OKW to deserve a seat. Several thousand men lucky enough to make it onto an outbound plane died on the way as massed anti-aircraft batteries and VVS fighter units scanned the sky for them, but those who did make it out considered themselves truly blessed.[7]

By the time of 6. *Armee*'s capitulation, the Luftwaffe in the East was exhausted. Excluding the few transport aircraft still in theatre, the Luftwaffe counted 1,657 aircraft in the East, with *Luftflotte* 4 – previously the jewel in the crown of the Luftwaffe's eastern armada – able to field just 240 aircraft, with serviceability rates at a miserly 38 per cent – about half what they were when *Blau* was launched. From now on the service arm that had been instrumental in the Third Reich's early years of victories was relegated to a junior role in Nazi Germany's war strategy.

The airlift was never going to be able to supply a force as large as 6. *Armee*. A German panzer division in 1942 needed around three to four hundred tons of supplies per day to function in an offensive role; some one to two hundred tons of ammunition, around 150 tons of fuel and assorted tonnage of food, spare parts, medical supplies and so on.[8] Food, and the lack of it, has become the *leitmotif* of Nazi Germany's Stalingrad disaster, but it was the lack of shells and jerrycans that was more decisive. A soldier can survive on little or no food for a few days if necessary and still fight, but without ammunition those same soldiers are simply casualties waiting for the bullet, and the panzers and heavy weapons that were vital to an aggressive defence of the Pocket needed fuel to move around the battlefield and counter Red Army attacks. Without supplies of fuel and ammunition the Germans couldn't fire back and couldn't manoeuvre, and that consigned them to miserable defeat.

The Germans had been seduced by the effectiveness of the earlier airlifts into Kholm and especially Demyansk. The latter was rightly judged a huge success with the Luftwaffe flying in some 24,303 tons of supplies at a daily average of over 265 tons, plus five million gallons of fuel and 15,446 replacements while bringing out 22,093 wounded. An average of a hundred to 150 flights a day had kept the 100,000 trapped men fighting for the three months between 20 February and 19 May 1942[9] when the encirclement was breached by troops led by none other than Walther von Seydlitz-Kurzbach.

What perhaps might have been more instructive for the Germans to consider was the siege of British and Empire troops in the city of Kut on the River Tigris by Ottoman forces in 1916. There, the British airlift conspicuously failed to supply the trapped men, leading to daily food rations as low as 170 grams of bread and 450 grams of horsemeat, with the defenders finally becoming the first ever troops to receive supplies dropped by air. The capacity of the aircraft at the time was just three sacks of supplies each, so that in total, by the time of the city's surrender, just five ounces of food per inhabitant had been flown in.[10]

Much has been made post-war about aircraft flying into the Pocket with containers full of condoms, Iron Crosses and thousands of right boots – but no left ones – among other such foul-ups, and yes, some of that is true. Paulus's Quartermaster, *Oberstleutnant* Werner von Kunowski, exploded when told one container was opened and found to be full of pepper and marjoram: 'Which ass was responsible for this load?' Milch himself stopped a consignment of fish meal being sent in, but the amount of useless items flown in was never large, and certainly not enough to make the difference between survival and defeat.

Back in the Reich, reaction to the calamity was one of chilled silence. The German people had not been properly prepared for the surrender, still being told as late as early January that 6. *Armee* was bravely holding out and would be relieved soon. When the tone of the news reels and radio broadcasts changed to that of stout defence and the heroism of a last stand, most civilians struggled to catch up. 'The press and radio were silent on the situation in Stalingrad, neither I nor the lower military command centres – and certainly not the German people, had any hint of the catastrophe that was building there.' The senior Army officer, Siegfried Westphal, said: 'The disaster of Stalingrad profoundly shocked the German people and Wehrmacht alike... Never before in Germany's history had so large a body of troops come to so dreadful an end.' The businessman, Hermann Voss, went even further: 'Only a fool could have shut his eyes to the ultimate outcome of the struggle. The German armies in North Africa were in full retreat, the occupied Balkan territories were in constant upheaval, and after the Allied landings in North Africa Germany's rulers expected an invasion of southern France.'[11] One *landser* was recorded as saying that 'Stalingrad was a terrific blow. It's impossible to estimate the proportions of that fiasco.'[12]

Even the Italian fascist dictator Mussolini, by now totally in thrall to his fellow tyrant, acknowledged the disaster, although his take on it was slightly different; '...[it] makes clear to the minds of the masses the great attachment of the Russian people to the regime – a thing proved by the exceptional resistance and the spirit of sacrifice.'

Another *landser*, a *Feldwebel* Schreiber, astonishingly still held out hope of final victory; 'If we don't finish the Russians off next year then we're done for.' For some it shook their faith in Hitler himself. British intelligence, eavesdropping on two captured Luftwaffe pilots in their cell at Trent Park in north London, overheard one saying, 'One begins to doubt him.'[13] This view was far from universal however, even after Stalingrad. Large-scale bugging of PoWs in British and American prison camps found that before 1945 there were precious few officers or soldiers who voiced criticism of the regime, and even fewer of Hitler himself. Far more representative than the doubting Luftwaffe *leutnant* of Trent Park was the unemployed sailor and Nazi brownshirt Fritz Muehlebach:

Stalingrad was a bit worrying, but the Führer himself explained it all ... it was only an apparent reverse because it would contribute to the achievement of final victory. Of course, to the ordinary soldiers it was a little hard to see what the Führer meant, but we all knew he knew what he was doing. After all, he had proven it often enough in the past.[14]

Extraordinarily, the likes of Muehlebach were given fresh resolve by the American President. Having concluded the Big Three conference in Casablanca in French Morocco a scant week before Paulus's surrender, Roosevelt declared to the world that he, Stalin and Churchill had agreed their joint war aim of Nazi Germany's 'unconditional surrender'. In fact, Churchill had made his view plain that this was a mistake and would only encourage Germany to continue fighting till the bitter end, but Roosevelt – flush with what he viewed as the achievement of a political understanding with the Soviet dictator – went ahead anyway. Goebbels's response was predictable and blared out to the German people: '...it means slavery, castration, the end of Germany as a nation.' Roosevelt also made mention of the controversial Morgenthau Plan to de-industrialise Germany after the war and partition her into several mini states, encouraging Berlin Radio to trumpet; 'The Jew Morgenthau [US Treasury Secretary Henry Morgenthau Jr] sings the same tune as the Jews in the Kremlin...'

For many Germans there seemed now little choice but to fight on and make even greater sacrifices in the hope of victory. But not all decided this was the best way forward. Dr Franz Wertheim – still serving in a field hospital in the occupied city of Odessa and living with his Russian mistress Olga – thought differently. 'I began seriously to wonder about the possible outcome of the war.' He decided enough was enough and claimed an earlier car accident was still badly affecting him and 'I was clearly suffering from the early stages of locomotor ataxia. It was made clearer by a discreet diet of barbital tablets.' On being discharged from service for his 'illness' he returned home to his private clinic where he survived a British air raid that 'dropped a few tons of explosives on my house which sent the clinic and 36 patients to hell.'[15] At the time he was staying the night at a lady friend's' house.

As for Friedrich Paulus, he was treated comparatively well by the Soviet authorities – as pretty much all the twenty-two captured German general officers were – but refused to collaborate with them in making public criticisms of Hitler and the Nazi regime. In private though, he reiterated his anger at being invited to commit suicide rather than give himself up, telling his fellow Stalingrad general Max Pfeffer, 'I had no intention of shooting myself for that Bohemian corporal.' Following the failed 20 July 1944 Bomb Plot to assassinate his Führer he changed his tune, joined the anti-Nazi *Nationalkomitee Freies Deutschland* (NKFD – National Committee for a Free Germany) and made broadcasts on their behalf encouraging members of the Wehrmacht to put down their weapons and join the Soviets. Appearing as a witness for the prosecution at the Nuremburg Trials he sought to lay blame for Stalingrad on pretty much everyone but himself, reserving much of his ire for Hitler and his henchmen.

Then, in perhaps one of his worst betrayals, he was asked by a journalist about the fate of his men in Soviet captivity. Annoyed to be asked such an impertinent question, he blithely declared that the wives and mothers of his men could rest easy in their beds as their menfolk were safe and being well looked after – one more calumny to add to the ledger of Friedrich Paulus. He was then allowed by Moscow to settle in Dresden in communist East Germany in 1953. Two years later the surviving former soldiers of 6. *Armee* were finally repatriated – there were barely 5,000 left alive of the 91,000 that had gone into captivity twelve years previously. Paulus died in 1957 and was ultimately buried next to his Romanian wife in West Germany. She had seen him last in 1942 when he departed for the Eastern Front and the advance on the Volga. Paulus had sent her his wedding ring aboard one of the last aircraft out of the Pocket.

MAPS

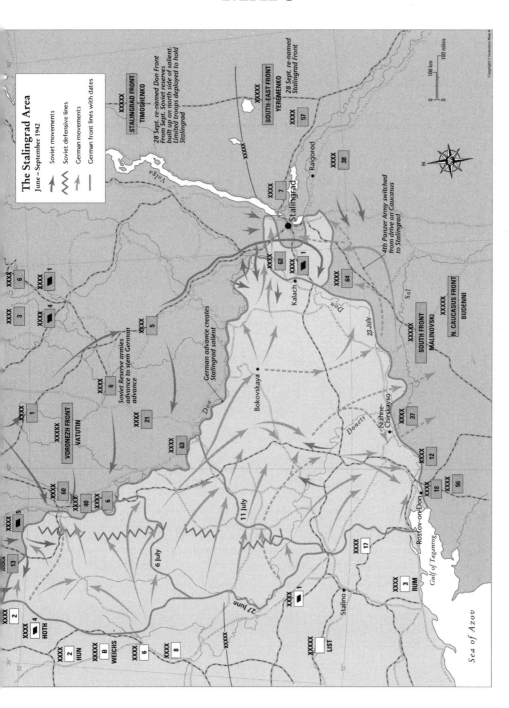

The Stalingrad Area
June – September 1942

- ↑ Soviet movements
- ∧∧∧ Soviet defensive lines
- ↟ German movements
- | German front lines with dates

STALINGRAD FRONT
TIMOSHENKO

28 Sept. re-named Don Front
From Sept. Soviet reserves
built up on north side of salient.
Limited troops deployed to hold
Stalingrad

SOUTH-EAST FRONT
YEREMENKO

28 Sept. re-named
Stalingrad Front

Soviet Reserve armies
advance to stem German
advance

German advance creates
Stalingrad salient

4th Panzer Army switched
from drive on Caucasus
to Stalingrad

VORONEZH FRONT
VATUTIN

N. CAUCASUS FRONT
BUDENNI

SOUTH FRONT
MALINOVSKI

HOTH

HUN

WEICHS

LIST

RUM

Volga
Stalingrad
Raigorod
Kalach
Don
Sal
Nizhne-Chirskayso
Donets
Don
Bokovskaya
Rostov-on-Don
Gulf of Taganrog
Stalino
Sea of Azov

6 July
11 July
27 June
23 July

100 km
100 miles

Copyright © Reservation Maps A

Operational German map of Stalingrad and surrounding area, autumn 1942.

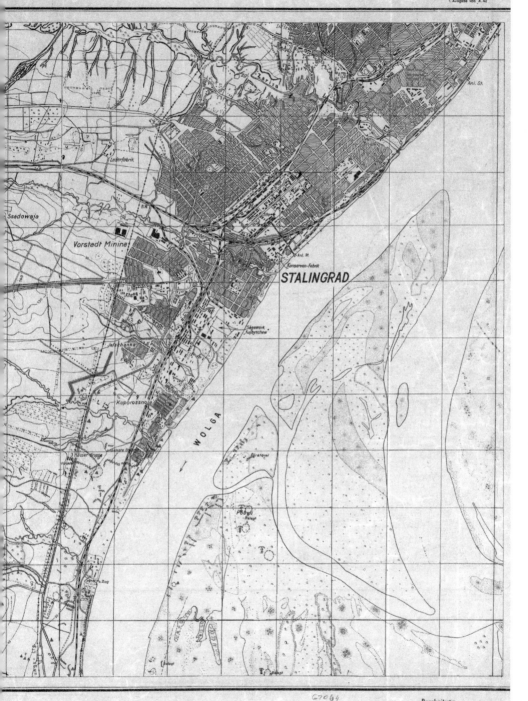

STALINGRAD

Befestigungen: Stand v. 12.X., 25.X., 27.X.42

67064
.1657
1942
.64

459113

Bearbeitung:
Korps-Kartenstelle 448
Armee-Kartenstelle 473
Druck: Armee-Kartenstelle 473

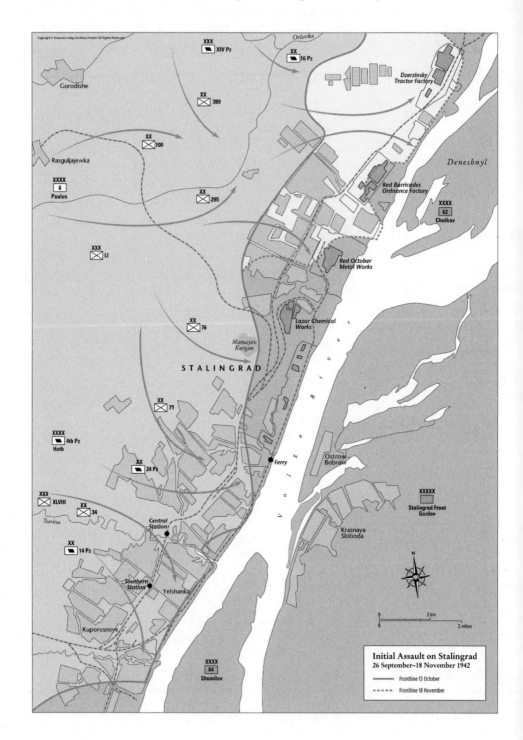

Orlovka

XXX · XIV Pz

XX · 16 Pz

Gorodishe

Dzerzinsky Tractor Factory

XX · 389

Deneshnyl

XX · 100

Red Barricades Ordnance Factory

Rasguljajewka

XXXX · 6 · Paulus

XX · 295

XXXX · 62 · Chuikov

Red October Metal Works

XXX · LI

Lazur Chemical Works

XX · 76

Mamayev Kurgan

S T A L I N G R A D

V o l g a   R i v e r

XX · 71

XXXX · 4th Pz · Hoth

XX · 24 Pz

Ferry

Ostrow Bobraw

XXX · XLVIII

XX · 34

XXXXX · Stalingrad Front · Gordov

Tsaritsa

Central Station

Krasnaya Sloboda

XX · 14 Pz

N

Southern Station

Yelshanka

Kuporosnoye

0 — 2 km
0 — 2 miles

Initial Assault on Stalingrad
26 September–18 November 1942

——— Frontline 13 October
- - - - Frontline 18 November

XXXX · 64 · Shumilov

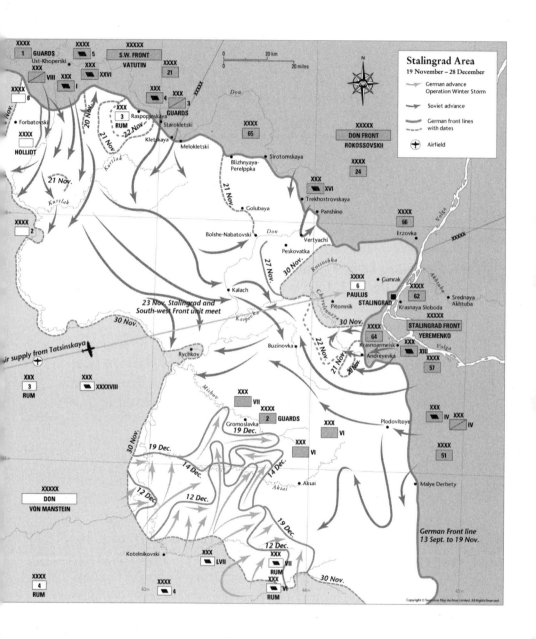

Stalingrad Area
19 November – 28 December

German advance
Operation Winter Storm

Soviet advance

German front lines
with dates

Airfield

APPENDIX A

The following is a list of some of the soldiers who are quoted in the text providing some additional biographical details.

Corporal István Balogh was a reluctant soldier in the *Magyar Királyi Honvédség* (Royal Hungarian Army) or *Honvéd* for short. His diary was taken from his dead body by a Red Army soldier and handed in for possible intelligence value. His tales of despair and low morale helped persuade the Soviets to target Nazi Germany's Axis allies and launch *Operation Uranus*. Balogh's war in Russia had lasted just three months. His diary was unearthed in Soviet archives by the British historian Antony Beevor.

Arthur Boje led the remnants of his once-proud regiment into captivity where he was separated from his men and forced to endure years of ill-treatment at Soviet hands. Transferred from camp to camp, he spent time in Moscow's infamous Lubyanka prison before being transported to the wilds of Kazakhstan. He refused to join the pro-Soviet NKFD and was finally released in January 1956, returning home as one of the very last former 6. *Armee* prisoners.

Gustav Böker was born in 1920 in Oberg in Lower Saxony. A Roman Catholic he trained as a commercial clerk after completing secondary school. A bachelor, Böker initially served in 111. *Infanterie-Division* as an anti-tank gunner. He fought in Ukraine and southern Russia, survived the Stalingrad fighting and was then killed in Russia in July 1943.

Ivar Corneliussen, a Danish Waffen-SS trooper in the *SS-Wiking*, was wounded during the fighting on the River Dnieper in 1943. He lost an eye but was able to re-join his unit and serve out the rest of the war in combat on the Eastern Front. He originally joined the Waffen-SS after being refused entry to the German navy for a suspected lung infirmity. He survived the war and finally passed away in 2019.

The grey-haired and bespectacled Helmut Groscurth resembled an academic rather than the professional field commander and staff officer he actually was. An early member of the anti-Nazi resistance in the Wehrmacht, he was born in Lüdenscheid, the son of a Protestant theologian and pastor. A devout Christian, he made himself hugely unpopular with the Nazi authorities by criticising atrocities both in Poland and then during *Barbarossa*. A staff officer in Stalingrad, he drafted Karl Strecker's last message for the surrender of the northern mini pocket of the city. He went into Soviet captivity at the final capitulation and died of typhus less than three months later in the Frolovo camp for captured officers.

The journeyman baker Karl Nünninghoff was born in 1920 in Mühlheim an der Ruhr. He came from a family of bakers before being drafted into the Wehrmacht and, specifically, *Artillerie-Regiment. 16*, part of *16. Panzer-Division*. Taken prisoner at Stalingrad, he died in captivity.

Fritz Pabst was born in Görmar, Thuringia, in 1906. A family man, he was married with children and originally a carpenter after graduating from elementary school. He was also a member of the Nazi Party. Drafted in August 1939 he became a member of 655 Construction Battalion, a part of *6. Armee*. He served in France, Greece and the Soviet Union and was promoted to NCO rank during the fighting in summer 1942. Posted as Missing In Action, nothing was ever heard of Pabst again after the surrender. He wrote over 370 letters to his wife and children from the front.

Born in Potsdam in 1908, Manfred Freiherr von Plotho was married and a landowner before joining the Army in 1937. Serving in *71. Infanterie-Division*, he fought in Belgium, France and then the Soviet Union. *Leutnant* von Plotho went into Soviet captivity at the end of the battle of Stalingrad. Imprisoned by the Soviets, he finally returned home in 1955.

Stephen Ritli survived 'the big run' and continued his service as a Hungarian army chaplain. He even performed a wedding at the front by proxy (as it was termed), although the new husband 'unfortunately never lived to see his new wife'. After the war he escaped Hungary before the communist takeover and emigrated to Australia for a new life. Years later, his Australian son-in-law wrote his memoir and had it published in 2020.

Felix Schneider from Büchel on the Moselle was married with children. An anti-tank gunner, he rose to the rank of *gefreiter* and fought in *6. Armee*. He went into captivity after the Stalingrad surrender and then all records of him cease.

The young officer who briefly held the high ground overlooking the River Volga by the Barrikady factory in late October – *Leutnant* Joachim Stempel – was a son of *Generalleutnant* Richard Stempel, commanding officer of *371. Infanterie-Division*. The son survived, being interviewed many years later for the BBC's 'War of the Century' documentary on the Eastern Front. His father Richard bade his son farewell on 26 January 1943 with the words, 'I'll see you up there, soon, where all brave soldiers go. Take care, my son.' He then committed suicide to avoid capture.

A Berliner, Karl Wagner was born in 1907 and went on to become a wholesale and retail salesman. After marrying he was drafted into the Wehrmacht in 1941 and fought with *6. Armee* across Ukraine and southern Russia on the advance to the Volga. A *gefreiter*, he survived the Pocket only to march disconsolately into captivity after the mass surrender. He died in the Saratov POW camp.

Paul Wortmann was born in Barcelona, Catalonia, in 1922. Single, a Roman Catholic and a student at a technical college, he entered the ranks of the Wehrmacht in October 1941. His specialist education marked him out and he became a member of the intelligence staff of Otto Kohlermann's *60. Infanterie-Division (mot.)*. He was killed in Stalingrad in January 1943.

APPENDIX B

6. *ARMEE* ORDER OF BATTLE 19 NOVEMBER 1942

IV Korps – General der Pioniere Erwin Jaenecke

29. Infanterie-Division (mot.) – Generalmajor Hans-Georg Leyser – Formed in 1934-35, its personnel were mainly drawn from Thuringia, Germany's so-called 'Green Heart'. A part of Heinz Guderian's *Panzergruppe 2* in *Barbarossa* it also fought in Poland and the Western campaign. As with most motorised infantry divisions it had just two infantry regiments instead of the standard three in non-motorised infantry formations but was still around 14,000 men strong. An outstanding and very experienced unit.

297. Infanterie-Division – Generalleutnant Max Pfeffer – Formed in spring 1940 as part of *Welle 8* from men in the 1940 draft class, it was in *6. Armee* from the beginning of *Barbarossa* and fought in the Kiev and Rostov battles.

371. Infanterie-Division – Generalleutnant Richard Stempel – A brand new division for *Blau*, formed as part of *Welle 19* it was intended for service in the occupied West, but having completed its work up training in France in May 1942 it was sent instead to *6. Armee* to help bolster its strength. An untried and inexperienced division.

VIII Korps – General der Artillerie Walter Heitz
76. Infanterie-Division – Generalleutnant Carl Rodenburg – Formed in the summer of 1939 from fully trained Prussian reservists, the division fought in France in 1940 and distinguished itself before joining *11. Armee* in southern Russia for *Barbarossa.*

113. Infanterie-Division – Generalleutnant Hans-Heinrich Sixt von Arnim – Formed in October 1940 it performed occupation duties in the Balkans in late 1941 before being ordered east to join *6. Armee* for *Blau.* An inexperienced division.

XI Korps – General der Infanterie Karl Strecker
44. Infanterie-Division - Generalleutnant Heinrich-Anton Deboi – based on the famous and historic *Hoch und Deutschmeister Regiment* from Vienna, the division was established in 1938 following the *Anschluss* with Nazi Germany and filled with former Austrian Army men. It fought in Poland and latterly France, where it had some issues with morale. It was in *6. Armee* from *Barbarossa* onwards.

376. Infanterie-Division – Generalleutnant Alexander Freiherr Edler von Daniels – Formed in May 1942 mainly from Bavarians, the division was fresh into combat during *Blau* with no prior experience.

384. Infanterie-Division – Generalleutnant Ecchard Freiherr von Gablenz – Formed in the winter of 1941-42 in Saxony, as with its sister division *376. Infanterie-Division* it had no prior combat experience before being sent to *6. Armee* to take part in *Blau.* Both the 376 and 384 were originally intended to serve as garrison troops in the West.

XIV Panzerkorps – General der Panzertruppe Hans-Valentin Hube
3. Infanterie-Division (mot.) – Generalleutnant Helmuth Schlömer – Originally the peacetime *Reichswehr*'s *3. Infanterie-Division,* the division fought in Poland and France before joining

Heeresgruppe Nord for *Barbarossa* where it took part in the drive on Leningrad. It was then sent south to join Bock's *Heeresgruppe Mitte* for the Moscow *Taifun* offensive before being reassigned once more to *6. Armee* for *Blau*.

60. Infanterie-Division (mot.) – *Generalmajor* Otto Kohlermann – Given the honorific title of *Feldherrnhalle*, the division was composed of the *Heimwehr Danzig* (Danzig Home Guard) and the brownshirt *Sturmabteilung Brigade Eberhardt*. The division fought in Poland and France before joining Ewald von Kleist's *Panzergruppe 1* for *Barbarossa*. A crack division and one of the best in *6. Armee*.

16. Panzer-Division – *Generalleutnant* Günther Angern – initially formed as an infantry division in 1935-36, it was recruited mainly from Westphalians along with a number of East Prussians. Converted into a panzer division in the summer of 1940 after fighting in France, it fought throughout the *Barbarossa* campaign in *Panzergruppe 1* under Hans-Valentin Hube's leadership. A well respected and admired division.

LI Korps – *General der Artillerie* Walther von Seydlitz-Kurzbach
71. Infanterie-Division – *Generalleutnant* Alexander von Hartmann – a fully trained reserve division from *Welle 2*, composed of men from the Hanover area in northern Germany, it fought with distinction at Sedan and the advance to Verdun in the French campaign before being sent to form part of *17. Armee* for *Barbarossa*. Sent back to France in the winter of 1941 to refit, it returned for *Blau* as an experienced and reliable formation.

79. Infanterie-Division – *Generalleutnant* Richard Graf von Schwerin – another *Welle 2* formation, it was mainly manned by trained southern German Swabian reservists, the division fought in France and then with *Heeresgruppe Mitte* during *Barbarossa*. An experienced and resolute formation, it distinguished itself in the fighting in Yel'nya and *Taifun* before its transfer south to take part in *Blau*.

94. Infanterie-Division – Generalleutnant Georg Pfeiffer – Raised as part of *Welle 5* just after the outbreak of war, the division was composed of reservists from Saxony and the former Czech Sudetenland. It joined *6. Armee* for the French campaign and then stayed with it for *Barbarossa*.

100. Jäger Division – Generalleutnant Werner Sanne – originally the *100. Leichte Infanterie Division*, this two-regiment formation was composed of two-thirds Austrians and one-third Silesians when established in December 1940. Designed for fighting in difficult terrain and for rapid movement warfare it formed part of *17. Armee* for *Barbarossa* and fought well at Uman and Kiev. Reinforced for *Blau* with an additional Croat regiment – Ivan Babić's *Verstärktes (kroatisches) Infanterie-Regiment 369* (Reinforced (Croatian) Infantry Regiment 369) – Sanne's division was an excellent formation.

295. Infanterie-Division – Generalmajor Dr Otto Korfes – Formed mainly with men from the 1940 draft class, this division was part of *Welle 8*. Assigned to *17. Armee* for *Barbarossa* the formation fought in Ukraine and the Donets.

305. Infanterie-Division – Generalleutnant Bernhard Steinmetz – a southern German formation formed in late 1940 as part of *Welle 13*, the division was originally intended for occupation duties in the West before being sent east to join *6. Armee* in May 1942. Prior to *Blau* it had no combat experience at all.

389. Infanterie-Division - Generalmajor Erich Magnus – Erwin Jaenecke's old division, it was formed as part of *Welle 18* – the so-called *Rheingold* divisions – and intended for use as a static garrison formation in the West. However, it was then decided to send it east and its original complement of Hessians received drafts of veterans to upgrade its capabilities.

14. Panzer-Division – Generalmajor Martin Lattmann – originally raised as the *4. Infanterie-Division* in the pre-war *Reichswehr*, the unit fought in Poland and France before converting to become a panzer division in the autumn of 1940. A Saxon formation, it fought in Yugoslavia and then joined *Panzergruppe 1* for *Barbarossa*. It was a well-trained and experienced outfit.

24. Panzer-Division – Generalleutnant Arno von Lenski – originally the *1. Kavallerie-Division* (the last cavalry division in the German Army) it was raised in Prussia and fought in Poland and the West in 1940 before transferring east for *Barbarossa* where it proved invaluable in the great encirclement battles including Kiev. Sent back West in the winter of 1941, it converted to become a panzer division before once more heading east to join *6. Armee* for *Blau*. One of the later panzer divisions to be formed it was still an excellent unit.

Independent of *6. Armee* but trapped in the Pocket with it was *Generalmajor* Wolfgang Pickert's *9. Flak-Division (mot.)*. A Luftwaffe unit, the division was formed in France in January 1941 before transfer to the central sector of the Russian Front for *Barbarossa*. The flak divisions were assigned sectors of responsibility but were not put under Army command, hence it operated separately from Bock's *Heeresgruppe Mitte*. A powerful formation with three motorised anti-aircraft regiments, it was assigned to southern Russia in early 1942.

Paulus also had a range of additional Army-level units he could call on including two mortar and two Nebelwerfer regiments, four regiments of artillery and a further seven artillery *bataillonen*. Two *pioniere bataillonen* were also originally assigned to *6. Armee*.

APPENDIX C

GERMAN ARMY AND COMPARABLE BRITISH ARMY RANKS

German Army	British Army
Schütze	Private
Oberschütze	Private
Gefreiter	Lance-corporal
Obergefreiter	Corporal
Unteroffizier	Lance-Sergeant (only used in the British Army in the Brigade of Guards)
Unterfeldwebel	Sergeant
Feldwebel	Colour/Staff Sergeant
Oberfeldwebel	Sergeant-Major - Warrant Officer Class 2
Hauptfeldwebel	Sergeant-Major - Warrant Officer Class 1
Leutnant	Second Lieutenant
Oberleutnant	Lieutenant
Hauptmann	Captain
Major	Major
Oberstleutnant	Lieutenant-Colonel
Oberst	Colonel
Generalmajor	Brigadier
Generalleutnant	Major-General
General	Lieutenant-General
Generaloberst	General
Generalfeldmarschall	Field-Marshal

ENDNOTES

Introduction

1. Hiwis – mostly former Red Army PoWs who volunteered to serve alongside their erstwhile captors carrying out a range of support tasks including carrying ammunition, maintenance, preparing food and digging trenches. Over time many became directly involved in the fighting as auxiliaries, and as German losses mounted their numbers increased to as much as 30 per cent of German unit establishments. By the end of the war almost two million Hiwis had served in the Wehrmacht.
2. Evans, Richard J., *The Third Reich at War,* p 421.

Chapter One

1. Detailed FHO assessment of Soviet strength dated 23 March 1942 and submitted to OKW.
2. Keller, Major Shawn P., US Air Command and Staff College Air University report: *Turning Point – A History of German Petroleum Production in World War II and its Lessons for the Role of Oil in Modern Air Warfare.*
3. Evans, Richard J., *The Third Reich at War,* p 341.
4. Hayward, Joel, S. A., *Stopped at Stalingrad – The Luftwaffe and Hitler's Defeat in the East 1942-1943,* p 5.
5. Response given by Antonescu to the Nazi Foreign Minister, Joachim von Ribbentrop, during the latter's visit to Bucharest on 12 February 1942.
6. Hayward, Joel, S. A., *Stopped at Stalingrad – The Luftwaffe and Hitler's Defeat in the East 1942-1943,* p 2.

7. Fromm would later be executed for his part in the failed *Valkyrie* plot against Hitler.

8. Turner, Jason, *Stalingrad Day by Day*, p 24.

Chapter Two

1. McNab, Chris (ed), *Hitler's Armies: A History of the German War Machine 1939-45*, p 216.

2. Cawthorne, Nigel, *Turning the Tide*, p 88.

3. Murray, Williamson, *A Strategy for Defeat: The Luftwaffe 1933-1945*, p 91.

4. Located in Berlin's Tiergarten district, the Bendlerblock was formerly the headquarters of Imperial Germany's Navy and the Weimar-era Reichswehr. Under Nazi rule it became the headquarters hub for much of the OKW, the OKH and the *Abwehr*.

5. Koschorrek, Günter K., *Blood Red Snow: The Memoirs of a German Soldier on the Eastern Front*, p 15.

6. Letter from Helmut Paulus to his family, dated June 1942, 3.2002.7209.

7. Letter from Rudolf Oehus to his family, dated June 1942, 3.2013.2829.

8. Klapdor, Ewald, *Viking Panzers: The German 5th SS Tank Regiment in the East in World War II*, p 42.

9. McNab, Chris (ed), *Hitler's Armies: A History of the German War Machine 1939-45*, p 219.

10. Kershaw, Robert, *Tank Men: The Human Story of Tanks at War,* p 213. Ludwig Bauer served in *Panzer Regiment 33* of *9. Panzerdivision*. Wounded an astonishing nine times, he nonetheless survived the war to tell his story.

11. Following the Battle of France in 1940 the Germans found themselves the masters of the defeated French Army's vast vehicle parks, within which were over 500 Lorraine artillery tractors.

12. Beringer, James, *A Hungarian Odyssey: The Life and Times of Dr Stephen Ritli*, p 33.

13. Hayward, Joel S. A., *Stopped at Stalingrad: The Luftwaffe and Hitler's Defeat in the East 1942-1943*, p 37.

14. Murray, Williamson, *A Strategy for Defeat: The Luftwaffe 1933-1945*, p 93.

Chapter Three

1. A *Welle* was the Wehrmacht designation for groups of infantry divisions raised at approximately the same time, with the same type of organisation and equipment, with similar tranches of trained personnel.

2. German men aged over 18 and fit for service were classified into nine categories, with *Reserve I* being fully trained men under 35 years of age.

3. Hayward, Joel S. A., *Stopped at Stalingrad: The Luftwaffe and Hitler's Defeat in the East 1942-1943*, p 126.

4. The Knight's Cross of the Iron Cross, to give it its full name, was worn on a ribbon around the recipient's neck, hence the term 'curing a throat ache'.

Chapter Four

1. Rehfeldt, Dr Hans Heinz, *Mortar Gunner on the Eastern Front*, p 174.

2. Evans, Richard J., *The Third Reich at War*, p 404.

3. Letter from Gustav Böker to his parents (3.2002.0966).

4. Eriksson, Patrick G., *Alarmstart East*, p 95.

5. Bergström, Christer, *Black Cross Red Star: Volume 3 Everything for Stalingrad*, p 28.

6. Letter from Rudolf Oehus to his parents (3.2013.2829).

7. Bergström, Christer, *Black Cross Red Star: Volume 3 Everything for Stalingrad*, p 145. *Unteroffizier* Walter Tödt.

8. Ibid – pp 35-36.

9. Beevor, Antony, *Stalingrad*, p 75.

10. Evans, Richard J., *The Third Reich at War*, p 407.

11. Eriksson, Patrick G., *Alarmstart East*, p 94.

12. Kaufmann, Johannes, *An Eagle's Odyssey: My decade as a pilot in Hitler's Luftwaffe*, p 151.

13. Hagen, Louis, *Ein Volk, Ein Reich*, p 53.

14. Rehfeldt, Dr Hans Heinz, *Mortar Gunner on the Eastern Front*, p 182.

15. Tsouras, Peter (ed), *Fighting in Hell: The German Ordeal on the Eastern Front*, p 184.

Chapter Five

1. Bock was extremely angry that he was still being named as the commander of the offensive as it became bogged down, as

he rightly believed his reputation would suffer. He never again held field command and died of his injuries in the final weeks of the war after his car was strafed by an RAF fighter in northern Germany. He was the Wehrmacht's only *generalfeldmarschall* to be killed by enemy action in the war.

2. Stargardt, Nicholas, *The German War: A Nation Under Arms, 1939-45*, p 305.
3. Klapdor, Ewald, *Wiking Panzers*, p 12.
4. De Giampietro, Sepp, *Blood & Soil*, p 173.
5. Ibid – p 189.
6. Klapdor, Ewald, *Wiking Panzers*, p 23.
7. Eriksson, Patrick G., *Alarmstart East*, p 103.
8. Rehfeldt, Dr Hans Heinz, *Mortar Gunner on the Eastern Front*, p 177.
9. Neitzel, Sönke, and Welzer, Harald, *Soldaten*, p 79.
10. Klapdor, Ewald, *Wiking Panzers*, p 23.
11. Kistemaker, Henk, *Wiking*, p 75.
12. Stargardt, Nicholas, *The German War: A Nation Under Arms, 1939-45*, p 317.

Chapter Six
1. Bergstrom, Christer, *Black Cross Red Star: The Air War over the Eastern Front volume 3*, pp 68-70.
2. Kaufmann, Johannes, *An Eagle's Odyssey*, p 161.
3. Letter from Rudolf Oehus to his parents, dated August 1942 (3.2013.2829).
4. Kaufmann, Johannes, *An Eagle's Odyssey*, p 161.
5. Bergstrom, Christer, *Black Cross Red Star: The Air War over the Eastern Front volume 3*, p 132.
6. Beevor, Antony, *Stalingrad*, p 115.
7. Letter from Karl Nünninghof to his parents, dated 27 August 1942, 3.2008.1388.
8. Bergstrom, Christer, *Black Cross Red Star: The Air War over the Eastern Front volume 3*, p 134. Diary of *Unteroffizier* Wilhelm Crinius.
9. Letter from Rudolf Oehus to his parents, dated 9 September 1942 (3.2013.2829).
10. Bergstrom, Christer, *Black Cross Red Star: The Air War over the Eastern Front volume 3*, p80.

Chapter Seven

1. Beevor, Antony, *Stalingrad*, p 119.
2. Bergstrom, Christer, *Black Cross Red Star: The Air War over the Eastern Front volume 3*, p 141.
3. Hoffmann, Wilhelm, *Diary of a German Soldier (1942)*.
4. Holmes, Richard, *The World at War*, p 286. *24. Panzer-Division* had been formed in late 1941 from the Wehrmacht's last remaining cavalry formation – *1. Kavallerie-Division*. Under that designation its officers and men had served in the *Barbarossa* campaign, including in the victory at Kiev.
5. Report written in December 1942 by Senior Lieutenant M.P. Polyakov, Red Army.
6. Hermann Graf, Alfred Grislawski, Ernst Süss and Heinrich Füllgrabe, were a remarkable group of fliers, soon dubbed the *Karaya Quartet* by their comrades in *JG. 52*.
7. Carruthers, Bob, *Voices from the Luftwaffe*, p 89.
8. Turner, Jason, *Stalingrad Day by Day*, p 107.
9. Letter from Rudolf Oehus to his parents, dated 27 September 1942 (3.2013.2829).
10. Busch, Reinhold, *Survivors of Stalingrad – Eyewitness Accounts from the Sixth Army, 1942-43*, p 17.
11. Bellamy, Chris, *Absolute War*, p 519.

Chapter Eight

1. Busch, Reinhold, *Survivors of Stalingrad – Eyewitness Accounts from the Sixth Army, 1942-43*, pp 64-5.
2. Hagen, Louis, *Ein Volk, Ein Reich*, p 53.
3. Tsouras, Peter (ed), *Fighting in Hell: The German Ordeal on the Eastern Front*, p 21. Paper written by Erhard Raus.
4. Holmes, Richard, *The World at War*, p 282. Interview with *Hauptmann* Ekkehard Maurer.
5. Wieder, Joachim & Einsiedel, Heinrich Graf von, *Stalingrad: Memories and Reassessments*, p 20.
6. Koschorrek, Günter, *Blood Red Snow*, p 29.
7. Vasily Zaitsev was played by the British actor Jude Law in the 2001 Hollywood film *Enemy at the Gates* about the Stalingrad battle and specifically a duel supposedly fought out between Zaitsev and an Olympic medal winning German marksman called Major Erwin König played by the American actor Ed Harris. The factual basis for the duel is dubious, with German

records having no mention of any Erwin König as a sniper and no Olympic medal winner of that name either. Interestingly, the Soviet authorities never repeated the story and it is difficult to imagine they would have passed up a propaganda opportunity of that magnitude, had it had any truth to it at all.

8. Busch, Reinhold, *Survivors of Stalingrad – Eyewitness Accounts from the Sixth Army, 1942-43*, p 128.
9. Cawthorne, Nigel, *Turning the Tide*, p 97.
10. Letter from Paul Wortmann to his brother Eberhard (3.2002.0935).
11. Letter from Paul Wortmann to his parents, dated 25 October (3.2002.0935).
12. Busch, Reinhold, *Survivors of Stalingrad – Eyewitness Accounts from the Sixth Army, 1942-43*, pp 248-9.
13. Carrell, Paul, *Hitler's War on Russia*, p 570.
14. Letter from Karl Nünninghoff to his family, dated 30 October (3.2008.1388).
15. Holmes, Richard, *The World at War*, p 286. Diary of *Leutnant* Reiner.
16. Lieutenant Nuto Revelli from 46th Company, *'Tirano'* Battalion, *Tridentina* Division.
17. Letter from Rudolf Oehus to his family (3.2013.2829).

Chapter Nine
1. Arthur, Max, *Forgotten Voices of the Second World War*, p 206.
2. Hagen, Louis, *Ein Volk, Ein Reich*, p 176.
3. Metelmann, Henry, *Through Hell for Hitler*, p 113.
4. Letter from Gustav Böker to his family (3.2002.0966).
5. Rudel, Hans-Ulrich, *Stuka Pilot*, p 68.
6. Hagen, Louis, *Ein Volk, Ein Reich*, p 53.
7. Hayward, Joel, S. A., *Stopped at Stalingrad – The Luftwaffe and Hitler's Defeat in the East 1942-1943*, p 231
8. McNab, Chris (ed), *Hitler's Armies: A History of the German War Machine 1939-45*, p 44.

Chapter Ten
1. Bekker, Cajus, *The Luftwaffe War Diaries*, p 238.
2. Hayward, Joel, S. A., *Stopped at Stalingrad – The Luftwaffe and Hitler's Defeat in the East 1942-1943*, p 257.

3. Taylor, Brian, *Barbarossa to Berlin Volume Two; The Defeat of Germany, 19 November 1942 to 15 May 1945*, p 9.
4. Wieder, Joachim & Einsiedel, Heinrich Graf von, *Stalingrad: Memories and Reassessments*, p 146.
5. Eriksson, Patrick G., *Alarmstart East*, p 97. Hener went on to become a fighter pilot with *JG 3*.
6. Letter from Rudolf Oehus to his family (3.2013.2829).
7. The classes were: Bread, Meats/soy etc, vegetables, puddings and milk, seasonings such as salt, mustard, vinegar, then spices such as cinnamon and cloves, fats, tea and coffee, sugar and lastly alcohol. Tobacco was in a category of its own.
8. Evans, Richard, J. *The Third Reich at War*, p 537.
9. Carrell, Paul, *Stalingrad*, p 171.
10. Evans, Richard, J. *The Third Reich at War*, p 416.

Chapter Eleven
1. Busch, Reinhold, *Survivors of Stalingrad – Eyewitness Accounts from the Sixth Army, 1942-43*, p 149.
2. Letter from Manfred Freiherr von Plotho to his wife (3.2008.2195).
3. Koschorrek, Günter, *Blood Red Snow*, p 100.
4. Irving, David, *Hitler's War*, p 478.
5. Hayward, Joel, S. A., *Stopped at Stalingrad – The Luftwaffe and Hitler's Defeat in the East 1942-1943*, p 272.
6. Letter from Paul Wortmann to his family, dated 24 December 1942 (3.2002.0935).
7. Letter from Karl Wagner to his wife (3.2002.7105).
8. Busch, Reinhold, *Survivors of Stalingrad – Eyewitness Accounts from the Sixth Army, 1942-43*, p 50.
9. Neitzel, Sönke, and Welzer, Harald, *Soldaten*, p 217.
10. Mitcham, Samuel W., *Hitler's Field Marshals and their Battles*, p 237.
11. Letter from Manfred Freiherr von Plotho to his wife (3.2008.2195).
12. Letter from Karl Nünninghof to his parents, dated 25 December 1942 (3.2008.1388).
13. Knappe, Siegfried, *Soldat: Reflections of a German Soldier*, p 254.
14. Busch, Reinhold, *Survivors of Stalingrad – Eyewitness Accounts from the Sixth Army, 1942-43*, p 242.

Chapter Twelve

1. Knappe, Siegfried, *Soldat: Reflections of a German Soldier*, p 254.
2. Trigg, Jonathan, *Voices of the Scandinavian Waffen-SS*, p 93.
3. Klapdor, Ewald, *Viking Panzers: The German 5th SS Tank Regiment in the East in World War II*, p 132.
4. Letter from Fritz Pabst to his family (3.2002.0306).
5. Letter from Felix Schneider to his wife, 1 January 1943 (3.2002.7369).
6. Letter from Karl Nünninghof to his brother Willi (3.2008.1388).
7. Beringer, James, *A Hungarian Odyssey: The Life and Times of Dr Stephen Ritli*, p 34.
8. Taylor, Brian, *Barbarossa to Berlin – volume 2*, p 26.

Chapter Thirteen

1. Taylor, Brian, *Barbarossa to Berlin – volume 2*, p 29.
2. Fowler, Will, *The Battle for Stalingrad*, p 170.
3. Hayward, Joel, S. A., *Stopped at Stalingrad – The Luftwaffe and Hitler's Defeat in the East 1942-1943*, p 288.
4. Wieder, Joachim & Einsiedel, Heinrich Graf von, *Stalingrad: Memories and Reassessments*, p 302.
5. Beringer, James, *A Hungarian Odyssey: The Life and Times of Dr Stephen Ritli*, p 49.
6. Trigg, Jonathan, *Death on the Don*, p 201.
7. Letter to Manfred Freiherr von Plotho from his wife, dated 24 January 1943 (3.2008.2195).
8. Letter to Karl Nünninghof from his parents (3.2008.1388).
9. *Signal* magazine report 'The Monument of Stalingrad' by *Major* Dr Wilhelm Ehmer.
10. Rosen, Richard von, *Panzer Ace*, p 130.
11. Neitzel, Sönke, and Welzer, Harald, *Soldaten*, p 244.
12. Wieder, Joachim & Einsiedel, Heinrich Graf von, *Stalingrad: Memories and Reassessments*, p 312.
13. Busch, Reinhold, *Survivors of Stalingrad – Eyewitness Accounts from the Sixth Army, 1942-43*, p 85.
14. Ibid – p 8.
15. Ibid – p 58.

16. Ibid – p 214.
17. Ibid – p 155.
18. Letter to the parents of Rudolf Oehus, dated 31 January 1943 (3.2013.2829).
19. Busch, Reinhold, *Survivors of Stalingrad – Eyewitness Accounts from the Sixth Army, 1942-43*, p 237.

Chapter Fourteen
1. Evans, Richard J., *The Third Reich at War*, p 329.
2. Ribbentrop, Rudolf von, *My Father Joachim von Ribbentrop*, p 388.
3. Casualty figures vary by dates used, with the German historian Paul Carrell giving the figure of 80,500 killed in the battle, Peter Young quoting 280,000 and Brian Taylor detailing 162,000. It is impossible to accurately state exact numbers, but Taylor's look about right and so those are the ones I have used.
4. Busch, Reinhold, *Survivors of Stalingrad – Eyewitness Accounts from the Sixth Army, 1942-43*, pp 85-6.
5. Young, Peter Brigadier (ret'd), *The Two World Wars*, p 396.
6. Eriksson, Patrick G., *Alarmstart East*, p 101.
7. Hayward, Joel, S. A., *Stopped at Stalingrad – The Luftwaffe and Hitler's Defeat in the East 1942-1943*, p 310.
8. McNab, Chris (ed), *Hitler's Armies: A History of the German War Machine 1939-45*, p 142.
9. Bekker, Cajus, *The Luftwaffe War Diaries*, p 277.
10. Rogan, Eugene, *The Fall of the Ottomans*, pp 262-63.
11. Hagen, Louis, *Ein Volk, Ein Reich*, p 109.
12. Neitzel, Sönke, and Welzer, Harald, *Soldaten*, recording of *landser* Faust, p 197.
13. Ibid, p 217.
14. Hagen, Louis, *Ein Volk, Ein Reich*, p 36.
15. Ibid, p 53.

SELECT BIBLIOGRAPHY

Alexander, Christine (editor) & Kunze, Mason (editor), *Eastern Inferno – Journals of a German Panzerjäger on the Eastern Front 1941-1943*, Casemate 2010

Arthur, Max, *Forgotten Voices of the Second World War*, Ebury 2004

Baumbach, Werner (translated by Frederick Holt), *Broken Swastika, The Defeat of the Luftwaffe*, Robert Hale 1986

Baxter, Ian, *The Destruction of 6th Army at Stalingrad*, Pen & Sword 2020

Beevor, Antony, *Stalingrad*, Viking 1998

Bekker, Cajus (translated by Frank Ziegler), *The Luftwaffe War Diaries*, MacDonald 1966

Bellamy, Chris, *Absolute War – Soviet Russia in the Second World War*, Macmillan 2007

Bergstrom, Christer, Dikov, Andrey, Antipov, Vlad, *Black Cross Red Star: The Air War Over the Eastern Front Volume 3*, Eagle Editions 2006

Beringer, James, *A Hungarian Odyssey: The Life and Times of Dr Stephen Ritli*, self-published 2021

Bidermann, Gottlob (translated & edited by Derek S. Zumbro), *In Deadly Combat: A German Soldier's Memoir of the Eastern Front*, University Press of Kansas 2000

Bullock, Alan, *Hitler: A Study in Tyranny*, Penguin 1962

Busch, Reinhold (translated by Geoffrey Brooks), *Survivors of Stalingrad: Eyewitness Accounts from the Sixth Army 1942-43*, Frontline 2018

Carell, Paul (translated by Ewald Osers), *Hitler's War on Russia*, George G. Harrap 1964

Carell, Paul (translated by David Johnston), *Stalingrad: The Defeat of the German 6th Army*, Schiffer 1993

Carruthers, Bob, *Voices from the Luftwaffe*, Pen & Sword 2012

Cawthorne, Nigel, *Panzer! Tank warfare 1939-45*, Capella 2003

Cawthorne, Nigel, *Turning the Tide: Decisive Battles of the Second World War*, Capella 2002

Clark, Alan, *Barbarossa: The Russo-German Conflict 1941-1945*, London 1996

Cloutier, Patrick, *Regio Esercito: The Italian Royal Army in Mussolini's Wars 1935-1943*, self-published 2013

Cloutier, Patrick, *Three Kings: Axis Royal Armies on the Russian Front 1941*, self-published 2012

Cooper, Matthew & Lucas, James, *Panzer – The Armoured Force of the Third Reich*, Book Club 1979

Craig, William, *Enemy at the Gates; the Battle for Stalingrad*, Reader's Digest Press 1973

Davies, Norman, *Europe at War 1939-1945: No Simple Victory*, Macmillan 2006

Erickson, John, *The Road to Stalingrad*, Weidenfeld & Nicolson 1965

Eriksson, Patrick G., *Alarmstart East: The German Fighter Pilot's Experience on the Eastern Front 1941-1945*, Amberley 2018

Evans, Richard J., *The Third Reich at War*, Allen Lane 2008

Everett, Susan & Young, Peter Brigadier, *The Two World Wars*, W. H. Smith 1982

Fischer, Wolfgang (edited & translated by John Weal), *Luftwaffe Fighter Pilot – Defending the Reich*, Grub Street 2010

Forty, Simon, *German Infantryman: The German Soldier 1939-45 – Operations Manual*, Haynes 2018

Fowler, Will, *The Battle for Stalingrad: The Turning Point of the Eastern Front*, Amber 2020

Galland, Adolf, *The First and the Last*, Blurb 2018

Geddes, Giorgio (translated by Natalie Lowe), *Nichivo: Life, Love and Death on the Russian Front*, Cassell 2001

Giampietro, Sepp De (translated by Eva Burke), *Blood and Soil: The Memoir of a Third Reich Brandenburger*, Greenhill 2019

Guderian, Heinz (translated by Constantine Fitzgibbon), *Panzer Leader*, Michael Joseph 1952

Hagen, Louis, *Ein Volk, Ein Reich – Nine Lives Under the Nazis*, Spellmount 2011

Hamilton, Hope, *Sacrifice on the Steppe: The Italian Alpine Corps in the Stalingrad Campaign, 1942-1943*, Casemate 2011

Harwood, Jeremy, *Hitler's War*, Quantum 2014

Haupt, Werner, *Army Group South: The Wehrmacht in Russia 1941-1945*, Schiffer 1998

Hayward, Joel S. A, *Stopped at Stalingrad: The Luftwaffe and Hitler's Defeat in the East 19422-1943*, University Press of Kansas 1998

Herrmann, Hajo (translated by Peter Hinchliffe OBE), *Eagle's Wings: The Autobiography of a Luftwaffe Pilot*, Guild 1991

Holmes, Richard, *The World at War*, Ebury 2007

Holmes, Tony (editor), *Dogfight – the greatest air duels of World War II*, Osprey 2011

Hooton, E.R., *Eagle in Flames – The Fall of the Luftwaffe*, Arms & Armour 1997

Hoyt, Edwin P., *199 Days: The Battle for Stalingrad*, Tom Doherty 1993

Hozzel, Paul-Werner, *Conversations with a Stuka Pilot*, Verdun Press 2014

Jukes, Geffrey, *Stalingrad, the Turning Point*, Ballantine 1968

Kaufmann, Johannes (translated by John Weal), *An Eagle's Odyssey; My Decade as a Pilot in Hitler's Luftwaffe*, Greenhill 2019

Kershaw, Robert, *Tank Men: The Human Story of Tanks at War*, Hodder & Stoughton 2008

Kistemaker, Henk, *Wiking: A Dutch SS-soldier on the Eastern Front*, Just Publishers 2019

Klapdor, Ewald, *Viking Panzers: The German 5th SS Tank Regiment in the East in World War II*, Stackpole 2011

Knappe, Siegfried (translated by Ted Brusaw), *Soldat: Reflections of a German Soldier, 1936-1949*, Bantam Doubleday Dell 1999

Koschorrek, Günter K. (translated by Olav R. Crome-Aamot), *Blood Red Snow, The Memoirs of a German soldier on the Eastern Front*, Greenhill 2011

Lucas, James, *Hitler's Mountain Troops – Fighting at The Extremes*, Cassell 1992

Lucas, James, *Kommando – German Special Forces in World War II*, Cassell 1985

Mahlke, Helmut, *Memoirs of a Stuka Pilot*, Frontline 2013

Malaparte, Curzio, *The Volga Rises in Europe*, London 1958

Matthews, Rupert, *Hitler: Military Commander*, Capella 2003

McNab, Chris, *Hitler's Armies: A History of the German War Machine 1939-45*, Osprey 2015

McNab, Chris, *The Luftwaffe 1933-45, Hitler's Eagles*, Osprey 2012

Messenger, Charles, *The Last Prussian*, London 1991

Metelmann, Henry, *Through Hell for Hitler*, Spellmount 2001

Michaelis, Rolf, *Panzergrenadier Divisions of the Waffen-SS*, Schiffer 2010

Mitcham, Samuel W. Jr, *Eagles of the Third Reich*, Stackpole 1988

Mitcham, Samuel W., *Hitler's Field Marshals and their Battles*, Guild 1988

Mitcham, Samuel W., *Hitler's Legions: German Army Order of Battle World War II*, Leo Cooper 1985

Munk, Jan, *I was a Dutch Volunteer*, self-published 2010

Muñoz, Antonio J., *For Croatia & Christ: The Croatian Army in World War II 1941-1945*, Europe 2003

Murray, Williamson, *Strategy for Defeat – The Luftwaffe 1933-1945*, Chartwell 1986

Neitzel, Sönke and Welzer, Harald, *Soldaten*, Simon & Schuster 2012

Nowarra, Heinz, *Heinkel He 111 – A Documentary History*, Jane's 1980

Pabst, Helmut, (translated by Andrew & Eva Wilson), *The Outermost Frontier – A German Soldier in the Russian Campaign*, William Kimber 1957

Perrett, Bryan, *Knights of the Black Cross*, Robert Hale 1986

Prüller, Wilhelm, *Diary of a German Soldier*, Faber 1963

Ribbentrop, Rudolf von, *My father Joachim von Ribbentrop*, self-published 2015

Roland, Paul, *Nazi Women of the Third Reich: Serving the Swastika*, Arcturus 2018

Roland, Paul, *The Nazis: The Rise and Fall of History's Most Evil Empire*, Arcturus 2019

Stargardt, Nicholas, *The German War: A Nation Under Arms, 1939-45*, Vintage 2015

Taylor, Brian, *Barbarossa to Berlin Volume One: The Long Drive East, 22 June 1941 to 18 November 1942*, Spellmount 2003

Taylor, Brian, *Barbarossa to Berlin Volume Two: The Defeat of Germany, 19 November 1942 to 15 May 1945*, Spellmount 2004

Tsouras, Peter (editor), *Fighting in Hell: The German Ordeal on the Eastern Front*, Frontline 2012

Turner, Jason, *Stalingrad Day by Day*, Windmill 2012

Wieder, Joachim and Einsiedel, Heinrich Graf von (translated by Helmut Bogler), *Stalingrad: Memories and Reassessments*, Arms and Armour 1993

Williamson, Gordon, *Loyalty is my Honor*, Motorbooks 1997

INDEX